RONALD S. GABRIEL

AMERICAN & BRITISH 410 SHOTGUNS

Our toll-free number to place an order or obtain a free catalog is
800-258-0929.

Published by

An F&W Publications Company

700 East State Street • Iola, WI 54990-0001
715-445-2214 • 888-457-2873
www.krause.com

Library of Congress Catalog Number: 2003108028
ISBN: 0-87349-679-5

Designed by Stanard Design Partners
Edited by Joel Marvin

Manufactured in Singapore

RONALD S. GABRIEL

AMERICAN & BRITISH 410 SHOTGUNS

DEDICATION

PHILIP LOUIS GABRIEL 1908-1993
IDALIA ORTIZ GABRIEL

For their constant moral compass by which I have tried to guide my life.

TABLE OF CONTENTS

ACKNOWLEDGMENTS

he photography is an important part of this book. Each of the photos is duly credited. Five photographers deserve special mention. R.J. Clark of Cameo, Norwich, England, did many of the British guns. G. Allan Brown of East Haddam, Connecticut, and Mike Levasheff of Los Angeles, California, did a number of American and a few of the British guns. Glenn Campbell of Los Angeles, California, photographed a potpourri of important guns, papers and cartridges. Paul Goodwin of Newport, Kentucky, did the largest number of guns and accouterments including the front and back cover. The quality speaks for itself.

Virtually all the individuals who provided information for this work are referenced accordingly. The generosity of the gun companies who opened their ledgers to me is especially noteworthy since the gun trade in general and their clientele in particular tend to be especially reserved in divulging information.

Donna Bledsoe, CMT has been my professional secretary, researcher, editor and transcriptionist for over 33 years. This work, as well as others, could not have been sustained without her skills. The course of my last three decades owes much to her ability, humor, loyalty and charity. Stacy Ann Winters has provided over two decades of support, affection and much more for my various professional and avocational endeavors. Pamela Jane Hobbs took in hand my life and provided the organization and tranquility to finish this project. I am well aware of my heavy debt to Idalia, Donna, Stacy and Pamela.

PREFACE

t is unlikely that a work of this kind, with its vast use of numbers and dates, will be errorless. Such errors brought to my attention will be corrected in future editions, if any.

The extensive use of references and communications is to credit the knowledge and work of others. If I have fallen short on this account, it was not willful.

The valuation of guns, though of great interest to all, has been studiously excluded. In some quarters of western life, "the excess of price over value is the true test of success in life," an unworthy fact of life. However, in the case of rare or unique guns, the intrinsic value is seldom the price negotiated between buyer and seller. Why? Because the human culture surrounding these artifacts of wood and steel has a value of its own, often far greater than the work itself.

When it comes to valuation, knowledge is the coin of the realm, and, in some measure, this book may help.

Ronald S. Gabriel
Los Angeles, California, August 2003

CHAPTER ONE

THE GENESIS OF THE 410 GAUGE

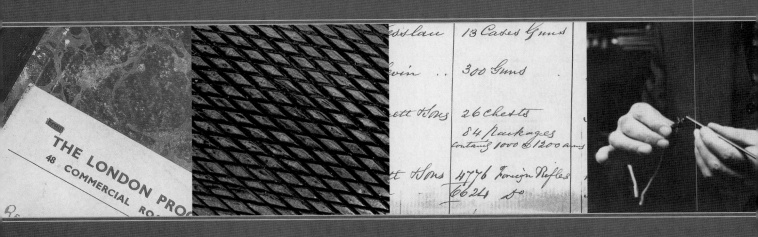

The 410 is not a bore or a gauge but a caliber that measures the internal diameter of the barrel in thousandths of an inch. Gauge or bore is based on the inside diameter of the barrel at 9 inches from the breech. It is calculated from the number of "pure lead spherical balls"—each of which fits the bore—"that makes up one imperial pound in weight [1]." For example, it takes 12 balls for the 12 bore and 20 for the 20 bore. However, in this book, we will always refer to the 410 as either a bore or a gauge.

The precise origin of the 410-gauge shotgun is unknown. Jack O'Connor believed that the gauge in America was a "direct descendant" of the 44/40 rifle cartridge. It was initially loaded using the standard 44/40 bottleneck case with the shot housed in a paper container. Indeed, at one time the shell was called the 44 XL. This was followed by the 2-inch straight brass case. The brass case was succeeded by the 2-inch paper case. Circumstantial evidence for this recently surfaced in a possible Annie Oakley-pedigreed Harrington & Richardson smoothbore hammer gun marked "410-44 cal" on a 26-inch barrel, made after 1900 and before 1903.

Based upon review of the British Proof House documents and gunmakers' records, it would appear that the first documented conventional 410 appeared in the 1870s (Photo 1). According to John Wilkes' memory of a gun passing through for repairs years earlier, the first Wilkes 410 was manufactured circa 1870s [2]. It was a 2-inch hammer side-by-side back-action shotgun. By the turn of the century, 410s, at least in England, were being made in measurable numbers. They were either of the hammer or hammerless configuration and the important actions included the boxlock and the sidelock. The latter action was usually back-action, rarely bar-action before World War II.

By 1925, the 410 gauge dotted the British Empire. This far-flung colonial leviathan, the likes of which was never seen before and will never be seen again, included Africa, Asia, Middle East, Australia, North America, the Caribbean, etc. Administering these vast territories required a modestly sized but very efficient British civil and military population. Many British subjects took with them a sporting gun and, for small camp and roadside game, a 410 was often included.

This was usually an inexpensive hammer back-action sidelock or Anson & Deeley (A&D) boxlock and, rarely, a "Best" quality boxlock or bar-action sidelock. Many such guns were sold through Army-Navy Cooperative Stores that were developed by overseas' officers in such then God-forsaken places as Khartoum, Bombay, Calcutta, and Fort Said. Conversely, Boothroyd noted in the 1920s that the United Kingdom imported a number of "Tukaway" double-barrel 410 pistol smoothbores made in Belgium, with "Tukaway" stamped on the barrel [3].

The 410 was generally a modestly priced boxlock, but it was produced to a high quality by such great firms as Holland & Holland, Watson, Greener, Churchill, Westley Richards, John Wilkes, William Evans, Webley & Scott, Cogswell & Harrison, and W.J. Jeffery, often for their export trade. Many manufacturers often had 410s made by small artisans and then "shot and regulated" them and placed their own name on the guns. Smaller firms, such as the Watson and Wilkes firms, were distinguished in that many components of their boxlock 410s were made in their own factory, with the frequent exception of the action. The action, usually an A&D boxlock, was supplied by such firms as Webley & Scott, Midlands, Carr & Son, A.A. Brown & Sons, and John Harper.

According to Richard Moore, lately of Greenfield, Ltd., Salisbury, England, Mr. Joseph Asbury ("JA" on the barrel flats before the lug), Midland Gun Company and Webley & Scott forged and machined the actions of a majority of all boxlocks made for the trade [4]. Both Moore and Tate [5] report that some of Watson Bros. A&D actions were made by George and Sidney Holloway; W.J. Jeffrey's by Webley Scott or John Saunders, and, for best quality, D. Leonard & Sons; and Holland & Holland's Northwood boxlocks after World War II by a Vic Simmons-led consortium. Watson, Jeffery, and Holland & Holland, all London firms, relied upon Birmingham artisans for the heart of their boxlock smoothbores.

There is some evidence in the British Proof Houses that a single firm, the Midland Gun Company, made a good majority of all the back-action 410s for a substantial period of time before and after the turn of the century, and sold them to other gunmakers for their regulating, precise fitting, and naming [6].

By 1910, Greener, in discussing the small bore 24- and 32-gauge guns, was able to say, "they are mostly exported to the Brazilian and Argentine markets" and, together with the 410 bore, are principally used by naturalists or used for such weapons as a "walking stick gun" [7].

Greener argued that the small-bore shotgun is not a toy and is, in the hands of a good shot, an efficient weapon. He discusses those who championed the 28 bore in the 1879 London Field Trials. He also lists game shooting testimonials for the 28 bore but none for the 410. Apart from the brief comments noted above, the 410 goes unnoticed in the 9th and last edition of Greener's compendium [7].

Indeed, it may have been Greener's comment that "the 28 bore is the smallest caliber of any practical use as a game gun" that led to the general disapproval suffered by the 410 gauge over

Photo 1: London Proof House records.

Paul Goodwin photo ∨

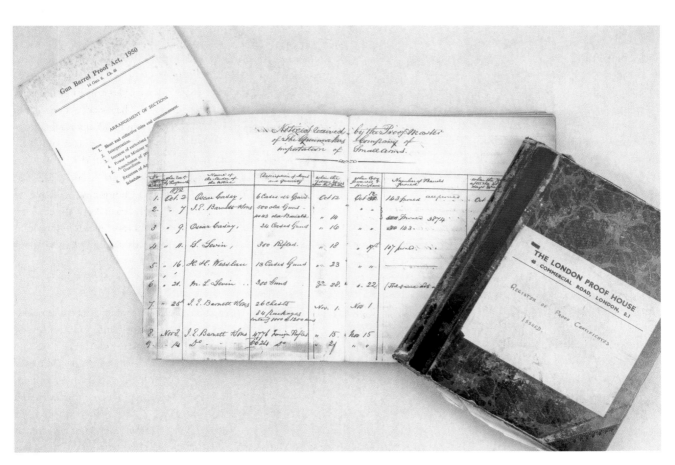

the next 50-odd years [8]. Greener did say that the small bore should be used by "either a first-rate shot or by a boy beginning to practice." Attesting to the lowly state of the 410 gauge in bygone times was the phrase "410s as vermin destroyers."

Ultimately, the extremes of society generated the interest in the 410 bore: the gamekeeper and poacher for predator control and "fast" food and the aristocrat and gentleman landowner for collecting birds and ground game for taxidermy and self-protection.

In America, the 410's traditional use as a rat and wildcat killer, buttressed by its otherwise presumed impracticality, was condescendingly celebrated by a generation of American shotgun writers including Elmer Keith, Jack O'Connor, and Charles Askins. These writers, all big-bore shotgun enthusiasts, dealt with the wide-open spaces of the American West with long-range upland game and waterfowl shooting of big birds including pheasant, chukar, grouse, partridge, duck, and goose.

America

Colt Firearms Company made a 410 smoothbore revolver for export to Great Britain and Europe as early as 1877, according to London Proof House research [6].[1] In America, the introduction of the 410 gauge during and just after the Great War was in the form of the inexpensive and mass-produced single-barrel shotgun. For example, the Iver Johnson Company introduced the 410-gauge Champion in 1916. Other American companies also made the 410 by this time. Geoffrey Boothroyd reports a British "Remington" catalog of 1915 offering a single-barrel hammer top-lever breech opener 410 smoothbore [9]. In 1919, Winchester introduced the Model 20, which was a single-barrel, break-open, boxlock, hammer shotgun. These shotguns were truly meant as a "kid's gun, a woman's gun, or a pot gun for the barn and camping trip..." [10]

However, by the middle 1920s, skeet shooting as a recreational phenomenon had developed to such an extent that the expensive double shotgun manufacturers found an enthusiastic market. Hence, in the middle and late 1920s, Parker, L.C. Smith, and Ithaca introduced the 410 bore, initially in their less expensive grades but eventually in virtually all grades.

Parenthetically, it was in this era when Purdey made its first modern hammerless bar-action sidelock double in the 410 bore, personally manufactured and assembled by perhaps the greatest shotgun artisan of his generation, Harry Lawrence [11].

The earliest American 410s, introduced at the time of the Great War, were chambered for the 2 1/2-inch shell. This continued into the early 1930s for all 410s including one of the most interesting ever produced, the Marlin 410 lever action, manufactured from 1929 to 1932.

In 1933, Winchester introduced the Model 42 with 2 1/2- and 3-inch chambers, the latter for the new Winchester Western 3-inch 410 shell. Winchester pioneered the longer shell in the early 1930s, with 3/4 ounce of shot and designed the Model 42 Winchester pump shotgun for it. The earlier 2- and 2 1/2-inch shells were loaded with 3/8 and 1/2 ounce of shot respectively.

The explosion of interest in target shooting coincided with increased opportunities for both women and children to participate in the sport of shotgunning. The initial assumption was that the 410, because of its small size and light weight, was an ideal gun for a beginning shotgunner. In time, however, it became apparent that the 410 was instead a gun for the expert marksman. It is not difficult to appreciate that the smaller the pattern and firepower, the larger the need for accuracy and judgment in the use of a 410.

By the middle 1930s, the tremendous popularity of target shooting compelled manufacturers (especially Parker and other double-barrel gunmakers who appealed to shotgun target shooters, a generally affluent middle-class lot) to introduce a shotgun choked Skeet & Skeet to serve the needs of the amateur and professional shooter. A philosophical change in American society transformed hunting into more of a recreational pastime and less of a mode for survival. This change resulted in shotgunning becoming, in part, the province of the target shooter and the finesse game bird gunner, rather than the subsistence hunter.

The development of the double gun served the purposes of conservation as well as recreation and the introduction of the 410 bore increased the challenge of shotgunning. An additional phenomenon was the developing American taste for a sense of aesthetics in her guns that was grandly realized in the delicate, subtle, and svelte lines of the 410.

However, its apparent refinement proved to be a most difficult characteristic for the typical shotgun writer in the middle 50 years of the 20th century to cope with. Indeed, machismo was a *sine qua non* for a successful gun writer who wished to flourish during this era.

Major Charles Askins groaned as early as 1929 that the 410 was "fit only for women and children," because it "kicks" like a 22-caliber rifle. He further observed that the 410 has become "strangely popular" for a "full-grown man" who wished to use it to bag game. Such a man "had really never grown up" or "nature made a mistake in fixing his sex." He did allow that a boy could use the 410 until his mid-teen years without contempt from his elders [12].

An Askins' progeny still laments "the tragic mistake" to introduce shotgunning to a beginner with a 410 [13]. The American skeet-shooting mindset, where you have to shatter 100 successive targets to have a good time, reflects this attitude.

Elmer Keith represented an archetypical example of such attitudes when he huffed that no bore smaller than the 20 gauge should ever have been made. He mocked Frank Pachmayr's 410 "close range" and "easy shooting" of pen-raised and liberated chukars in an alfalfa field. "Trying to shoot big upland birds with a 410 bore" he growled, is like using a "270 on elk." Yet, he describes

---

1 There is now emerging evidence that some of these guns were made in a Colt factory established in England.

having patterned a "3-inch" cartridge with the lever-action Marlin 410 with 7-1/2 shot. "No bird the size of a pheasant or mallard could have gotten through this 30-inch circle without receiving three or four" hits. "Just the same," he "never could see any earthly use for the 410" except for the taxidermist [14]. By the way, the Marlin 410 was never chambered for the 3-inch cartridge.

It was a mistake, Keith carries on, to ever "arm anyone for game shooting with a 410 bore." He went on endlessly about never seeing "any reason for the tiny 410 gauge." "The 410 is all right for shooting rats in the barn or in the basement, but that about lets it out, to my notion." Even the fair-minded Jack O'Connor, when describing the origins of the 410 shell, considered it an embryonic form in the shape of "such little pest cartridges" as the 44 XL [10]. He acknowledged it was a "gun for skeet shooting" but then lamented that it was "not a man's gun." In a delightful O'Connor hagiography, a listing of over 20 "favorite" shotguns listed the smallest bore as a 28 [10A].

Even a modern premier gun writer offers a similarly caustic refrain but with a tincture of fondness. He refers to the 410 as a "Little Bitch" (a term of endearment normally reserved for female dogs and human harlots) [15]. He complains, "it's bad news for beginners." He further laments that, "Boys have given up shooting forever" because the 410 was their first bore. This is haughty nonsense. His first bore was his granddad's single-shot 410, and shooting his first quail with it is "as clear now as it was then." He waxes on proudly recalling, "rabbits and squirrels were dead meat."

McIntosh's nostalgia finally overwhelms his prejudice and ends in affection, as it does for many American and British gun writers. Though big bore shooters as hoary adults, they started as 410 shooters and look back wistfully and with profound sentiment in the pages of their books and magazine essays.

With these early endorsements, it is a wonder that the 410 gauge survived its maiden voyage in America. Although the writers' antipathy may reflect their degree of marksmanship, it more likely reflects the ambivalence, even aversion that the American male had toward those aesthetic characteristics traditionally attributed to the feminine domain. Yet, how many of us started shooting with a single-barrel hammer 410, wisely selecting our targets for an effective kill and to husband precious cartridges? The 410 gauge forced us to be accurate, disciplined, and quiet stalkers of small game. All of these attributes were traditionally male.

Today, certainly, the collector/investor interest in the 410 gauge is testimony to its existence as the ultimate embodiment of beauty and function in a double shotgun. This, together with its rarity in all makes and grades, makes the 410 vulnerable to the verbal extravagances of the aficionado. It certainly has "come a long way" from a pest control walking stick to its present day financial and artistic apogee.

In summary, the earlier single-barrel and well-made American 410s, made in the second and third decades of the 20th century, were in response to the needs of predator hunters, pot shooters, bird collectors, and the young. These were guns such as

the Iver Johnson Champion, introduced in 1916, and the Winchester Model 20, introduced in 1919. The expensive doubles responded to the desires of the increasingly affluent American target and small game shooter who wanted a challenge wrapped in a mechanical work of art.

The 410 Collectable Side-by-Side

This phenomenon began to occur in America in the 1950s and 60s among the 410 game and skeet shooters and the rare pure collector. Such a collector was Leon Kelly who had at one time over 30 Parker 410 shotguns, many upgraded models by the Robert Runge and Larry DelGrego cottage industry [16]. Shooting small-winged game with a 410 became sporting and challenging. Simultaneously, the 410 collector began to have an impact upon and, at times, to dominate the gun-collecting fraternity, by setting new market trends aesthetically and economically. By the 1970s, the 410 collector fancied himself among the elite.

Early 410 collectors such as Otis Odom of Georgia, William Jaqua of Ohio, Leon Kelly of Alabama, and Alan Phillips of California, set the agenda. These men were of such high repute and credibility that their knowledgeable opinions informed the next generation of collectors. Their dicta often assumed near biblical importance to those they mentored.

The press and professional shotgun writers in the 1980s began to catch up with what the shooter and collector had known for several decades. Don Zutz, now deceased, was one of America's greatest modern shotgun writers. He waxed deliriously when he described the 410 as the "epitome of line, proportion, grace, elegance, fit, balance, and finish." He called it the "gunmaker's toughest challenge and his greatest pride" [17]. In fact, Harry Lawrence, Great Britain's great gunmaker of the middle half of the 20th century, built Purdey's first hammerless bar-action sidelock 410 in 1927 and, together with his building three miniature working guns for King George V, called it "my greatest gunmaking feat" [18].

Zutz, the man with the big-bore name and a technical mastery of the American shotgun scene, continued poetically on behalf of the 410 in which smallness becomes appealing, "... something apart from the gross, the bulky, and the ordinary ... a collector's dream, an investor's hedge and a hunter's joy." His recent death leaves a large void in popular shotgun writing. He wrote about shotguns with such joy that he filled his readers with a great emotional satisfaction.

There are two reasons why the collectable 410 began to sell at a premium. First, is its rarity. The era when the quality double 410 was being built favored the big bore. In part, this was because of the attitude of an earlier generation of gun writers and in part because it remained for many a hunter a time of hunting out of necessity and quality double 410s were an unnecessary luxury. Furthermore, the 1930s was not an extravagant time. Just ask the many still-living sons and daughters of agricultural produce pickers of the California Imperial and Central valleys who lived in tents in the blistering hot summers. Many of them supplemented the meager family table with small game shot with their single-shot, single-barrel 410.

In America, the double 410 did not make its appearance at Parker, Ithaca, and L.C. Smith until the mid to late 1920s. This was soon followed by the economic straits of the 1930s in which few could indulge in an expensive small-bore shotgun. By the early 1950s, the great American double shotguns, with the exception of Olin-Winchester's Model 21, had essentially ceased production.

A second reason the collectable 410 sells at a premium is that the aesthetic aspects of this bore are most compelling. As Zutz continued in his own hyperbolic prose, "gun fanciers cherish the small bores." It is "a matter of profile, trimness, and size." The "artistry of gunsmithing, assemblers and finishers and engravers" is "truly electric"—all on behalf of the 410.

Personalities and Influences

One of the most important 410 collectors in the world has been William Jaqua, the fabled shotgun dealer from Ohio. At one time, he had, without question, the finest 410 collection in the world, encompassing American, English, and European shotguns. This included perhaps the greatest high-grade original Parker 410 that can be confirmed with factory records, a CHE, number 241429. It features a ventilated rib, a single trigger, and a beavertail forend (see Parker chapter). As the dean of American shotgun dealers, Jaqua represented the best in knowledge and honesty and their application to the treacherous field of shotgun collecting.

Alan Phillips, president of the Gray Truck Company turned gentleman gun dealer, had a deep and varied collection of shotguns including unique Parker and Model 21 410s. He also shares Jaqua's value system. Kelly, at one time, had the major collection of Parker 410s, several of which were upgrades that he had commissioned by Runge and DelGrego (see Parker chapter). Other Parker 410 collectors include the remarkable Otis and Ruby Odom who became, by the 1970s, the pre-eminent Parker collectors with a subspecialty in the 410 bore. This uniquely traditional and unsurpassingly hospitable couple acquired a singular expertise in all phases of the Parker, especially the 410.

A number of dealers and gun writers highlighted the desirability of 410 collecting, especially the Parker. These include writers Peter Johnson and Larry Baer and the prolific dealer and universally known Herschel Chadick. In recent times, Chadick has managed to raise shotgun dealing to a near religious experience. Current shotgun dealers, known for their reliability and large fund of knowledge of the 410, include Michael Weatherby and Don Criswell of California, William Larkin Moore of Arizona, and Marshall Field of New York.

Two articles appearing in *Arms Gazette* gave specific impetus to the world of 410 collecting in the 1970s. Alan Phillips' article on the Model 21 Winchester 410 was well researched and succinctly written. It has stood the test of time now that complete factory data have surfaced.

A second article on the Parker 410 further stimulated popular interest in this gauge as an important objective for the serious shotgun collector. However, it is a minefield of data requiring considerable critical scrutiny, particularly with respect to the guns pictured and identified as original high-grade 410 Parkers. At one time, to this writer's knowledge, not a single factory-documented original Parker 410 bore on a triple 0 frame above a CHE grade had surfaced publicly to allow for a consensus and/or record authentication. In fact, Charles Parker, a grandson of the founder who oversaw the sale to Remington in 1937, has stated that Parker never made a 410 that was originally in a grade above CHE [19]. This, at times acrimonious debate, has had some closure now that the Remington-Parker records have been fully collated (see Parker chapter).

These important collectors, dealers, and writers, and those that followed, have developed a love affair with the 410 because of the gun's inherent quality, rarity, and beauty. Above all other gauges, the 410 has been most vulnerable to embellishment, alteration, re-finishing, and upgrading. The Parker and the Model 21 Winchester have been most subject to this peculiar but understandable post-World War II development in the aesthetics of shotgunning. Fortunately, Winchester kept very detailed records of the Model 21, and it is possible to identify virtually every 410 that has been altered, upgraded, or otherwise changed from the original. In the case of the Parker, public access to the historical records was denied for decades. Authentication of specimens relied upon the word of experienced dealers and collectors and whatever records that fraternity could develop. Virtually every other manufacturer of the 410 in this century has kept excellent and available records. Their guns are relatively impervious to the machinations of those engaging in the craft of shotgun "upgrading" for either aesthetic, impulsive, and/or economic exploitation (see Parker chapter).

The Great American side-by-side double 410 ceased to exist when the various companies liquidated. Even the Model 21, the last fine side-by-side double 410 introduced in America and the last to be discontinued, is no longer made by Winchester. In fact, Winchester discontinued the Model 21 410 in the 1960s, except for very special circumstances (see Model 21 chapter). They sold the rights of the Model 21 in the early 1980s to the U.S. Repeating Arms Company who began to advertise the 410 and 28-bore Model 21 in the middle 1980s. This appears to have been a short-lived effort for as of 1992, they were no longer offering these gauges.

Recently, however, this version of the Model 21 410 bore has resurfaced on the commercial market through the efforts of Tony Galazan and his Connecticut Shotgun Company. Galazan, who is now America's premier gunmaker, has resurrected Fox and the Winchester Model 21 and has patented a unique over and under, all available in the 410 bore.

The Browning over/under double 410, an American invention made in Belgium, is a unique story. It had a quarter century run from 1959 to 1983 and produced some of the most spectacular 410s in existence (see Browning chapter).

Great Britain

In Great Britain, the 410 smoothbore has a much longer and more revered early history. The naturalist, the taxidermist, the small bird collector, the poacher, and the gamekeeper used it readily and pleasurably as early as the last quarter of the 19th century.

It seems quite clear that the 410 smoothbore is not mentioned prior to 1874 in the surviving gun literature. However, small-gauge smoothbores were produced in antiquity. A 32-bore shotgun was produced by London gunmakers in 1660 and Joseph Manton made a 22 bore in 1785 [20]; however, not a 410. A Surrey, England, dealer had for sale in 1992 a beautiful "John Manton" 32 smoothbore made in 1785. It is a muzzle-loading flintlock with a splinter forend and a straight stock. There is a reported Holland & Holland 69-bore smoothbore musket. If anyone has discovered that a 410 smoothbore shotgun appeared prior to the last quarter of the 19th century, please enlighten me.

The Beginning [21,22,23]

The non-trigger matchlock gun with its "glowing smoking mouth" appeared in 1300, followed by the trigger matchlock in 1450 [24]. These included the Snap Matchlock.

The wheellock gun, first described by Leonardo de Vinci, appeared in 1530, and the flintlock in 1550. The matchlock and wheellock guns had essentially vanished by 1725.

The flintlock was mainly a muzzleloader; however, by 1775 a breechloader ensemble had been developed but unsuccessfully marketed. There was a perceptible space of time between ignition of priming and the explosion of the main charge. A piece of flint striking steel immediately over the priming pan generated the sparks necessary to ignite the priming powder.

In the early 1800s, Alexander Forsyth paired the flintlock with the percussion ignition system he developed in 1807. This ignition system utilized the detonating powers of a fulminating powder (fulminate of mercury) to ignite the charge in the barrel. The falling hammer detonated a small quantity of fulminate and the flash was then diverted into the touchhole. This led to the 1850 to 1870 era, a cradle of modern shotgun development. Throughout this period, various smoothbores were described from 4 bore to 32 bore. Yet, there was complete silence on the 410.

The artistry that so beguiles the present generation of writers and aficionados is all the more remarkable when its progenitor is explained [25]. "Barrel setting" or straightening was done by visual examination, a technique discovered in 1770 by an unknown Birmingham, England, artisan. He used natural daylight and interior barrel surface shadows to achieve the necessary result.

This method is still in use for quality doubles in the great gun houses of England. Through the 1850s, the locks and plates were handmade at the forge and anvil. This, the most difficult task for the gunmaker, was followed by the hand filer. Then the fitter, assembler, polisher, engraver, and hardener completed the task. After the 1850s, the steam hammer and stamp started to replace the forge and anvil, and the milling machine, the filer.

After the 1860s, machine-equipped factories emerged simultaneously with the acceptance of the breechloader gun. No wonder the 19th-century doubles are valued often as much for their history as for their intrinsic value.

The 19th-century muzzleloaders ranged from the 10 bore to the 30 bore, according to old auction catalogs in the Sotheby and Christie archives. Yet, no 410 smoothbores are listed.

From 1850 to 1870, an explosively active period in shotgun development, the centerfire, the breech-loading, and the hammerless shotguns were developed. During this time, there is no mention of the 410 smoothbore in the historical shotgun record, the British Proof Houses, or the cartridge/ammunition literature [26].

However, during the period of 1871 to 1890, the 410 finally emerged in the British Proof House records, in shotgun and cartridge literature, and in the production records by British gunmakers of serial-numbered shotguns that are traceable to their production dates.

Although Kynoch, a leading cartridge maker, was not offering the 410 bore cartridge in an 1882 poster, the British Proof House records showed that the 410 bore was available by importation from Europe as early as 1874 [26,27]. In the "London Notices of Importations" in August 1874, William Whitmore imported "410 guns." On September 30, 1874, Robert Hughes brought in 16 walking stick 410 smoothbores from Europe. In April 1877, 100 Colt 410 smoothbore revolvers were shipped from Colt Firearms Company in America. In December of 1878, Thomas Bland & Sons imported 410 smoothbore pistols from the continent.

Cogswell & Harrison, a prolific gunmaker in the late 19th and early 20th centuries, records its first 410 smoothbore in 1880, serial number 10311, a "410 walking stick" [28].

A 410 hammer gun by Charles Osborne of Seven Whitehill Place, London, was traced by Boothroyd to a production date of between 1885 and 1892 [29]. This was a typical Victorian bird collector's gun used for taxidermy. Brass 410 cartridges were introduced in the 1880s. An Eley Ammunition Display Chart, circa 1890, showed 410-bore cartridges [30].

Edward Booth, the greatest of the Victorian bird collectors with 236 species to his credit, used a 410 air rifle and a 410 smoothbore walking stick sometime between 1865 and 1884 [31].

William Evans, who started in 1883, made his first 410 in 1884 and his second in 1885. Both were "walking stick" guns with "moveable butt" and "patent safety trigger" priced at two pounds, five shillings. His first breech opener 410 had a side-lever and was made in 1887 [32]. Greener first lists the bore in his 2nd Edition of *Modern Shotguns* in 1891 [33].

The marriage of the walking stick with the percussion ignition in an 1876 patent led to a "410 walking stick gun" manufactured by a French gunmaker, Celestin Dumonthier, and sponsored in England by A.M. Clark. With this gun, the barrel sleeve is pushed forward to open the chamber in the side of the barrel. It is then pulled back to close the chamber. Releasing the firing pin occurred by one of several methods. One involves blowing the firing pin against the base of the shell as you would a "peashooter"! [34] This comes under the author's chapter heading "Interesting Types of Smoothbore 410s." Remember that Greener's reference to the 410 was under "Odd Size." Such is the literary ontology of the Zutz' "Truly Electric" bore, a "collector's dream."

The pinfire breech-loading shotgun, introduced by LeFaucheux at the Great Exhibition of 1851, was manufactured as late as 1896 in Great Britain. Dickson & Sons produced the last one in Britain, but manufacturing continued in Europe into the early 20th century [35,36]. However, no English-made pinfire 410 has surfaced in the records or in the marketplace.

The pinfire cartridge, patented in 1836 by LeFaucheux, was manufactured well into the 20th century, at least until 1935, by Eley. It was available in the 410 bore by 1895.

Daw introduced the centerfire cartridge in 1861 and Greener describes many centerfire field trials comparing 12, 16, 20, and 28 bores under varying conditions. These took place from 1879 through to the end of the 19th century without mention of the 410 bore.

In 1885, G. Fosbery, a Victoria Cross winner, Great Britain's highest award for valor under fire, patented a Paradox barrel. This allowed a shotgun barrel to fire a solid bullet accurately by rifling only the constricted muzzle portion of the barrel. It stabilized the solid bullet without distorting the pattern of the shotgun cartridge. By 1899, Holland & Holland had produced approximately 5000 Paradox guns from 8 to 28 bore, with and without exposed hammers, almost always a back-action sidelock for added stock strength, both black powder or nitro [37].

410 Cartridge (see 410 Cartridge chapter)

Exploring the cartridge and gun barrel literature helps in dating the time period for the advent of the 410 bore. In 1882, Kynoch Ammunition Company offered shotgun cartridges from the 8 bore to the 28 bore and 36 caliber (.36-inch), pinfire or centerfire, brass or paper bodied. A recapitulation of this literature emphasizes the nearly nonexistent use of the 410 bore in conventional shooting circles prior to 1882. It also illustrates that because the pinfire 410 cartridge exists—and they do in small numbers—one cannot conclude that the 410 pinfire shotgun cartridge dates back to the 1860s.

In fact, Eley offered a pinfire 410 shell in a 20th century pre–World War II flier supplied by Boothroyd. At least one pinfire 410 shotgun is known (see Interesting Types of Smoothbore 410s chapter). It has European proof marks but no maker's name and the date of production is unknown. Alas, the provenance of this gun cannot be traced. It is clear though that the pinfire shotgun and/or cartridge were made in Europe well into the 20th century.

410 Transition

From 1870 to 1890, the sale of British gun licenses almost doubled from over 90,000 to over 170,000, and many 12 bores were downsized from 7 pounds to under 6 pounds [34]. These two facts certainly reflected the advent of the breech-loading centerfire gun and cartridge that enormously simplified and made safer the art of shotgunning. It also reflected increasing numbers of women and boys entering the recreational shooting arena. The downsizing in weight of a given bore and improved ballistics of cartridges and barrels eventually led to a smaller bore acceptable to the game and target shooter. This gradually led to the acceptance of the use of the 410 bore in both pursuits. Indeed, Purdey sold a few wonderfully crafted "E"-grade 410s in the late 1880s and early 1890s, both in single- or double-barrel hammer back-action smoothbores (see Purdey chapter).

Before the turn of the 20th century, the system of serial numbering guns in England was as follows: "Best" quality guns had no letter with the serial number; "B"-grade guns were made in the "trade" (local artisans and gunmakers) but were finished and regulated by the principal firm; and "C"-grade 2nd quality and "E"-grade 3rd quality guns were similarly produced for such firms as Purdey, Westley Richards, and Holland & Holland on occasion (see appropriate chapters). Alternatively, the gun may have been made entirely "in the trade" and sold as a "gun made for" a specific firm such as Cogswell & Harrison (see Cogswell & Harrison chapter). This designation would appear on the rib of the barrel.

In virtually all cases, the specifically serial-numbered and named 410s of the 1880s and 1890s era were single- or double-barrel back-action sidelock hammer guns or were "walking stick" guns. It would appear that the manufacture of great hammer or hammerless bar-action sidelock and "Best" quality A&D boxlock guns in the 410 bore did not begin in earnest until after the turn of the 20th century. For example, Greener manufactured its first bar-action sidelock 410 in 1914 (see Greener chapter). This was a double-barrel hammer gun.

The first hammerless bar-action sidelock "Best" quality 410s built by the London firms essentially began in the 1920s when Harry Lawrence created Purdey's first "Best" quality hammerless sidelock bar-action 410. He called this his greatest achievement in conjunction with the three miniature guns that he built for King George V's 1935 Silver Jubilee. Parenthetically, these three miniature guns were 1/6 the size of the 12-bore hammer guns that were used by the King in his recreational pursuits. All three work and fire cartridges specifically made for the miniaturized guns (Photo 2). Lawrence's ranking of Purdey's first hammerless 410 with the Silver Jubilee accomplishments is quite an accolade [18].

Photo 2: Harry Lawrence and ∧ one of the three working miniature guns for King George V.

Purdey photo

The American high-quality double-barrel 410 introduced in the late 1920s had a different genesis. This great American shotgun story, bought to fruition by the classic American manufacturers of double guns, does not begin until the late 1920s. Unlike their British brothers, the American double 410 bore was in response to the demands of the clay target and upland game bird shooter. Four companies manufactured these quality 410 double guns: Parker Brothers, Ithaca, L.C. Smith, and Winchester. The 410 story of each company, to the extent known, will be discussed along with those of other companies in lesser detail.

410 Rook Rifle Conversion (see Rook Rifle chapter)

An interesting side note is the evolution in the last three decades of the 19th century of the Rook & Rabbit rifle. These were made by virtually all quality gunmakers including Purdey, Holland & Holland, Westley Richards, Boss, and Rigby. William Tranter invented this centerfire rifle in 1866. They were bored for various cartridges from 200 to 300+ calibers. When the cheaper 22 rimfire cartridge came along, this class of rifle vanished [38]. Many of these Rook rifles, particularly those in 300+ bore, were converted to 410 shotguns. Very few Rook rifles remain today in their pristine and original form.

The Tranter connection is of further interest since the Rook & Rabbit rifle was sold by W. Watson & Son who appear to be the forerunner of the Watson Bros., a firm that specialized in small-bore guns.

Boxlock and Bolt-Action 410s

Before World War II, the British imported many low-priced 410s from Belgium as folding single-barrel or double-barrel boxlock guns with 2-inch chambers. For the most part, these were neglected, wrecked, or destroyed [1]. Between the two world wars, the British boxlock A&D 410 was a well-crafted high-quality double for local consumption and for exportation to Indian, African, and Australian markets. Makers such as Churchill, Jeffery, Wilkes, Westley Richards, Cogswell & Harrison, Webley & Scott, and many provincial firms such as Gallyon & Son, made the occasional 410 on the A&D action.

During World War II and after, cheaply priced European imports accounted for a large percentage of 410s in Great Britain, for the average shooter. These were used by young beginners, vermin and rabbit shooters, taxidermists, and during World War II to "feed the troops" [39]. Correspondence to the *Shooting Times & Country Magazine* frequently mentions with warmth the use of the 410 to "shoot a mink" [40] and to shoot "thousands of rabbits" for decades, and once mastered after "years of practice," is a "brilliant little gun" [41].

In the immediate post-World War II era, the 410 shotgun made up 6 percent of annual sales of all shotguns in Great Britain. The large majority were single-barrel bolt-action guns built by such firms as B.S.A. and Webley & Scott.

Boxlock A&D double 410s continued to be made, though rarely, after World War II by the above-mentioned gunmakers. For example, the Webley & Scott A&D 410, which was started in the first quarter of the 20th century as a 400 series gun, found a market for only three 410s after World War II. It was by then called a 700 series gun, reflecting modest cosmetic advances (see gunmaker chapters).

Sidelock Guns

It was not until after World War II that the expensively made bar-action sidelock 410s became well known, mostly catering to the American market. The large majority of Purdey's hammerless bar-action 410s were manufactured after World War II (see Purdey chapter). Holland & Holland manufactured its first recorded bar-action hammerless sidelock in 1963 (see Holland & Holland chapter). Large majorities of the rare "Best" quality 410s by Westley Richards, Wilkes, and Boss have been manufactured since World War II, again for the American market. The Westley Richards "Best" quality drop-lock is a singular exception in that they made several for export trade to an affluent clientele in India between the two world wars (see Westley Richards chapter).

Conclusion

We have seen several transitions in the 410 bore. In England, they had been initially made as a walking stick and then as a back-action hammer sidelock gun. This was followed by the hammerless sidelock and boxlock doubles. There was a corresponding transition from a 2-inch to eventually a 3-inch shell. A further evolution occurred in the quality and in the nature of the action such that the post-World War II era 410s, most of the "Best" 410s of British manufacture, were bar-actions. This is not to say that they did not make a high-quality boxlock 410 for the domestic and export trade, especially by firms such as Webley & Scott, Churchill, Jeffery, and Westley Richards.

In America, the 410 was introduced as a single-barrel inexpensive gun during and just after World War I. The high-grade double 410s introduced in the middle to late 1920s in America were not manufactured to any significant extent after World War II. Various very well made 410s continue to be available in the American market from several popular manufacturers including Browning, Winchester, Remington, Mossberg, Stevens, and Marlin.

It was in the early 1950s when Ithaca and Smith ceased their double gun production of all gauges. The Winchester Model 21 410 was introduced after World War II and ceased effective production in the mid-1960s (see Winchester chapter). A Browning over/under, manufactured in Belgium, represented a high quality double and is still being manufactured under special circumstances (see Browning chapter). As in England, the shell progressed from a 2-inch to a 2 1/2-inch, and finally to a 3-inch shell with continued use of a 2 1/2-inch shell in skeet shooting.

In the following chapters, I will make an effort to detail and summarize existing knowledge of the 410 gauge for various important manufacturers. This will include the American and British firms with additional sections on the Browning Belgium 410. The intent of this book is to provide a substrate of documented and reliable data upon which others can build in the future. The hope is to provide some evidentiary basis for what is otherwise a pure art form of 410 shooting and collecting.

The final purpose of the book is to persuade the reader that the beauty of shooting a 410, especially for the young, is that the rewards of patience and good form are a broken target and harvested game.

The Genesis of the 410 Gauge References

1. Cradock, Chris, *Cradock on Shotguns*, 1989, B.T. Batsford, Ltd., London.
2. Personal communication, 1985.
3. Personal communication, 1995.
4. Personal communication, 2001.
5. Tate, Douglas, *Birmingham Gunmakers*, Safari Press, Inc., 1997.
6. Author's review, London Proof House records.
7. Geeener, W.W., *The Gun and Its Development*, 9th Ed., 1910, Cassell & Company, Ltd.
8. Greener, W.W., *The Gun and Its Development*, 2nd Ed., 1884, Cassell & Company, Ltd.
9. Personal communication, 1996.
10. O'Connor, Jack, *The Shotgun Book*, 1965, Alfred A. Knopf, New York.
10A. Anderson, Robert, *Jack O'Connor*, 2002, Safari Press, Inc., Long Beach, California.
11. Personal communication, 1981.
12. Askins, Charles, *Modern Shotguns and Loads*, 1929, Small Arms Technical.
13. Askins, Bill, *Petersen's Hunting*, December 1988, Petersen's Publishing Company.
14. Keith, Elmer, *Shotgun*, 1967, Bonanza Books.
15. McIntosh, Michael, *Shotguns and Shooting*, 1995, Country Sport Press.
16. Personal communication, 1979.
17. Zutz, Don, *The Double Shotgun*, 1985, Winchester Press.
18. Personal communication, 1982.
19. Personal communication, 1978.
20. Boothroyd, Geoffrey, *Sidekicks and Box Locks*, 1991, Sandlake Press.
21. Hastings, MacDonald, *The Shotgun*, 1981, David & Charles, Newton Abbott, London.
22. George, J.H., *English Guns & Rifles*, 1947, Small-Arms Technical Publishing Company.
23. Pollard, H.B.C., *A History of Firearms*, 1926, Geoffrey Bles, London.
24. Blackmore, H.L., *Hunting Weapons*, 1971, Barrie & Jenkins, London.
25. Bailey, Dewitt and Nie, Douglas A., *English Gunmakers*, 1978, Arms & Armour Press, London.
26. Author's review, London & Birmingham Proof House Records.
27. Crudgington, I.M., *The British Shotgun*, Vol. One 1850-1870, 1979 Barrie & Jenkins, London.
28. Maker's record books examined by author.
29. Personal communication, 1996.
30. Akehurst, Richard, *Game Guns and Rifles*, 1969, G. Bell & Sons, London.
31. Jackson, Tony, *Shooting Times & Country Magazine*, 1990, June 21
32. Maker's record books examined by author.
33. Greener, W.W., *Modern Shotguns*, 1891, Cassell & Company, Ltd.
34. Crudgington, I.M. and Baker, D.J., *The British Shotgun* Vol. Two, 1871-1890, 1989 Ashford.
35. Boothroyd, Geoffrey, *The Shotgun History & Development*, 1985, A. & C. Black, London.
36. Boothroyd, Geoffrey, *Shotguns and Gunsmiths*, 1986, A. & C. Black, London.
37. Maker's record books examined by author.
38. Boothroyd, Geoffrey, *STCM*, 1990, May-June.
39. *STCM*, May 9-15 1991.
40. *STCM*, May 2-8, 1991.
41. *STCM*, November 21-27, 1991.

CHAPTER TWO

THE 410 CARTRIDGE

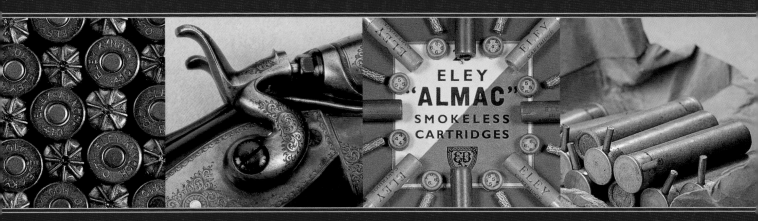

One way of researching the origins of the 410 shotgun is to review the history of the 410 cartridge. The cartridge may have germinated from the old 44-40 caliber rifle cartridge used famously in the Winchester Model 1873, the Winchester Model 1892 lever action, and the Marlin Model 1894 lever action rifles. The very rare Colt Model Ring Lever used the caliber in 1837, as did the somewhat more common Colt-Burgess Lever in 1883. The Remington Sporting Rifle, beginning in 1888, and the Remington Rolling Block Carbine of 1892 both used the 44-40 cartridge.

Jack O'Connor argued the 410 smoothbore cartridges evolved in America from the 44 XL that were "shot shells in rifle cases" and used for small game [1].

The 410-bore diameter is .410 inch or 10.414 millimeters, and therefore, differs from all other gauges in its nomenclature. Gauges 4 through 32 are derived from the number of pure lead balls fitting a given diameter, whose total weight equals one pound. According to Boothroyd, this comes from the days of muzzleloading artillery when the size of a gun was measured not by its internal diameter but by the weight of the spherical shot [2].

Photo 1: E.J. Churchill 36-gauge smoothbore, SN 4964, a 1934 gun with heavy but worn engraving.

Paul Goodwin photo

Photo 4: 36-gauge centerfire cartridges, circa 1890-1910.

Tom Grange photo

Photo 2: E.M. Reilly 36-gauge smoothbore, SN 23746, black-powder proofed, a pre-1900 back action.

Paul Goodwin photo

For example, 12 balls for the 12 bore equals one pound and 28 balls for the 28 bore equals one pound. In this normative classification, the 410 bore is a 67 gauge, very much smaller than the next larger gauge, the 36 (.506 inch). The 12 bore has a .729-inch diameter and the 28 bore a .550-inch diameter or approximately 14 millimeters. The British Proof Houses accept as the 410 gauge a bore internal diameter varying from .405 to .415 inch.

It should be noted that an even smaller smooth"bore", the very rare "36-gauge" smoothbore, was in fact a .36-inch (9.14-millimeter) gun, smaller than the 410. Churchill built such a *centerfire* gun, as did Bland, E.M. Reilly, and Greener on a very rare occasion for the small bird collector (Photos 1-3). Also pictured is a group of .36-inch centerfire cartridges, circa 1890 (Photo 4). These cartridges were 1 3/4-inch length with 3/16-ounce shot propelled by black or smokeless powder.

In 1967, Webley & Scott had built a "No. 3-bore garden gun" in 9-millimeter caliber, which shot a *rimfire* cartridge (Photo 5). Rimfire .36-inch cartridges were first available in 1890 for handguns for pest control. In America, the Winchester Model 36, made from 1920 to 1924, was a rimfire 9-millimeter bolt-action smoothbore for pest control (see Webley & Scott chapter).

Crudgington & Baker document a 12-millimeter blackpowder walking stick gun patented in 1876, which may have been made at that time [3]. However, the first reference to a 12-millimeter cartridge is in 1886 as indicated below.

Photo 5: 9-millimeter (#3) rimfire shell shot cartridges, circa 1900-1910.

Tom Grange photo

In Geoffrey Boothroyd's resume of the four cartridge types historically known—centerfire, pinfire, rimfire, and basefire—only the first two were ever produced for 410 shell shot [4]. The knowledge that pinfire 410 cartridges exist does not imply that the gauge existed in the mid-1800s when the pinfire shotgun was first developed in England and Europe. In fact, the pinfire gun was in common use into the early 1900s, especially in southern Europe (Spain, Italy, Greece, etc.). These included a rare 410 (see Interesting Types chapter). There is no evidence for the existence of a British 410-gauge pinfire shotgun.

The pinfire 410 cartridge, along with the .36-inch shotshell seems to have disappeared in both Great Britain and Europe after World War I as a catalog item. However, there is evidence that it continued in use up until World War II, at least in Italy, and was manufactured by local European firms.

England

Tom Grange of Bourne, England, an authority on the British cartridge, has unearthed a box of short 7/8-inch shotshell 410 cartridges which may be of "just after" 1880 vintage [5] (Photo 6). These were intended for a smoothbore 410 handgun.

Peter McGowan and Jim Buchanan, two other well-known British cartridge collectors, assisted this writer in researching British cartridge catalogs. This proved to be both fascinating and helpful in establishing the temporal origins and evolution of the 410 cartridge.

The Kynoch and Eley Brothers posters, boards, and catalogs of the 1860s and 1870s do not mention the 410-gauge cartridge. With the help of C.W. Harding, the Birmingham Proof House historian and archivist, two 1880's references were unearthed [6]. In a June 1882 advertisement, a 410-shotgun cartridge is listed for use in Rook rifles. Described as "Perfect" and "Gastight", it is a 2-inch cartridge with black powder loading.

Photo 3: These Reilly (top) & Churchill (bottom) 36-gauge guns make a unique pair.

∨   *Paul Goodwin photo*

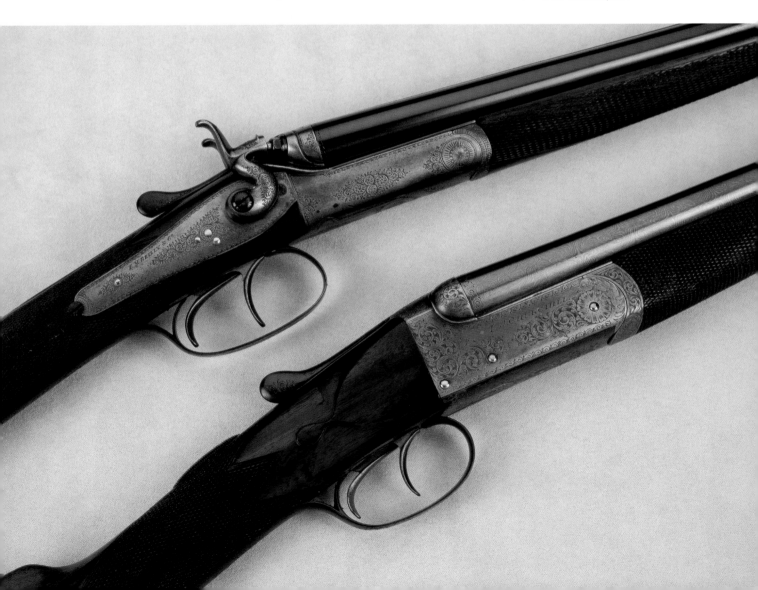

<

Photo 6: Very short (7/8-inch) 410 shot cartridges.

Tom Grange photo

Photo 7: Eley pinfire cartridges, circa 1885.

Cameo photo ∨

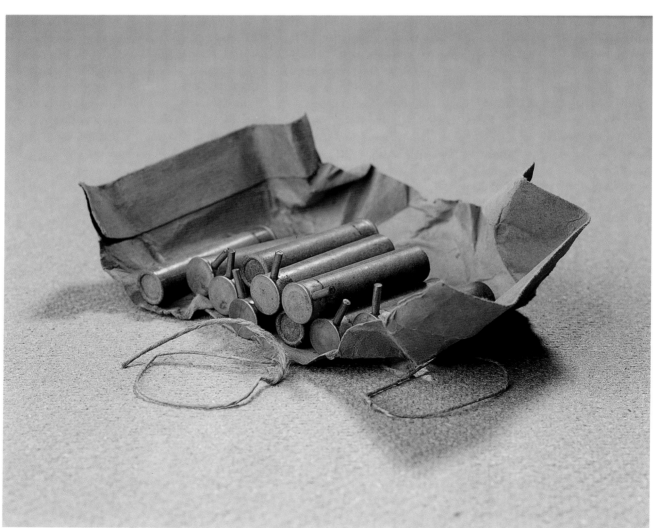

>

Photo 8: "Crimped" all brass Eley cartridges of the late 1920s. According to Tom Grange, a British cartridge specialist, crimping was not used in Great Britain on paper cartridges until after World War II.

Cameo photo

An 1884 catalog lists a "Perfect cartridge, which includes the gauge .410".

In the European cartridge literature, a French catalog from 1886, *Societe Francais de Munitions*, describes a 12-millimeter shotshell. The 12 mm is slightly larger than the .410-inch caliber but has been considered the European equivalent of the British-American 410 gauge. (I have safely shot 410 cartridges through several 12-millimeter smoothbores; however, before anyone else does so, a gunsmith should verify the safety of each 12-millimeter smoothbore for the 410 cartridge.)

The 410 cartridge appears in magazine advertisements as early as 1882 in the *Shooting Times* and *The Field*. An Eley green, gas-tight, 2-inch 410 cartridge of 1885 confirms this gauge's production in England in appreciable numbers by the mid-1880s. A packet of ten green pinfire 410 shell shot casings produced in 1885 further supports the 410 gauge production in this configuration (Photo 7).

An F. Joyce catalog of 1891 lists a 410-revolver cartridge that may have been a shotshell. The 1891 Kynoch catalog lists the 410 and the 12-millimeter cartridge "for rook rifles"; yet they are loaded with 3/8-ounce shot, clearly shotshell cartridges. The 2-inch cases are described either as "Gastight" in maroon or green, or as 12-millimeter Solid Thin Brass cartridges, re-loadable "100" times.

The 1892 Eley Brothers catalog describes a green Extra Quality Gastight, 2-inch, 3/8-ounce, 410 cartridge and a similar pinfire 410 cartridge. The 1893 Eley Brothers catalog includes a Solid Drawn Brass 410. An 1897 Kynoch catalog duplicates its 1891 literature.

Eley Brothers catalogs of 1896 and 1901 offer 410 shotgun cartridges with either "Extra Quality" green paper or brass.

Notwithstanding the 1880s and 1990s catalog information regarding the 410 cartridge, a major compendium of experiments with gunpowders and cartridges of the last two decades of the 19th century does not reveal a single 410 study [7]. The data had been published in scientific journals and then summarized in *The Field*, the definitive gun publication of the 19th and early 20th century. They detailed all bores from 4 through 32, but contained not a word about the 410.

There is a particularly interesting set of ballistic studies published in 1885 regarding the "bursting of small—bore guns" causing a "great amount of mischief." Small-bore barrels were made thinner and did not stand up despite a corresponding reduction in powder charge. This is now a well-understood aspect of ballistic physics. Then, experimental trial and error discovered that with the smaller bore diameter, the tons of pressure per square inch inside the barrel is greater than in a larger bore (despite a sharp reduction in drams of powder), ranging from 1 to 5 tons per square inch.

Returning to the cartridge study, an 1898-99 Kynoch price list and the 1899 Eley Brothers catalog list respectively the 410 "Perfectly Gastight" centerfire "Warranted" 2-inch Paper or "Metallic" cartridge and the 410 "Thin Brass". The latter catalog offered a pinfire 410 cartridge to accommodate the rare pinfire shotgun imported from southern Europe. The 1901 Eley Brothers catalog is the same as the 1899, but the 1902 shows a new "Improved Gastight" with double heads. Both the 1902 and 1905 catalogs list a 410 pinfire gauge.

The three Kynoch 1901 through 1905 catalogs are essentially unchanged. Then the 1908 Kynoch drops the 410 brass cartridge. The 1908-1909 Eley Brothers catalog has a one-fourth-page advertisement listing both the 410 and the .360-inch shot cartridges. It describes the 410 as 2 inches in length with 3/8-ounce shot and "Black Powder" or "Smokeless" priced at 5 shillings per 100 loaded cartridges. There is a colored picture of the 2-inch "Fourten". No longer listed at this point is the pinfire 410.

The 1910-1911 (No. 83) Eley Brothers catalog reintroduces the "Gastight" pinfire 410 and the "Thin Brass" is replaced exclusively by the "Solid Drawn Brass". Nobel's Explosives catalog of 1911-12 lists a 410 2-inch cartridge with Black or Smokeless Powder.

Harding reports that an Eley Factory Loading Manual lists a 2 1/2-inch 410 cartridge in January 1911 [9]. A Kynoch 1911 catalog, for the first time, offers a 2 1/2-inch 410 cartridge. This appears to be the introduction of the 2 1/2-inch 410 cartridge. A Bonehill catalog of 1909-1913 introduces a 2 1/2-inch purpose built smoothbore 410 gun. I am unaware of an earlier 2 1/2-inch 410 smoothbore offering.

A 1913 Curtis & Harvey catalog, *The Powdermakers*, advertised a 410 2-inch "Smokeless" cartridge. The Eley 1914-15 catalog (No. 85) offered the "Fourten" 2-inch and the "Fourlong" 2 1/2-inch 410 cartridge. Solid Brass and pinfire 410 cartridges were still available at that time. The Nobel Industries 1925 brochure lists the 2-inch "Fourten" and the 2 1/2-inch "Fourlong".

The Eley Brothers 1919 catalog (No. 86) drops the pinfire and all brass shells. Here, two points are worth elaborating. First, brass 410 cartridges were still made from 1927 to 1939 under the imprint of "ICI". The "crimping" of these brass shells under "ICI" specifically signals the dates of production [8] (Photo 8).

Secondly, the production of pinfire 410 shellshot cartridges raises the possibility of this smoothbore gauge gun having been produced before the 1880s after the origination of this ignition system in 1836. However, all existing cartridge literature

Photo 9: Cartridges matching the vintage 410 "Best" Watson.

∨   *Glenn Campbell photo*

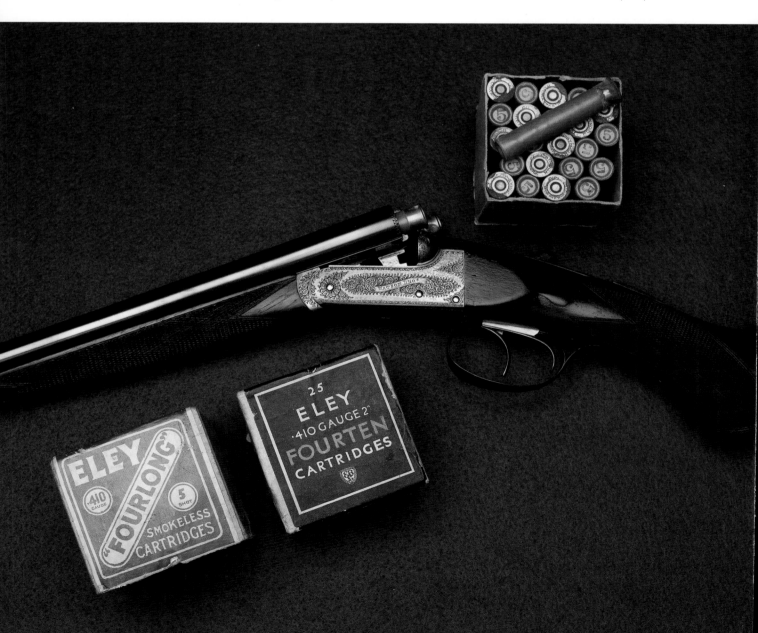

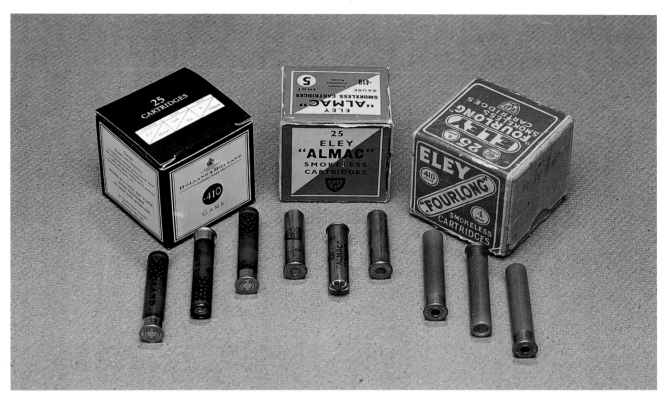

Photo 10: An array of brass, vintage paper and modern 410 shot shells.

Cameo photo

Photos 11 & 12: 410 loading equipment and various cartridges.

Cameo and Tom Grange photos

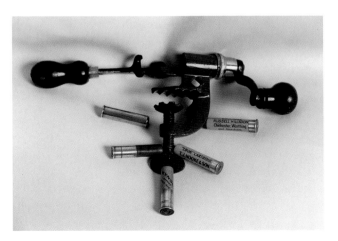

indicates that the pinfire 410 cartridge was introduced after the centerfire 410 in the Eley Brothers and Kynoch catalogs and flyers. Furthermore, as C.W. Harding observed, the pinfire construction, given the "protruding pin and high rise hammer", would not be practical on a cane gun because of, among other reasons, lack of concealability [9].

It is worth noting here that the Eley 2 1/2-inch "Fourlong" contained 7/16-ounce shot and was recommended for small ground and wing game. The 2-inch "410" was a "collector's cartridge" for shooting without "damaging" small birds by the naturalist for taxidermy (Photos 9 and 10).

Typical British 410 loading equipment pre-World War I illustrates the variety of personalized and types of cartridges made throughout the early 20th century (Photos 11 and 12).

Photo 13: A wooden box of 2 1/2-inch 410 (12 mm) cartridges. Note the mistaken use of the "36 GA." under "410."

Glenn Campbell photo

Photo 14: Boxes of "Super X" shot shells, single ball and non-corrosive primers.

Glenn Campbell photo >

Photo 16 (bottom, right): More brands of 410 shot shells.

Glenn Campbell photo

Photo 15: Full boxes of cartridges under different brands.

Glenn Campbell photo >

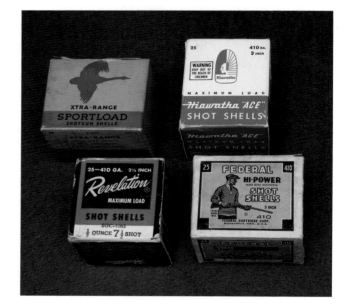

America

The European and American 410 cartridge story is far more obscure for the former and more recent for the latter. Geoffrey Boothroyd suggests that the 410 originated in Germany as the 12 millimeter. However, no specific European data could be found to provide further specifics except for the previously noted French ammunition list *Societe Francais de Munitions* of 1886, which offered a 12-millimeter shotshell.

As for America, a "Colt Firearms and Cartridge" catalog of 1888 did not offer a 410 shotshell. A series of "Winchester Arms and Cartridges" catalogs of 1875, 1878, 1891, and 1893 did not list the 410-gauge shell. Although Winchester began making 410 cartridges in 1916 and included a 2-inch shell in a 1916 catalog, the first detailed catalog listing appears to be in 1925. They described the gauge as a "410 caliber 12 m/m" with "bulk powder only" and "chilled shot only" in either 2 or 2 1/2-inch shells, a quaint but descriptive promotion (Photo 13). Interestingly, Boothroyd has a Remington cartridge head stamp that says both 410 and 12 millimeter [10].

A 1905 "Union Metallic Cartridge Co." catalog lists cartridges from 4 through 28 bore, but nothing for 410. The "United States Cartridge Company" catalogs of 1881, 1891, 1908, and 1917 make no mention of a 410 gauge. An 1885 and 1910 Remington gun and cartridge catalog makes no mention of the 410, and did not list the cartridge until 1915 when they advertised a 1 1/2-inch shell.

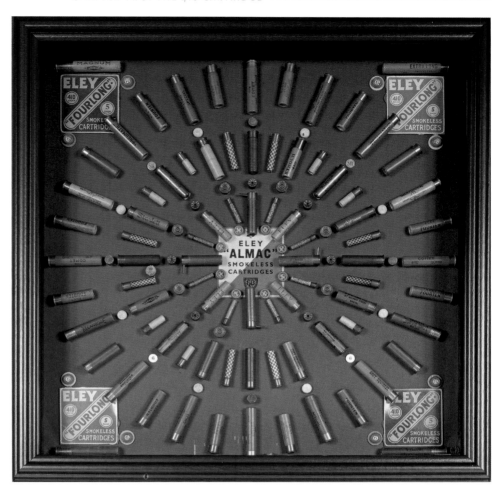

>

Photo 17: A cartridge board of 410 and smaller cartridges by Ronnie Crowe.

Ronnie Crowe photo

A wide variety of makers, types, and labels of 410 cartridges have appeared on the American market. The "Western Super X" brand dominated the pre-World War II era (Photo 14) and illustrates the early use of non-corrosive primers in America. This has resulted in greater survivability of American 410 barrels over that seen in the British Isles. In Britain, the use of fulminate of mercury and potassium chlorate as primers in the 410 cartridge well beyond World War II into the early 1950s, unlike bigger bore cartridges, resulted in a high rate of destruction of 410 barrels due to the deposition of the highly corrosive mercury/potassium salts. Illustrated are pre- and post-World War II boxes of

cartridges of different makers and types. Note Remington's misuse of the 410 cartridge as a "36 ga" (Photos 15 and 16).

Today, 410 cartridge collecting is a serious endeavor. A unique cartridge board, which includes many paper, brass, and pinfire 410 cartridges and a number of smaller cartridges such as the .36-inch shell, illustrates the remarkable variety and decorative beauty of the historical very small bore shell (Photo 17). This was made by Ronnie Crowe, an authority on the British cartridge, and once an owner of a European made pinfire 410.

The 410 Cartridge References

1. O'Connor, Jack, *The Shotgun Book,* Alfred A. Knopf, 1965.
2. Boothroyd, Geoffrey, *Boothroyd on British Shotguns,* Sand Lake Press, 1993.
3. Crudgington, I.M. and Baker, D.J., *The British Shotgun* Vol II, 1871-1890, Ashford, Southampton 1989.
4. Boothroyd, Geoffrey, *Shooting Times & Country Magazine,* August 18-24, 1994.
5. Grange, Tom, 2001, *Shooting Gazette,* December.
6. Hedlung, Dale J., *Kynoch,* Spectrum Books, 2000.
7. Cox, Horace, *Sporting Guns and Gunpowders,* London 1897.
8. Grange, Tom, personal communication 2002.
9. Harding, C.W., personal communication 2002.
10. Personal communication 1990.

CHAPTER THREE

BALLISTICS OF THE 410 CARTRIDGE

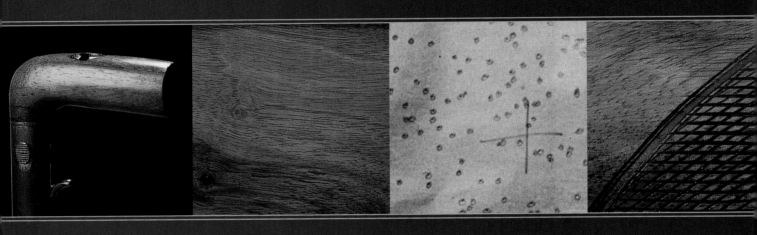

History

HAlthough the 410 shotgun appears in British Proof House records as early as the 1870s, Greener did not mention this bore in 1884 [1]. He discussed Rook rifles from 295 through 380 caliber with box or back-action locks, hammer or hammerless, breech opening, usually single-barrel guns. He discussed the Express rifles up to 600 caliber. He discussed all smoothbores from 4 through 28, but not the 410. He discussed "walking stick guns" but not in the 410 bore.

In 1891, Greener again reviewed in detail all bores up to the 28 and, once again, was essentially silent on the 410. However, he did list in a chart the 410 bore as requiring a 2-inch cartridge with 3/8-ounce shot and 3/4-dram powder [2].

The "Archives of The Guild" at the London Proof House reveal a set of "Instructions to Proof Master" for the 410 bore [3]. A February 23, 1887, instruction ordered "the 410 bore for nitro proof to be proofed with 1-1/4 drams* (34 grains) of powder** and 1/2-ounce shot." A September 29, 1903, document reports that the London Proof House proofed the walking stick 410 in the "same manner" as at the Birmingham House. The provisional proof used 2-1/4 drams with 3/8-ounce (164 grains) shot. The definitive proof used 3/4 dram with 3/8-ounce shot, and 1-1/2 drams (41 grains) with 1/2-ounce (218 grains) shot.

An August 4, 1904, letter from Mr. Turner of the London Proof House to Mr. Athol Purdey, discussed the 410 being "bored up" from 400 to 405, 410, or 415 with the .005 allowance for this bore "quite enough." A firm English directive typically couched in velvet. At this time, the 1904 Rules of Proof required for nitro proofing 1-1/4 drams (34 grains) of "T.S. No. 2 Powder" and 9/16-ounce (245 grains) shot. This is confirmed by Greener in 1910 in which proofing the 410 bore required 1-1/4 drams of powder for 9/16-ounce shot charge. This was modified November 2, 1911, when the drams were increased to 1-1/2 for both 2-inch and 2 1/2-inch cartridges for nitro proofing.

Six days later, on November 8, 1911, perhaps after a bottle of claret plentifully stocked in the bowels of the London Proof House, the 2-inch cartridge proofing was changed back to 1-1/4 drams for the 9/16-ounce shot. The 2 1/2-inch cartridge was kept at 1-1/2 drams for a larger 11/16-ounce (302 grains) shot—clearly an empirical decision!

It appears that in England the 410 cartridge is a direct descendant of the 44-40 rifle cartridge [6]. This cartridge is analogous to the American 44 XL pest cartridge that O'Connor claims is the progenitor of the 410 smoothbore cartridge [7]. Remember, the 410 bore is a caliber .41 inch and is equivalent to a 67 gauge. For example, the 12 gauge has a bore diameter of .729 inch, the 28 gauge .550 inch, and the 410 gauge .410 inch or 10.414 millimeters.

Breech-loading Walking-stick Gun.

Photo 1: Greener's illustration of ∧
a cane 410 smoothbore.

Glenn Campbell photo

Originally a bottleneck configuration with a paper shot container, it was followed by a 2-inch straight brass case. This led to a 2-inch paper case with 3/8-ounce shot and by 1900 to a 2 1/2-inch case with 1/2-ounce shot. In early 20th century America, shotgun shooters were making 410 brass shot shell cases from 444 Marlin rifle cartridges [5].

The smallest bore Greener discusses in his subchapter on "Small Bore" game guns is the 28 gauge. He recommends this bore as a first gun for boys or young women. It is "the smallest caliber of any practical use as a game gun" [6]. This observation may be the genesis, in part, for the 410 phobia retailed by the gun gurus of the middle third of the 20th century in America such as Askins, Keith, and O'Connor.

Later gun writers described the 410 as a "misunderstood" gun, using the language of psychology to explain a utilitarian concept. Namely, that this gauge is not a beginner's gun but one for the expert and its use is limited to taking game for the pot or for shooting clay targets [5].

So, the 410 "hasn't much use"? Did anyone not start with a 410 and bag plenty of game or clay targets? Even more recently, and by someone who knows better, McIntosh confesses to a "bad attitude" towards the 410 as a game gun. The cartridge is a "patchy-shooting, bird-crippling piece of ballistic crap." In partial atonement, he admits that 410 skeet shooting is "great fun" [8].

Greener's one allusion to the 410, as late as 1910, is its use "by naturalists or for such weapons as walking stick guns." He shows one such walking stick 410 (page 517), which is identical to one that recently surfaced in Scotland [6] (Photos 1 and 2). This reference, by the way, under section entitled "Odd Size", recalls Askins' reference to gender ambivalence! [9]

The Cartridge and Gun

Notwithstanding his contempt for the 410 bore, Askins discussed the ballistics of a 2-inch cartridge with 3/8-ounce shot for small wing game [9]. For quail shooting, he thought it best to use No. 8 shot with a full choke barrel. Of 150 pellets in the charge, 105 will be in the pattern at 40 yards with 0.85 pounds of energy per pellet delivered to the bird and a kill requires 2.25 pounds or three hits. For snipe, he recommended No. 10 shot giving 366 pellets in the charge, of which 329 will be in the pattern at 35 yards and 225 at 40 yards. Energy delivered to the bird, in this instance, is 0.54 pounds per pellet, and a kill requires 0.89 pounds or two hits.

*"**Dram**" is a term of measurement equaling 27.34 grains (1/16 ounce) and originates from the black-powder days of the 19th century. The use of the term in modern smokeless cartridges is a misuse. For example, a 3 1/4-dram 12-gauge load contains less than one dram of smokeless powder. Joseph Manton's typical 12-gauge shot shell load in 1800 consisted of 1-1/4 ounces of shot and 3-1/2 drams of blackpowder. Today, the use of "dram" is, in fact, "dram equivalent," meaning the amount of smokeless powder used that is equivalent in propellant powder to the number of drams required of black-powder. For example, one dram of blackpowder performance significantly differs from that of 27.34 grains of smokeless powder. The term is of historical and aesthetic interest and should be honored by its retirement.

"Powder**" has an extraordinarily simple history in comparison to the complex destruction wrought by its use in the good hands of the human species. By the 9th century, the Chinese were producing stable explosives and propellants from a combination of saltpeter, charcoal, and sulfur [4]. Saltpeter, as potassium nitrate, created oxygen and charcoal and sulfur provided the fuel.[1] The elimination of potassium salts, very corrosive to barrels, was accomplished by the nitration of glycerin in the 1840s. The result was nitroglycerin. Later other organic substances replaced glycerin such as wood pulp and cotton. When cotton, a cellulose, was treated with nitric and sulfuric acids, the result was nitrocellulose.[2] This propellant, a single base powder, is the primary American powder [5]. The British historically have tended to use a double base powder, a combination of nitrocellulose and nitroglycerin, otherwise known as cordite. The British powders have been very corrosive on barrels. When combined with primers compounded of fulminate of mercury, which turned to salt when combusted, the result was deep pitting of barrels. A primary reason why so few vintage 410 British shotguns exist today is that the 410 cartridge was the last to eliminate mercury from the cartridge and did not do so routinely until after 1950.

---

[1]This is the basis for blackpowder, which generated force by heat expansion.
[2]This powder, smokeless, generated force by gas escaping under high pressure.

<

Photo 2: Action and stock of an English cane 410 smoothbore.

Cameo photo

Interestingly, as he wrote this, the 1920s had been the decade when the 410-bore cartridge was dominated by the 2 1/2-inch case with 7/16-ounce shot for small game and 1/2-ounce shot for American skeet shooting, of which Askins was apparently oblivious [10].

O'Connor called the 2 1/2-inch cartridge the "sub-small bore" and the 3-inch case with 3/4-ounce shot, pioneered by Winchester-Western in the early 1930s, the "small bore" [7]. These cartridges were chambered by a wide variety of American 410s in the 1920s and 1930s.

The American 410 bore in the late 1920s and 1930s included the premier double-barrel side-by-sides such as Parker, L.C. Smith, and Ithaca. Lesser quality but well-made doubles included Ithaca's Grade A Lefever manufactured from 1934 to 1942, L.C. Smith's Hunter Special, The Fulton manufactured from approximately 1930 to 1951, and the Marlin Model 90 over/under manufactured from 1939 to 1952.

A number of cheaper 4l0s were developed prior to and subsequent to the classic doubles in boxlock, bolt, pump, hammer, or lever action and in various single- and double-barrel configura-

tions built for the 2 1/2- and 3-inch cartridges. These included the famous but short-lived Marlin 410 lever action, the Remington 11/48, the Noble 410 semi-automatic, the Stevens over/under 410/22, and the Savage Model 99 takedown with interchangeable 410-smoothbore and 300-caliber rifle barrels.

These also included the post-World War I Winchester Model 20, a boxlock hammer gun manufactured between 1919 and 1924; the Winchester Model 37 top-lever break-open action manufactured between 1936 and 1963; the Winchester Model 41 bolt-action single-shot 410 manufactured between 1920 and 1934; and the Iver Johnson Champion single-barrel hammer with auto ejectors manufactured from 1909 to 1956. Iver Johnson also made a Hercules-grade 410 double-barrel hammerless boxlock from post-World War I to 1948. Savage-Stevens made a boxlock side-by-side double. Crescent made a serviceable back-action sidelock between the two world wars. In the 1930s, the premier single-barrel 410 was the Winchester Model 42 (for details of the above guns, see relevant chapters).

Barrel chambers were available for the 2 1/2- and 3-inch cartridge. The latter cartridge proved to be very effective in the field for small wing and ground game.

It is estimated that 4 to 10 percent of all shotguns sold in America in the middle third of the 20th century were 410 bore [7]. Eley, who currently supplies 60 percent of cartridges in Great Britain, reports that in a sample 3-year period in the 1970s, 6 percent of all cartridges sold were 410 bore, second to the 12 bore which was 87 percent.

Keith, after many caustic comments such as its use to "bag game shows damn little intelligence", concedes that the 410 can be used effectively under 30 yards for quail, dove, woodcock, snipe, and ruffled grouse if a 3-inch, 3/4-ounce cartridge is employed [11]. He patterned a 2 1/2-inch, 7 1/2-shot cartridge using the lever-action Marlin 410. At 40 yards, using a 30-inch pattern, three or more pellets would hit a pheasant or mallard. Using a Marlin over/under Model 90, with the same cartridge, at 40 yards, four or five pellets would hit a big bird. At 35 yards, there would be enough force to kill a grouse or a duck. He recommended a full choke for greater kill density and a No. 8 shot for a denser pattern.

By the 1960s, a resurgence of interest in the 410 occurred in target shooting, and the 1970s saw a maturing development of interest in 410 collecting. In the 1980s, there was widespread use of the modern 410 for appropriate small wing and ground game by the sportsman shot gunner.

Today

William Hovey Smith, an American moviemaker, wrote enthusiastically about the hunting and ballistic capabilities of the 410 [12]. He, like other shotgun writers of the 1980s and early 1990s, extols the merits of the 410 as both a practical gun for close-range shooting (15 to 30 yards), producing minimal game destruction, as well as a challenging bore for the shooter who fancies a challenge. Smith's first 410, as for so many of us, was the Stevens over/under 410/22. From this, he progressed to the Savage-Stevens side-by-side 410.

Smith argued for modified and full chokes to minimize cripples and escaped but wounded game. The 3-inch cartridge with 11/16- to 3/4-ounce shot gives a maximum effective killing range of 25 yards for 8 shot and 30 yards for 7-1/2 shot. He uses the same ounce of shot with 5 or 6 shot for rabbit and squirrel that loads 117 and 151 pellets respectively. For quail, dove, or woodcock, he prefers 7-1/2, 8, or 9 shot that loads 234, 280, and 392 pellets respectively. Interestingly, the 392-pellet No. 9 shot 410 cartridge compares favorably with the 400-pellet No. 8 shot cartridge in bigger bores.

The 410 has become more than a "misbegotten" gauge reserved for the taxidermist or small kids.

A recent ballistic assessment for the modern 410 loads proves very reassuring for the game shooter [13]. The striking energies of 6- and 7-shot 410-gauge cartridges at velocities of 800 and 900 ft/s at 25 yards are over the 1 ft/lb of minimum ener-

gy necessary to effectively kill small wing and ground game. At maximum powder loads, a 3-inch 11/16-ounce 410 cartridge of shot sizes 5 through 9 has a muzzle velocity of 1135 ft/s, slower than any gauge from 12 to 28, but sufficient for an effective kill.

This compares favorably with Askins' original data. The 2-inch cartridge contains 3/8-ounce shot and is effective up to 20 yards with a pattern density of 80 to 90 percent. The 2 1/2-inch shell with 1/2-ounce shot is effective up to 25 yards with a density of 80 percent. The 3-inch shell with 3/4-ounce shot is effective up to 30 to 35 yards with a density of over 90 percent. The pellet count at 30 to 35 yards in a 30-inch circle for the 3-inch 410 cartridge is superior to the shorter shells at shorter ranges.

Short of wild pheasant, big duck, and geese, the 3-inch cartridge is effective in the hands of a good shooter for all wing game under 30 to 35 yards. Recent essays on self-loading the 410 cartridge illustrates the many variables in producing a custom load [14,15].

Chris Cradock, once the grand man of British clay target shooting, started shooting with a 410 as a 10-year-old boy [16]. Despite the obvious advantages for a beginner—small size, small recoil, small price—he couldn't refrain from recalling that "not for nothing do our American cousins dub these guns the 'idiot sticks'" [17]. He is certainly referring to earlier American shotgun writing by big bore aficionados such as Askins, Keith, and O'Connor.

Commentary

This is fair enough when we consider that for upland game shooting in the wide-open American West—"rough shooting" not dreamt of in Britain or Europe—long-range accuracy is at a premium. Anyone who has hunted wild chukar among the rocky outcrops and mesas in the California and Nevada high deserts, offering but a small handful of shooting opportunities over a long and hard day of trekking up, down, and around inhospitable terrain, will so attest. All who have tried to walk or run down the wild ruffled grouse in the broad undulating plains of South Dakota will quickly agree that big bore shotgunning, especially for meat or survival hunters, will always dominate certain shooting or hunting venues.

Nothing could be more inappropriate than a 410 bore for large wild upland wing game or for smaller game that flushes at 30 or more yards. It is equally inappropriate for waterfowl, pass, or decoy shooting at almost any range. Greener acknowledged that for the naturalist, the taxidermist, and the gamekeeper, the 410 was in demand because of its portability and stock detachment but that "its killing range" was up to only 25 yards.

Shooting instructors dislike teaching a beginner with the 410, especially if the 2-inch cartridge with 3/8-ounce shot is used. This yields a meager number of pellets, and because many guns were full choked, a pattern "like thrown by a rifle bullet" occurs. This results in many more missed than hit targets, a demoralizing experience for a novice. This also raises the issue of how does the choke affect 410 ballistics.

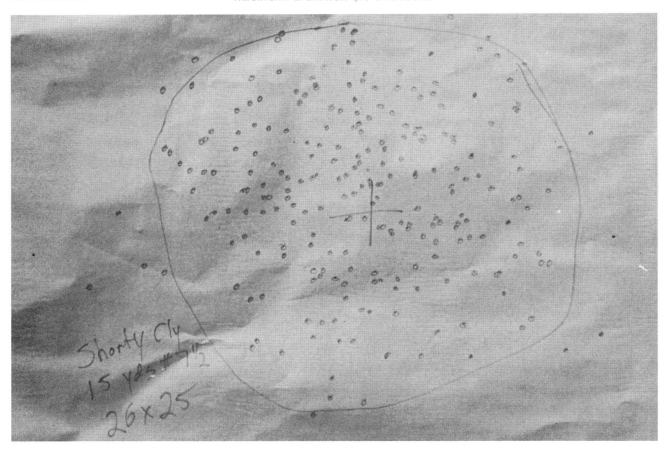

Shorty Cly
15 yds # 7½
26 x 25

Photo 3: A typical very effective ∧
pattern of a cylinder-choked
410. Photo courtesy of *Shotgun
Digest,* 4th Edition, 1993.

The Effects of Choke

Choke boring was patented in England by W.R. Pape in 1866 but
may have been developed earlier by Fred Kimble of Illinois [11].
Greener brought it to its first commercial success in the 1870s by
holding a number of clinics and trials to demonstrate its value [6].

Choke is defined as the amount of constriction at the barrel
muzzle in thousandths of an inch. It is generally accepted that 40
thousandths is full choke, no constriction is true cylinder.

Although it is demonstrable that the degree of choke is
relatively unimportant in determining pattern density under 15
yards, in the 15 to 35 yard range, choke becomes increasingly
important. Moreover, there is considerable controversy as to
what choke is appropriate for game shooting.

This writer, a 410 shooter all of his life, argues that a full
choke reduces the number of cripples; hence lost birds. This is
especially true with wild Valley and Gambel's quail in California,
Gambel's and Scale quail in Arizona, Scale in Texas, and the three
major quail species in Mexico. The problem of crippled
"runners" is nearly insoluble without dogs, and much western
quail hunting is done without our canine companions.

This is less a problem for snipe, woodcock, mourning dove,
or whitewing dove shooting. They are not "runners" and a crip-
ple can usually be retrieved with or without dogs. Southeastern
bobwhite hunting in America is always done with dogs, and
"runners," therefore, are not a problem. With retrieval dogs, wing
game can be shot with a more open choke, improving the kill-to-
cartridge ratio without a significant loss of crippled birds.

A recent essay in *Shotgun Digest* presents a powerful argu-
ment for a straight cylinder choke when hunting in thick woodcock and quail coverts where shotgunning is fast and close [18]. At
15 yards, the 3-inch 11/16-ounce load 410 cartridge with the
cylinder choke will open more uniformly, faster, and wider than
any other choke and gauge duo does. Photo 3 illustrates pattern
uniformity and density at 15 yards with a cylinder 410 cartridge.

Furthermore, based upon Askins' pounds of energy per pellet, only two or three 8 or 7-1/2 shot will take down any small
game bird. Modern powder will propel the shot at over 1100 ft/s.

The essay does agree that rabbit, squirrel, and pass shooting
for high dove requires a more restricted choke, notwithstanding
the problems of a long shot string and shot deformation with
patchy perimeter pellet hits.

Cradock points out that a full choke is problematic for even
an experienced shot. At 25 yards, in all bores 12 through 410, the
full choke shot pattern has a diameter of 21 inches (340 square
inch area). At 25 yards, the improved cylinder choke in the 410

bore has a shot pattern diameter of 32 inches (800 square inch area). This latter choke is a more practical choice for some small wing and ground game species. There is still sufficient pellet density to kill, depending upon cartridge length and range [17].

A recent paper has recommended full-length plastic wads and slow burning powder giving an approximate velocity of 1200 ft/s of hard quality shot [19].

Physics

There is a well-known and interesting characteristic about the 3-inch 410 cartridge that results in its being called a "ballistic abortion" [13]. This is because this cartridge has the longest shot "string" or "column" of all cartridges in all bores, due to the soft lead shot and to a poor velocity-to-pressure ratio.

For example, the 410 shot column (the amount of shot deformed by contacts with the cone of the choke) is 2.175 inches long, compared with the 12 bore at .69 inch and 28 bore at 1.21 inches. This "rifle bullet" or "balling of the shot" effect results from the deformation of pellets and may throw the charge out to 100 to 150 yards. In general, the smaller the gauge, the longer the column and the less dense the pattern.

This was first described by Burrard in 1888 [20] and this phenomenon of a long shot "string" appears to have two physical causes. First, under high pressure, the soft lead shot column results in the welding together of the lead pellets. Second, hot gasses get past the wadding and into the shot charge causing fusion of the pellets. This is called poor "obturation." Poor obturation also occurs when 2-inch cartridges are fired from 3-inch chambers, because of the difference in case length and chamber depth.

Ultimately then, the long shot string is due to poor velocity-to-pressure ratios. The proof is in the high proof pressures required for the 3-inch 410 bore. The 2-inch 5/16-ounce load and the 2 1/2-inch 7/16-ounce load in the 410 bore require proof pressures of 3-1/4 tons per square inch. For the 12 bore 2 1/2-inch cartridge, it is 3 tons. But, for the 410 bore 3-inch 10/16-ounce load cartridge, the proof pressures are 5 tons per square inch! This may also be expressed in "bars," whereby one bar equals 14.5 pounds of pressure per square inch. Therefore, one ton equals approximately 138 bars.

Personal Note

This writer graduated from the Stevens under/over 410/22 to the Marlin 410 lever action. This was followed by the Webley & Scott 400 series boxlock side-by-side, and finally rested with the Belgian-made Browning Superposed over/under. A variety of configurations have been used with clay targets and wing game from the single-shot hammer Purdey with 2-inch cartridges to the Winchester Model 42 single-barrel 3-inch cartridge to the classical 410 doubles made by Parker, Boss, Purdey, and Winchester.

Each has its own style, quirks and enjoyments. My workhorse is the Browning in full choke with a 3-inch cartridge for game and a 2 1/2-inch cartridge for targets. Seldom is a hit bird not retrieved. Furthermore, the gap between human technology and nature is somewhat narrowed, making for a more rigorous stalk, hunt, and shoot. Even at appropriate game and ranges, these may still be "idiot sticks"; however, the "idiots" are more content with the bigger challenge and the greater satisfaction. Furthermore, the state of idiocy connotes irrational choices. The 410 use is non-rational rather than irrational. That is, it is emotional, intuitive, and aesthetic, gender ambivalence be damned. Let the big-bore apologists wrestle with that ambiguity. The beauty of shooting the 410, especially for the youngster, is that good form and patience are usually rewarded with a broken target or harvested game.

Ballistics of the 410 Cartridge References

1. Greener, W.W., *The Gun and Its Development*, 1884, 2nd Edition, Cassell & Company, Ltd., London.
2. Greener, W.W., *Modern Shotguns*, 1891, 2nd Edition, Cassell & Company, Ltd., London.
3. British Proof House records (London), researched on site 1985 to 1990.
4. Jackson, Tony, *ST&CM*, 1995, February 9-15.
5. Wallack, L.R., *American Shotgun Design & Performance*, 1977, Winchester Press.
6. Greener, W.W., *The Gun and Its Development*, 1910, 9th Edition, Cassell & Company, Ltd., London.
7. O'Connor, Jack, *The Shotgun Book*, 1965, Alfred A. Knopf, New York.
8. McIntoch, Michael, *Shooting Sportsman*, 1994, July-August.
9. Askins, Charles, *Modern Shotguns and Loads*, 1929, Small Arms Technical, 1929.
10. Hastings, MacDonald, *The Shotgun*, 1981, David and Charles, Newton Abbott, London.
11. Keith, Elmer, *Shotgun*, 1967, Bonanza Books.
12. Smith, W.H. *The American Shotgunner*, February 1983.
13. *ST&CM*, 1990, September 27-October 3.
14. Greevy, Les, *Shooting Sportsman*, 1999, July-August.
15. Williams, Marshall, *Shotgun Sports*, 1999, January-February.
16. *ST&CM*, 1991, March 14/20.
17. Cradock, Chris, *Cradock on Shotguns*, 1989, B.T. Batsford, Ltd., London.
18. Christian, Chris, *Shotgun Digest*, 4th Edition, DBI Books, Inc., 1993.
19. Woodhouse, Tim, "Fun With a 410," *The Shooting Gazette*, April 2002.
20. Burrard, Major Sir G., *The Identification of Firearms and Forensic Ballistics*, 1934, 1st edition.

CHAPTER FOUR

VARIOUS ACTIONS USED TO BUILD THE 410

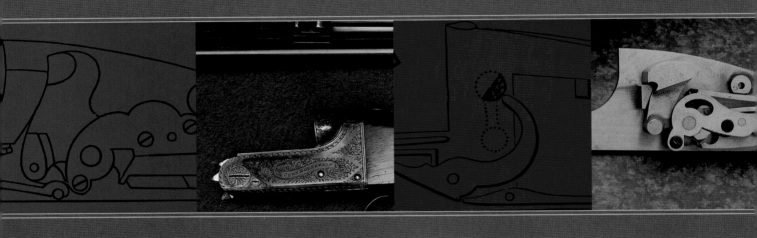

nother approach in sketching the evolution of the 410 bore is to review the different actions used in their construction.

There is no record of a 410 smoothbore having been made before the development of the breechloader, which goes back to Pauly's 1812 hinged breech lifted gun that exposed the chambers for loading. LeFaucheux developed, in 1834, drop-down barrels, which then led to the pinfire gun. This was followed by Needham's invention of the needle fire breechloader action after Daw, in 1862, sparked the commercial success of the hammerless breech. Murcott invented the first lever-cocking hammerless sidelock in 1871. Needham, an inventive genius, patented the first ejector and barrel cocking system in 1874, improved by Greener in 1881 [1].

During this era, action locks slowly evolved in satisfaction and reliability in the form of bar- and back-action sidelocks. However, in 1875, a truly revolutionary action was developed, the hammerless boxlock.

Actions are the heart of a shotgun, the source of its single greatest expense, and the cause of much inflamed debate over the merits of the various action locks. As part of the discussion of the 410 bore's application to these actions, a summary of the essential components of this history and debate may be illuminating.

1. Sidelocks

The sidelock action is the oldest and has been in continual use since the muzzleloaders of the pre-flintlock era. In rudimentary form, they are found in matchlocks and wheellocks of the late medieval centuries. External hammers, the money part of the lock, go back into the mists of the early second millennium.

The sidelock action comes in two forms, the bar action and the back action. All parts of the action are attached to the sideplate. The back action has the apex of the "V"-shaped mainspring pointing towards the shooter and the mainspring is located behind the hammer (called tumbler if not exposed and, therefore, inside the lock) and trigger. The lock mechanism is behind the axle. The bar action has the apex of the "V"-shaped mainspring pointed forward or away from the shooter. The mainspring is located in front of the hammer and trigger along the "bar" of the action in front of the breech face. This lock mechanism is in front of the axle upon which the hammer swings.

The external plate appearance of the bar action is symmetrically rounded in its posterior aspect (see Figure 1 per Purdey catalog circa 1900).

The back action has two configurations. The 19th century and early 20th century back-action sideplate is characterized by a long, lean, tapered elegance. A later appearance in the back-action external plate duplicated the bar-action geometry, except that the visible pins are in a different place on the lockplate. For example, with the bar action, the visible stud or pin of the "V" mainspring is located at the most anterior portion of the external plate, the "shoe" of the action body. The back action has no such pin location.

The bar action requires deep inletting along the action bar, reducing frame strength in comparison to the back action. The latter has more metal in the frame at the angle of the breech and under the water table and is the action of choice for large caliber double rifles. Using one of three top bolts (doll's head, Greener's crossbolt, or Purdey's third fastener rotary bolt) gives added support to the bar action.

Boothroyd, one of the greatest of all shotgun historians, describes the term, "bar-in-the-wood," in which the "metal of the bar is recessed and the wood of the butt stock is carried forward over the metal." He cites the MacNaughton "Edinburgh" action as a decorative example [2]. Beauty does not necessarily expense strength.

One of the important assets of the sidelock is the intercepting safety. This helps to maintain its popularity despite cost and complexity and remains part and parcel of a "Best"-quality back- or bar-action sidelock. This safety blocks the fall of the tumbler (internal hammer) in case the sear is accidentally jarred loose from its notch in the tumbler. Thus, this safety blocks both the effect of the trigger pull and accidental sear dislodgement.

The classical boxlock action has no intercepting safety for the sear. The boxlock safety simply blocks the trigger pull. It is noteworthy that the original Anson & Deeley boxlock patent in 1875 showed the safety blocking the tumbler and not the trigger pull. Greener made some boxlocks with the intercepting safety device [3]. Interestingly, the few American sidelocks, either bar- or back-action, made by Baker and L.C. Smith, did not have the intercepting feature, no doubt due to complexity, and hence, cost.

The back action is considered stronger than the bar action because the action bar is not cut away for inletting of the "V" mainspring as it is for the bar action, and the back-action locks are narrower. With less wood removed, this sidelock in hammerless configuration was and remains a preferred choice for many professional African hunters and for most quality gunmakers such as Holland & Holland and Rigby for the early 20th century Express double rifle. These back-action guns are nearly a solid unit with the barrels as there is little or no clearance between the action and barrel invaginations. Today's large caliber Express double rifles by the great British makers are more for collectors for the guns' decorative value, and are made with the bar-action sidelock.

Additional assets attributed to the sidelock are its superior balance and the most mechanically efficient angle between tumbler and sear resulting in superbly crisp trigger pulls [4]. These advantages may be more apparent than real, as any shooter of the round- or trigger-plate action in the Dickson or Perazzi or any user of a quality boxlock such as the Parker, the NID Ithaca, or the Westley Richards droplock will attest.

A further advantage in the sidelock action is its accessibility

Figure 1: Lock diagram from a sidelock action.

1. Lock Plate
2. Tumbler or Hammer
3. Bridle
4. Sear
5. Intercepting Safety Sear
6. Mainspring
7. Swivel
8. Sear Spring
9. Intercepting Safety Sear Spring

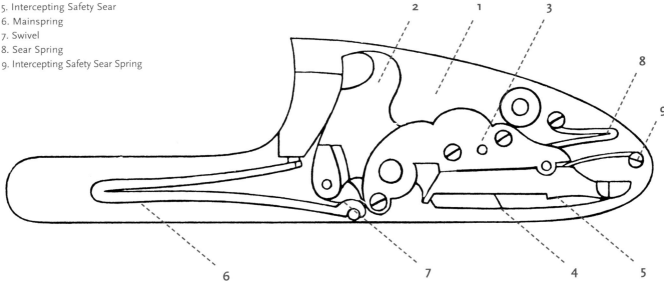

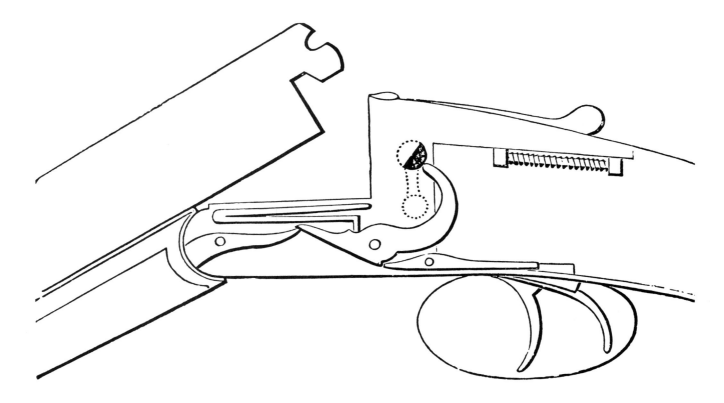

for cleaning and lubricating. Holland & Holland did develop for its bar-action sidelocks a hand-detachable variation in the first decade of the 20th century that immensely improved accessibility and subsequently became popular in "Best"-quality guns of many English gunmakers. Its ease of servicing is matched only by the Westley Richards droplock, patented in 1897, in which each lock is mounted on a floor plate, and this unit is then inserted into the bottom of the action box.

Among the hammerless bar-action locks, there were definable differences. The Purdey action, patented by Frederick Beesley in 1880, is an integrated system in which cocking the hammers, firing, and opening the breech ("self opener") are powered by a single "V" spring. Conversely, the Holland & Holland action, initiated in 1883 by John Robertson, the gunmaking inventor who saved Boss from oblivion, was not an integrated power platform but was easier to build. This action is now seen in sidelocks throughout the world, especially high quality Spanish, Italian, and some British sidelock side-by-side doubles. Woodward's Rogers action, based upon a John Rogers patent of 1881 in which the fall of the barrels "cocks a sidelock hammerless gun," and Boss' own creation represent significant variations [5].

Although the great British gun houses made many of their own locks, there were and continue to be individual lock makers of great repute. The past includes Brazier, Chitten, Saunders, Stanton, and Harper. The present includes A.A. Brown and York & Wallin, all of whom have supplied best quality locks to virtu-

Figure 2: The original form of the famous Anson and Deeley hammerless action, where the tumblers are cocked on the fall of the barrels. This is a particularly strong action that is notable for its economy of parts. It was first produced by Westley Richards, Birmingham, in 1876 and almost all modern boxlock guns are based on this model.

ally every maker of best quality bar-action sidelocks in England.

A final consideration is an aesthetic one. The sidelock, because of its configuration, whether a bar or back action, remains the paragon of grace, elegance, and beauty among the double shotguns of the world.

2. Boxlocks

As the sidelock may be considered an evolutionary development beginning with the match- and wheellock in the 15th century, the boxlock was clearly revolutionary (see Figure 2 per Geoffrey Boothroyd).

This hammerless action, patented by Anson & Deeley in 1875

for Westley Richards (A&D action), was simplicity itself in which all parts were attached directly to the frame. It became and remains, given a certain standard in materials and workmanship, the most popular and cost-effective action for double guns in the world. All the quality American 410 doubles used this action or a variation, save the L.C. Smith back-action sidelock. And the vast majority of quality English and European 410 doubles use the boxlock action including great makers such as Holland & Holland, Webley & Scott, Churchill, Watson, Jeffery, Lancaster, Westley Richards, Cogswell & Harrison, Merkel, etc. Greener's "box-like" action (Facile Princeps) was actually quite different and was patentable but was similar in effect, simplicity, and cost (see Greener chapter).

In fact, Webley & Scott and Midland supplied the boxlock action for many of these gunmakers in the first 70 years of the 20th century. Total numbers dwarf the comparatively few bar-action sidelock guns built in the 410 bore in the 20th century. Conversely, many back-action hammer 410s were made in the late 19th and early 20th centuries, especially by Watson and Cogswell & Harrison.

The hammerless boxlock has five main components consisting of the cocking lever; the sear; the tumbler, including the firing pin; the mainspring; and the ejector, which was added in 1886 by Deeley with modification in 1893 by Southgate. The action was cocked by the fall of the barrels, the first successful design to do so. This compares with the usual 22 parts in the finest bar-action sidelock. Its essence is simplicity and ease of manufacturing and maintenance. Its strength must compare favorably with the back-action sidelock. W.J. Jeffery Company chose the boxlock for its 600-bore Express double elephant rifle [6]. The A & D action, when combined with the Scott spindle and top-lever and the Purdey underbolt, became the world standard [7]. In fact, this action was "popular" in America, according to Tate, until the McKinley tariff of 1890 made the "importation prohibitive."

The lock components are supported by and contained within the action frame. The boxlock removes more metal from the action bar to accommodate the lock. The tumbler or hammer pin extends through the action body from side to side just below the 90-degree "angle" created by the action water table and the action face (standing breech). This angle point is the boxlock action's greatest vulnerability. This is a decided weakness in comparison to the bar- and back-action sidelocks that will leave more metal in the frame. Parenthetically, this distinction relates only to the strength at the frame "angle." For example, in comparison to the boxlock, the amount of wood removed for the sidelock action fit to wood renders the sidelock stock vulnerable where it meets the frame. The intercepting safety, a William Anson patent in 1882, was added to the better quality A & D boxlock guns to prevent the gun's discharge absent a trigger pull!

The mainspring is "V" shaped in English guns and "coiled" in many American guns such as the Parker. The "V"-shaped springs are thought to be faster, stronger, and more durable than the "coil" spring.

Greener's good words on the boxlock include "faster firing" than the sidelock and more opportunity for a cosmetic effect using "sham sidelocks" [8]. These are plates applied to the wood stock just behind the action body, now known as "sideplates" or inexplicably called the "third type of sidelock" by the dean of shotgun historians, G. Boothroyd [9]. They can be distinguished from sidelock actions by the absence of any lock pins seen through the plates and by the forward position of the trigger. Greener pictures a round-action Dickson with highly engraved sideplates manufactured before the turn of the century. In modern times, Browning, Francotte, and other American and European companies have popularized these sideplates for decorative purposes.

A variation of the Anson & Deeley boxlock is the Westley Richards droplock designed by Leslie Taylor and patented in 1897. Each lock is mounted on the floor plate of the action box. It can be inserted and removed from the action at will and without tools save one's fingers.

Before leaving the sidelock and boxlock actions, three topics should be mentioned: bolts, hammers, and springs.

Bolts

A digression to discuss bolts for a moment is important because this development influenced the use and acceptance of the various actions. The bolting system is essential on breech openers to counter the three firing forces:

1. Axial (horizontal arrow to the right)
2. Radial (curved arrow pointing upwards and curved to the left)
3. Bending (arrow pointing vertically upwards)

Underbolts or barrel lugs (bites) are powerful thick extensions from the under flats of the barrels. They may be single, like LeFaucheux's pinfire of 1834, the first breechloader to spark the conversion from muzzleloaders. Most subsequent quality American shotguns such as the Parker had a single bolt. Double bolts (two lugs), an invention by Purdey, are seen in most British and European shotguns and in the Winchester Model 21. In the quality double shotgun, these bolts or lugs are intrinsically forged with the barrels, called the chopper-lump construction. Other such lug assemblies included the dovetail in which the lug is brazed between the breech ends of the barrels. This was seen especially in the blackpowder hammer guns. A third assembly is the sleeved-on "monobloc" style as done today in Italy or Japan and rarely in British doubles.

The top bolt, which complements the underbolt, holds the barrel face to the standing breech and is of four basic types:

1. The doll's head
2. Purdey's "secret" extension, the so-called third fastener
3. The Greener crossbolt
4. The American-developed rotary bolt

The doll's head reinforces the bar of the action and was developed by Westley Richards in 1864 and is widely used in American smoothbores such as the Parkers and many Lefevers. The Purdey "secret" or top extension (third fastener) supports the barrel underbolt and is used in many quality British and European double guns. The Greener crossbolt, patented in 1867, reinforces both the action bar and the underbolt and is seen in many continental guns, especially Germany's Merkel, which uses a double crossbolt with over/under doubles, the so-called "double Kersten." The rotary bolt also reinforces both the action bar and the barrel underbolt and is seen in L.C. Smith, A.H. Fox, and NID Ithaca guns. The New Ithaca Double is bolted solely by a top bolt, a tribute to the bolt's effectiveness [10].

Hammers

A brief comment about hammers is necessary here. Prior to the 1870s, all hammers were exposed. These hammers were non-rebounding until John Stanton's 1867 invention of the rebounding variety. Both types have three positions: cocked, half-cocked, and fired. The non-rebounding hammer's firing pin remained indented in the cap of the cartridge, blocking the opening of the breech. The advantage of Stanton's rebounding hammers, which quickly superseded the earlier type, was that the fired or down position is only momentary in the act of firing. Immediately following firing, the hammers rebound instantly to the half-cocked position. Then by fitting the firing pin with a coil spring, which caused the pin to withdraw from the cap after firing, the breech was easily opened. The half-cocked position is also a position of safety from an accidental discharge by an external blow or inadvertent trigger pull.[1]

The historical record does not reveal a sidelock hammer 410 with non-rebounding hammers. This is consistent with the first 410 being manufactured after the 1870s when this type of hammer apparently ceased to exist.

Springs

In 1888, Burrard described the source of kinetic energy for the functioning of a gun as the release of distorted matter allowing it to return to its more natural state. Matter, or in this case "V"-shaped coiled or flat springs, has been geometrically deformed by applied energy from the shooter, taking advantage of the principle of leverage, and locked in that state of deformation. When the shooter's energy releases this bit of matter, it returns to its more natural state and the gun's rationale is realized. It is essential that this matter, the springs, are worked into the proper molecular configuration by craftsmen so that its geometry, both natural and unnatural, does the necessary work of safety cocking,

firing, ejecting, and opening the breech [12].

In the second half of the 19th century, the "V" spring was used in virtually all British guns, however inexpensive [13]. Conversely, the coiled spring was used in most American guns regardless of expense, including the Parker, Ithaca, Fox, Winchester, and Remington [14]. European gunmakers were more eclectic.

Today the "V" spring is used primarily in the best grade British guns, while the modern American gun uses coiled springs. One of history's greatest artists in gun engraving, the late Lynton McKenzie, started out as a master spring maker [15].

3. Other Actions
A. Trigger Plate

The next action of importance in the evolution of the shotgun is a variation of the boxlock called the "trigger plate" or "round action" and in Germany called the "Blitz." In fact, this action, in primitive form, probably originated in Germany. Because of strong commercial ties between northern Europe and Scotland, this action, in modified form, was nourished in the industrial belly of southern Scotland, Edinburgh, and Glasgow.

All lock parts are connected to the trigger plate that fits the bottom of the frame. John Dickson and James MacNaughton, the two premier Scottish gunmakers, pioneered or developed this action between 1879 and 1887. Three advantages were apparent. The frame was very strong because no machining of the action body was necessary. The ensemble was very accessible for cleaning and repair. In addition, the aesthetics were compelling with a diminutive action body covered in wood [16].

No other British company used this action, and records of both Scottish companies reveal that the 410 bore was never built or attempted to be built until recently. Dickson attempted a single 410 round-action double in the 1990s, unsuccessfully, for they were unable to build a scaled-down 410 action. More recently, McKay Brown has built a 410 round-action double (see Dickson chapter).

In America, a variation of the action has been used in the Winchester 101 and the Remington 3200 in all bores. In Germany, where it is called the "Blitz," Merkel uses the action. In Italy, Perazzi uses this action for its over/under because of its great frame strength. The Franchi 2000 series uses a variation. For decorative, stylistic, and engraving purposes, sideplates may be added as illustrated by a 1910 Dickson gun [8].

B. Bolt Action

This action, patented by Joseph Needham in 1852, with a later variation by Francis Bacon in 1870, was popularized in rifles and shotguns built by Rigby of Dublin and later London. There are no known double bolt-action 410s. However, the single-barrel bolt 410 became a popular gun for the gardener, taxidermist, and youth by 1900 with a high volume manufactured up to and after World War II.

Companies making them in England included Webley & Scott, BSA, and Midland. Webley & Scott's single-barrel 410 bolt action, of which many thousands were built, was manufac-

---

1 Throughout the 20th century, firing pins have been made of steel with varying mixtures of manganese and carbon for strength without brittleness. More recently, many are made of titanium, which has the strength of steel and the weight of aluminum [11].

tured in lots of up to several hundred. With every lot or so, they would make a single "Deluxe" version. Today a "Deluxe" 410 is extremely rare and commands admiration and a handsome price (see Photo 1 in Webley & Scott chapter). In America, Mossberg, Stevens, and Marlin built many such guns.

C. Lever Action

This action became famous for its use in the preeminent rifles on the American frontier. My father used a 300-caliber lever-action Savage to hunt big game in the western United States for four decades from 1925 to 1965, as did many of his generation. Before that, it was used for sustenance and protection to survive and tame the American frontier. John Browning, the American firearms inventive genius, appears to have developed the first successful lever-action repeating shotgun, brought out by Winchester in 1887, in the 10 and 12 bore. The revised 1901 model was made until 1920 in the 10 bore. Kessler built a lever-action shotgun after World War II. Winchester, in the Model 89, and Remington built a single shot "falling (rolling) block" action shotgun, a version of the lever action [17].

The first lever-action 410-bore shotgun was built by Marlin from 1929 to 1932 and is described in detail in Chapter 10.

D. Sliding Barrel or Sliding/Rotary Breech Action

This action has a most distinguished pedigree. Starting with Pauly's 1812 hinged-breech fixed-barrel ensemble, a number of great names in mid-19th century gunmaking are associated with this action type. Its development continued in Europe and in England with the names of W.J. Harvey (1860), Joseph Needham (1862), Jeffery (1862), and James Purdey (1865) dotting the landscape [3]. Purdey built such an action for a 32-bore rifle in the mid-19th century.

It is clear that this action was developed earlier in Europe, and it appears that France was the only country where it was able to sustain a commercial life. Darne, the great gunmaking company of St. Etienne and considered the gunmaker's "Birmingham" of France, produced such guns from 1881 to 1980. They first started with a rotary breech and then converted to a sliding breech with its long tapered look. They built all gauges with the exception of the 410 bore, according to available records. In 1984, Paul Bruchet, a former Darne production manager, resumed production and now will build a 410 bore in any grade on a custom basis. The gun is eccentric, elegant, highly functional, and recommended for the adventurous shotgunner.

E. Miscellaneous Actions

These are best illustrated by the various cane and walking stick guns made in Europe and England beginning before the turn of the century [18] (see Interesting Types of Smoothbore 410s chapter).

Commentary Applicable to the 410 bore

In England, the sidelock started its evolution long before the 18th century. Both the bar- and back-action guns slowly emerged towards greater refinement until the end of the 19th century with the final development of the Beesley bar-action ejector hammerless sidelock made by Purdey under patent. Apart from the possibility of a John Wilkes back-action 410 of 1876, there are no 410s recorded with either action until the 1880s. For example, Purdey produced at least one 410 with each the bar- and the back-action sidelock at that time (see Purdey chapter). There are few recorded best quality sidelock bar-action 410s from any of the great British gunmakers until the 1930s. It was in the late 1920s when Harry Lawrence built Purdey's first bar-action hammerless 410.

The 1920s was the decade when the great American gunmakers began to build the 410 bore in their side-by-side configuration. Other British quality gunmakers did not begin their bar-action hammerless 410s until later. Boss built its first bar-action hammerless in the 1930s while Holland & Holland as well as Westley Richards waited until after World War II to do so.

After the Anson & Deeley revolution in 1875, the 410 with the hammerless boxlock action was made with increasing frequency by high-volume firms such as Webley & Scott and by local artisans and provincial gunmakers for the general public and young shooter. Often these firms and individual makers would send their product to one of the quality London gunmakers such as Holland & Holland, Churchill, Evans, Jeffery, and Cogswell & Harrison to be "shot and regulated" and sold under the firm's name. There is no record of an in-house production of a boxlock 410 by such firms as Purdey, Boss, and Holland & Holland. Firms such as Greener, Watson, Beesley, Westley Richards, and Webley & Scott had their own in-house production of the 410 boxlock action, although even these firms often used components such as actions and barrels produced by "out workers" or local parts makers. Boxlock 410s manufactured by local artisans or high-volume firms—to be then precisioned and refined by the quality firm under whose name the gun would be sold—usually would have the inscription "Made for ... " on the barrel rib.

In 1897, Westley Richards developed a refined variation of their boxlock, the droplock, of which there are six recorded in the 410 bore prior to 1990. They have resumed production of the 410 droplock within the past few years (see Westley Richards chapter).

In America, the 410 bore was made by the best quality firms from the mid-1920s onwards. Hence, this bore enjoyed the most advanced lock design of each manufacturer. For example, Ithaca did not begin 410 production until their latest and last configuration had started in 1926, the NID model. All quality companies except L.C. Smith made the 410 with their most advanced boxlock. The Smith 410 was a back-action sidelock with a coiled mainspring.

L.C. Smith, the only sidelock firm in America of any volume, did not start to manufacture the 410 until 1926 when its back-action hammerless sidelock was at its peak. Interestingly, L.C. Smith did build a number of bar-action sidelocks before the 20th century. However, they converted entirely to the back-action hammerless sidelock by 1900 because this type appeared to be stronger and simpler to build (see L.C. Smith chapter).

The more cheaply made 410s in America, such as those by Iver

Johnson or Winchester, were started in or just after the 20th century's second decade and were invariably hammer or hammerless boxlock actions. They were made in some volume. For example, the Iver Johnson single-barrel hammer 410, the Champion, started in 1916 and had a production run of over 5000, of which very few are now in existence. By today's standards, it was a well-made gun, but in that day, it was treated as a barnyard tool and most did not survive the ravages of time, use, and abuse. The Winchester Model 20 was made from 1919 to 1924 with a total production of at least 23,616. This was an especially well-made boxlock in today's terms.

By the end of World War II, most of the quality American manufacturers had virtually ceased production of the 410. The Browning's Superposed, made under the fine standards of Belgium's Fabrique Nationale (FN) Factory, made a 410 bore starting in 1959 and ceasing in 1983 when two American dealers brought into the United States the last of the FN-built 410 guns (see Browning chapter). The boxlock Olin Winchester Model 21 410 bore was brought out in 1952.

The British socialized economy of post World War II accelerated the hitherto gradual decline of the great British gunmakers. Some ceased to exist, some amalgamated with other firms, and some, such as Holland & Holland, Purdey, Westley Richards, and Boss limped along in a post-World War II atmosphere of envy, sloth, and hatefulness, the triple engines of British socialism. During this time, the high-quality bar-action sidelock 410 would appear rarely from one of these great makers, usually custom made for an American swell or an Arab potentate. Holland & Holland's Northwood model and Webley & Scott's Model 700 series continued to make a rare high-quality hammerless boxlock priced at least 75 percent cheaper than a comparable "Best"-quality British sidelock.

Today we look back upon the 1980s as a time when some of the pre-eminent British gunmakers such as Purdey, Holland & Holland, and Westley Richards began once again to thrive in Margaret Thatcher's market-driven economy. Increased numbers of custom-made special-order bar-action

410s were made, usually for the American market. The 1990s, with these gunmakers retooling and with some being bought by large industrial or commercial multinational firms, ushered in a renaissance of quality gunmaking. Additionally, today the greatest volume of quality double 410s is being produced in Europe. The Spanish, Italian, and Belgium gunmakers are producing 410s in sidelock and boxlock actions with and without exposed hammers.

Except for the brief Browning Superposed interlude, a high quality American double 410 had not been made in many years. Very recently, the Connecticut Shotgun Mfg. Co. has resurrected the classic A.H. Fox shotgun in greater splendor and workmanship than the original [19]. They will now build small bores including the 28 and 410 bores, not built by the original firm.[2]

Tony Galazan, the mechanical wizard behind the Connecticut Shotgun Mfg. Co., has designed and is now building a unique over/under shotgun offered in the 410. David Winks, the former Holland & Holland gunmaking expert, describes it as "brilliant" [20].

---

2 The 410-bore Fox Model B and Fox Sterlingworth guns were built after Savage Arms acquired the A.H. Fox Co. in 1929. These were relatively inexpensive boxlocks. The Model B 410 was cataloged in 1940.

Various Actions Used to Build the 410 References

1. Boothroyd, Geoffrey, *British Shotguns*, 1993, Sand Lake Press, Oregon.
2. Boothroyd, Geoffrey, *S.T.C.M.*, 15 Feb. 1996.
3. Boothroyd, Geoffrey, 1985, *The Shotgun*, A&L Black, London.
4. Keith, Elmer, *Shotguns by Keith*, MCMLXVII, Bonzana Books, N.Y.
5. Baker, David, *Sporting Gun*, March 2002.
6. Gough, Thomas (G. T. Garwood), *Shotguns & Cartridges*, 1975, Adam & Charles Black, London.
7. Tate, Douglas, *Shooting Sportsman*, July/August 1996.
8. Greener, W.W. *The Gun and Its Development*, 9th Ed., 1910, Cassell & Company, Ltd.
9. Boothroyd, Geoffrey, 1986, *Shotguns & Gunsmiths*, A&L Black, London.
10. McIntosh, Michael and David Trevallion, "Top Fasteners," *Shooting Sportsman*, Nov./Dec. 1997.
11. DiGiacobbe, B.H., *Shotgun Sports*, October 2000.
12. Burrard, Major Sir Gerald, 1934 1st Edition, *The Identification of Firearms and Forensic Ballistics*.
13. Baker, David, *Sporting Gun*, July 1996.
14. McIntosh, Michael & David Trevallion, *Shooting Sportsman*, July/August 1996.
15. Personal communication 1991 with McKenzie.
16. Boothroyd, Geoffrey, *Guns Review*, January 1993.
17. O'Connor, Jack, *The Shotgun Book*, 1965, Alfred A. Knopf, N.Y.
18. Crudgington, I.M. and D.J. Baker, *The British Shotgun*, C. & B., Vol. 2, 1989, Ashford, South Hampton.
19. McIntosh, Michael, *A.H. Fox*, Country Sport Press, 1994, Traverse City, MI.
20. Personal communication 1999.

CHAPTER FIVE

THE BROWNING SUPERPOSED 410

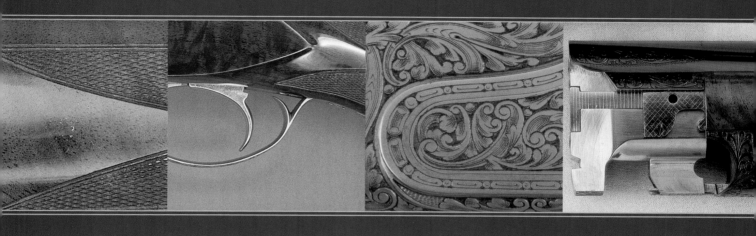

Perhaps the most used and beloved of the modern American double 410s for small winged game and clay pigeon shooting was and remains the Browning Superposed. This gauge was first intro-duced by Browning in 1960 in the Lightning model, and upgraded in 1967 to the Superlight version if the customer so chose. The 410 represents the pinnacle of John Browning's gunmaking genius, although he died long before he would see his Superposed produced for the American market [1].

Browning filed the original B25 action patents October 15, 1923, and September 29, 1924. The patents were granted March 30, 1926, numbers 1578638 and 39, a landmark in gunmaking history and the end of the era of the world's greatest inventive gunmaker for the ages, John M. Browning (1855 to 1926) [2].

Browning received 128 different patents for 80 different firearms in almost 50 years, from smoothbores to rifles, and from sporting arms to military automatic weapons. His gun designs were and continue to be made by many American and European firms, including Browning, Winchester, Colt, Fabrique Nationale (FN), Remington, Savage, etc.

FN of Liege, a Belgian Company and one of the premier continental gunmakers of this century, produced the Superposed in 1930. Proofing took place at the Liege Proof House and the guns were hand-assembled and finished in the FN custom shop. In 1931, the company began marketing the 12-bore Superposed in America under the "Browning Arms Co." name. Browning was never a production company, except in the late 1800s, when they made the 1885 single-shot rifle [3].

The 1932 Stoeger *Shooter's Bible* illustrates quality and pricing of the Browning vs. comparable doubles from 1931-1932. A Standard Superposed sold for $107.50 and a Midas grade for $374. This compared with the Model 21 Winchester standard grade at $65.50 and Trap grade at $98.45; a Parker VH at $74.80 or an A-1 Special at $825; an Ithaca Field at $40.55 or a 7E at $379.20; an L.C. Smith Field at $43.20 or a DeLuxe at $1203.30; a W. & C. Scott & Son Monte Carlo B sidelock $600; and an A.H. Fox Standard SP $48.50 or the FE at $500. The Midas price fell between the Crown and Monogram L.C. Smith, between the BHE and AHE Parker, and approximated the 7E Ithaca. It was priced equivalent to the W. & C. Scott & Son best boxlock and cheapest sidelock (Monte Carlo B) of the period.

From 1931 to 1936, Browning produced only the 12 bore in Standard, Pigeon, Diana, Midas, and Special Order grades. FN introduced the 16 bore in 1936. From 1938 to 1947, virtually all production ceased, resuming after the war in 1948. In 1949, Val A. Browning, John's son, introduced the 20 bore [4].

∧ **Photo 1:** A rare 410 P4, SN P83RN 1063, with its characteristic straight stock and Schnabel forend. This is a B25 gun built entirely in Belgium.

Paul Goodwin photo

The following year, 1950, the company changed the grade names to the prosaic nomenclature of Standard, 2, 3, 4, 5, and Special Order.

During the early years, the basic gun was continually improved. The Lightning model made its appearance in 1935 to accommodate the field hunter, giving him a 12 bore that was a half-pound lighter than the Standard. This was necessary to compete effectively with the Remington over/under Model 32 and the Winchester side-by-side Model 21.

The gold-plated inertia-shift selective single trigger, also developed by Val Browning, became standard in 1939. According to Schwing, it was "designed to fire the second barrel after recoil set the second barrel sear." The second pull initiated by the recoil disconnects the shifting trigger mechanism between the first and second shot, thus preventing doubling. Recoil disengages the first sear. The safety disconnects the trigger from the sears but does not lock the hammers themselves, in contrast to best-quality English sidelocks that have intercepting sears. By the 1970s, Browning had converted its inertia single trigger to a mechanical system, in large part because the 410- and 28-gauge recoil was not great enough to ensure complete reliability with the inertia system.

Like the Gebruder Merkel, and unlike the Boss, Woodward, and Beretta, the Browning is a high-frame gun. A sliding underlug and a knuckle pin locking the floor plate to the lower barrel elevate the barrel axes. Unlike the Merkel, there is no top fastener such as the Greener cross-bolt (Kersten fastener) or the doll's head.

Theoretically, this would allow the upper barrel to separate from the standing breech on firing due to bending pressure on the frame. However, frame angles have not failed on the Superposed due to the quality and mass of steel at critical points. This makes the Standard Superposed a heavy gun in comparison

to other over/under guns. However, the Browning locking system is as tough as the Utah mountains, where John Browning once owned a half million acres.

Superposed barrels were available from 26 to 32 inches long and they had chopper lumps (made in one piece of steel with the barrel). The ventilated rib became available by 1948 and standard by 1954.

Browning first marketed the 410, along with the 28 gauge, in 1960—although the first 410 came out of the FN plant in 1959. A single-selective trigger and ventilated rib were standard along with the aesthetically pleasing round knob pistol grip and long tang trigger guard. At this time, Browning returned to the more poetic grade designations of the 1930s: Standard, Pigeon, Pointer, Diana, Midas, and Special Order. Many a shooter told his wife he was spending the day with his "Diana," an all-consuming mistress.

The Exhibition grade was available by 1966 for the gun aficionado with more money than sense, and the Pointer grade discontinued. Dropping the Pointer grade from the line disappointed many because the engraving pattern had a singular beauty of scroll and game scenes.

In 1967, Browning introduced the last Superposed refinement for the walking hunter, the Superlight. This configuration was a special joy in the 410, adding to its sleek delicacy. The barrels and solid or ventilated rib were "taper milled" from breech to muzzle. They also slenderized and tapered the forend to match the barrels. Later they converted the forend to an upward sweeping Schnabel-tipped European ensemble. The latter change allows the shooter's leading hand to be more intimately mated to the barrels. During the production years from 1967 to 1976, the pistol grip stock went away and a straight stock took its place.

The familiar round knob pistol grip gave way to a flat knob in 1967, and a year later, in 1968, the long tang was shortened on the pistol grip model. Both changes, for economic reasons, were aesthetic degenerations and served no shooting purpose. The long tang was reintroduced in 1970 because the short version "was more prone to breakage," [5] one of the perils of tinkering with a good thing. The change from lacquered wood finish to polyurethane in the mid-1960s further reduced cost at the expense of beauty. Oil finish remained available on Special Order. The production decisions to convert to a flat knob (easier to carve and to checker), to shorten the tang, and to use salt-cured wood were all cost-cutting techniques in response to European labor conditions [3]. After World War II, the European trade unions became powerful and crippling strikes resulted. This drove up costs of production, spiraling prices upward. Penny-wise and dollar-foolish was the result as well as lost business.

The salt-wood problem, beginning in 1964, was publicly evident by 1966 and continued with the Superposed at least through the early 1970s. The use of salt-cured wood was a bizarre production decision as salt and metal are notorious antagonists. It crippled the reputation of Browning for a new generation of sporting shooters. In fact, the Exhibition and Pigeon grades disappeared in 1971 and 1972 respectively and the production of the Superposed in all grades ceased as a regular production gun in 1976 because of poor sales, in part due to the salt-wood fiasco. Browning has subsequently demonstrated

Photo 2: Close up of the engraving on the J.M. Debrus engraved P4 410.

Photo 3: Bottom view of the J.M. Debrus engraved P4 410.

Paul Goodwin photos ∨

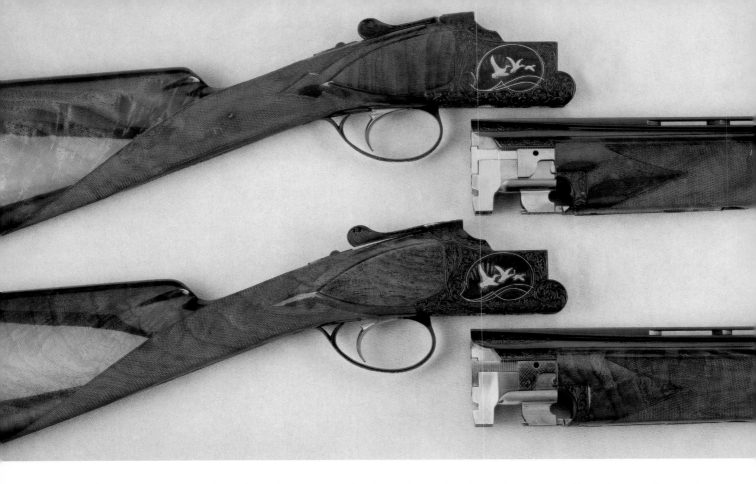

remarkable corporate responsibility by replacing the wood and refurbishing all returned guns of original owners and has done so for over 25 years without cost to the original owner.

After 1963, the letter S, V, F, or J standing for, respectively, a 12, 20, 28, and 410 gauges followed the numerical serial number on the Superposed. The last number of the year the gun was produced then followed this new letter. For example, J3 denoted a 410 made in 1963. In 1969, the last two numbers of the year were affixed (i.e. J69 for a 1969 410 gun). This identity system continued through 1974 in the bigger bores and through 1976 in the 410 and 28 gauges.

After 1974, a new identity system in the bigger bores included a numerical system followed by two alphabet letters to denote the year. This was not applicable to the production 410 because it ceased in 1976.

After the Browning family sold the company to FN in 1977, Browning attempted in 1977 to re-market the Superposed as the Presentation series in the P1, P2, P3, and P4 models. The P4 grade had sideplates for more elaborate engraving. The Superposed P series was cataloged from 1977 to 1984; however, most known guns were manufactured in the 1977-78 timeframe, hallmarked by RR for 1977 and RP for 1978. In 1985, Browning went back to the Pigeon, etc. grade nomenclature in 12 and 20 bore only and only by special order.

After approximately 2000 units were built in all gauges, many with multi-barrels, the P-series effort died quietly in 1983 [6]. Schwing records 1415 P-series sales; however, this does not

Photo 4: The two Midas 410s, SN 415J83 (top) and SN 614J83 (bottom), that bracket the final B25 run of 1983-1984.

Paul Goodwin photo ∧

Photo 5 (opposite, top): A Diana ＞ 410 Superlight, SN 315J76. Many Browning fanciers prefer the Diana engraving to the higher grade Midas.

Paul Goodwin photo

Photo 8 (opposite, middle): ＞ A Pigeon 410 Superlight, SN 327J76.

Paul Goodwin photo

Photo 6 (opposite, bottom): ＞ A Pointer 410 Superlight, SN 350J76, another favorite engraving among Browning owners.

Paul Goodwin photo

include many direct factory orders by other wholesale and retail entities [1]. It was possible to order these models with one, two, three, or four barrels, gray or blue actions, and Superlight or Standard configuration [6].

In 1977, FN went to partial chemical (acid) etching or laser engraving for many of their production lines, including the P series. Indeed, all P guns were partially decorated in this manner, except for the P4 and the 1977 P3 guns that were fully engraved and signed by the engraver (Photos 1-3).

Finally, with existing components at the FN factory, William Jaqua and Thomas Koessl imported the last of the small-bore Superposed in 410 and 28 gauges in 1983.

The Browning Collector Association reported that the FN Custom Shop would still make a Superposed in any configuration and in any gauge. In fact, one report stated that the company made 10 sets of 410/30-06 smoothbore rifle combinations in the Diana grade with a Schnabel two-piece forend, straight stock, and an oil-finished wood. Called the "Continental" set, they were engraved by the sister of Jose Baerton.

The 410 Gauge

In 1959, the 410 became available with 26 1/2- and 28-inch barrels, single-selective trigger, and weighed from 6 pounds 5 ounces to 6 pounds 9 ounces, depending upon barrel length. In the early 1960s, the stock was a hand-checkered, hand-rubbed walnut. Built on a 20-gauge frame, it was essentially a set of 410 barrels added to a 20-gauge frame, stock, and forend. By the time the 410 came on the market, FN had built 112,913 Superposed guns in 12, 16, and 20 bore.

The first 410, made in 1959, #9J1, has an unknown fate. The second 410 produced, 9J2, is a Pigeon grade (Grade II) skeet gun in beautifully used condition. The 410 alphanumeric serial numbering with the letter J denoting the 410 gauge was as follows: 1959 (9J____), 1960 (0J____), 1961 (1J____), 1962 (2J____), fall 1962 (J2____), 1963 (J3____), etc. In 1969, the system changed to J69, 1970 (____J70), 1971 (____J71), etc., ending in 1976. Some guns in 1969 were serialized with the prior numbering system (i.e. J9). Schwing notes that the "old series" of numbering ended November 29, 1971, with SN 3868J71. The "new series" started April 27, 1972, with number 1J72 and ended May 1977 with the last consecutive number 373J76 (the last number was SN 390J76 shipped September 1977). The 200 special-order Superlight 410s ordered in 1983-84 by William Jaqua and Thomas Koessl were numbered 415J83 to 614J83 with two Midas 410s bracketing this production run (Photo 4).

Browning reports that from 1960 to 1970, they produced approximately 3100 410s. This included all styles and grades except for the Superlight. From 1970 to 1976, they made an additional 414 410-gauge guns. Of this number, over 120 were Superlights, all with the suffix J75 or J76, and imported by William Jaqua. Jaqua is a remarkable gun dealer and collector from Ohio whose extraordinary integrity and business acumen are legendary.[1]

Photo 7: The detailed Pointer engraving.

Levasheff photo ∨

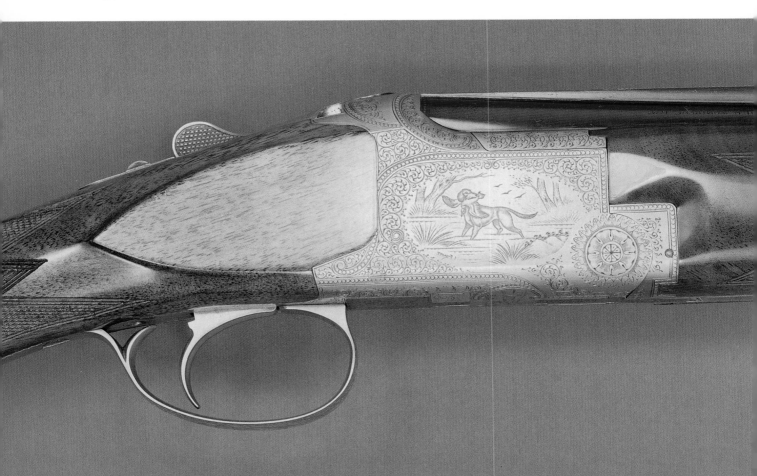

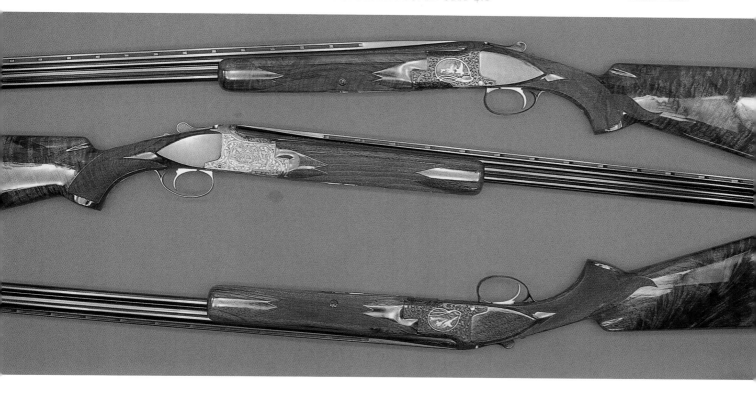

Jaqua ordered virtually all the 410 Superlights ever built, and reports the following Superlight production numbers: 26 Grade I, 18 Pigeon, 24 Pointer, 26 Diana, and 26 Midas (Photos 5-8). He also imported three Midas 410/28/20 gauge sets, three Midas 410/20 sets, six Diana 410/20 sets, and six Grade I 410/20 sets [7]. Thus, a total of 120 single 410s and 18 combination 410s were manufactured in the Superlight configuration with either the suffix J75 or J76.

Therefore, from 1960 through 1976, FN manufactured approximately 3514 of the 410 guns, of which 138 were singles or in sets in the Superlight configuration.

Browning collectors will be interested to know that Jaqua also imported virtually every 28-gauge Superlight manufactured with the suffix F75 or F76. The production totaled 44 single guns, only six of which were in Midas grade.

Schwing's brilliant and authoritative research provides production data not easily compared to other sources because of different timeframes [1,6]. According to Schwing, total world

Photo 9: A typical configuration ∧ of this era's Superposed with a Diana 410 bracketed by two Midas 410s.

Levasheff photo

sales of the 410 from 1960 to 1969 were 2804 guns. North America 410 sales from 1964 to 1969 were 2049 guns in Hunting or Skeet configuration.

Total North American 410 sales from 1964 to 1977 were 3427 guns: 1687 in Skeet, 1696 in Hunting, and 44 in "Special Order" models. There were, in this timeframe, 894 guns in grades above Standard, which included 373 Pigeon, 87 Pointer, 264 Diana, 147 Midas, and 23 Exhibition (Photos 9 and 10). One gun is unaccounted for in this data. According to Schwing, total world 410 production estimates from 1959 to 1977 were 3927 Browning and 331 FN guns.

In 1977, the P series began and continued into 1984 with the 410 suffix P83 denoting either the Superlight or pistol grip model. The 410 gun number is first coded as a P83, followed by the year coded with the two alphabet letters, and then the serial number. For example, P83 RP 1204 designates a P4 410 made in 1978. This gun has a three-piece Schnabel forend and an oil-finish stock. Browning reports building only 124 410 guns in this short production run [6]. However, Schwing's data reveals a 410 production of 178 guns from 1977 to the end of production in 1984, 163 in Lightning and 15 in Skeet. This was 12 percent of the total gun production. This information came from Browning

---

1 When Jaqua, in the fall of 1945, was mustering out of military service, his uncle, a gunsmith, wrote to him offering him a position in a retail shotgun business. He was home on Tuesday and in the gunshop on Friday on Main St., Findlay, Ohio. They started with fifteen guns in inventory. Within three years, the uncle had been bought out so he could retire. By the early 1950s, Jaqua started to carry the Belgium Superposed Brownings and was the first American dealer to inventory the Diana and Midas grades. He moved to a larger store, started an athletic dry goods section, and by the mid-1950s, began his famous gun list. The rest is well-known history.

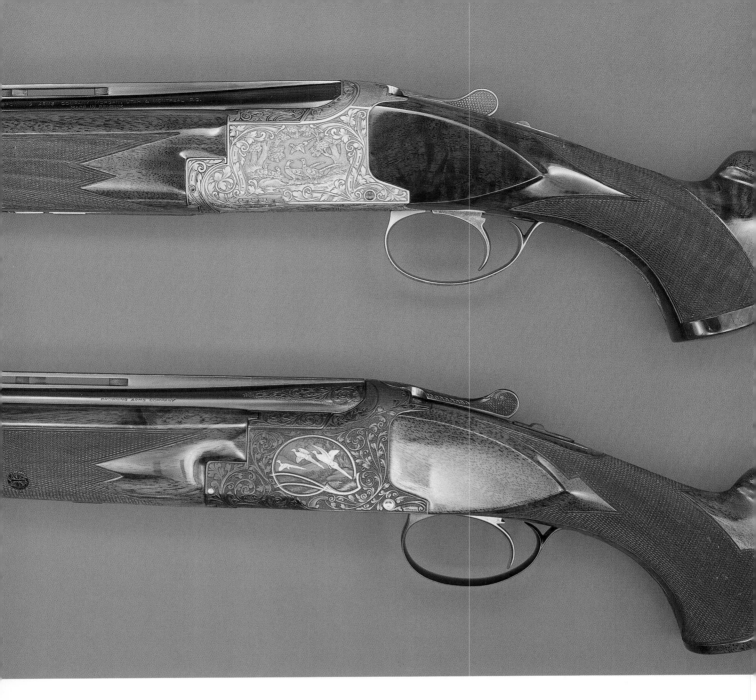

Photo 10: A detailed comparison of the Diana (top) and Midas 410 of the era.

Levasheff photo

Co. sales records and does not include P guns imported by other individuals or companies. There are 35 P4, 40 P3, 50 P2, and 53 P1 guns. There were 73 multi-barrel sets, with 410 barrels in a large but unknown percentage.

It is likely that the Browning collector will have a very active interest in this series, especially the P4 410s, of which only 35 were made. By comparison, the 28 gauge had a run of 156 P series guns, 20 in P4. The total number of P4 in all gauges is 176. The P4 is characterized by side plates with deep-scroll engraving similar to the Diana guns, but with the addition of birds in gold. P83RN1063 with "RN" denoting a 1979 production is one brilliant example (Photos 2 and 3).

Finally, in 1983, Jaqua and Koessl received the last of the Superposed 410 guns, all in Superlight configuration on 20-

gauge frames. FN made these guns from the remaining parts at the factory. All had the suffix J83 and ranged from SN 415J83 to SN 614J83 for a total of 200 410 guns. The two guns that bracket the J83 series are Midas grade with 28-inch barrels and Schnabel forend with exquisite epoxy-finished wood with a straight stock. A rounded action and a tapered ventilated rib together with signed hand engraving complete these exquisite guns (Photo 4).

In this final series, 15 sets of five guns in all grades—Standard, Pigeon, Pointer, Diana, and Midas—were made, 10 with 28-inch barrels and five with 26 1/2-inch barrels for a total of 75 410s. The remaining 125 single 410s included 100 with 28-inch barrels and 25 with 26 1/2-inch barrels. They also included SN 500J83 and SN 600J83, "Special" Midas grades with special engraving by Jose Baerton. They all have the Schnabel forend, straight stock, and are hand engraved, not chemically etched. Either feather-crotch or fiddle-back grain patterns characterizes the stocks on these guns. Interestingly, because all 410s were on 20-gauge frames, the 410, having more metal in the barrels, is heavier than the 28 gauge that, in turn, is heavier than the 20 bore.

Today

Clearly, the 410 story does not end with the J83 production run. Today, the FN factory in Herstal, near Liege, Belgium, through its Custom Shop, will build a customer almost anything.

The factory is now offering several B models.

The original, the B25, was a handmade gun. It had all its components manufactured and assembled in-house. The B125 had its components fabricated in Japan's Miroku factory and the parts shipped to FN for assembly and finishing by the Custom Shop. It also differs from the B25 in that the single trigger relies on recoil from the first barrel to cycle an inertial force. The B25 model converted from an inertia trigger to a mechanical system by the early 1970s. Importantly, the B125 also has a safety for the intercepting sears, unlike the B25, an important safety feature if the gun happens to be dropped or jarred.

The Browning Arms Company has been retailing a totally Miroku-built Superposed with a detachable forend since 1973. Called the Citori, Browning marketed the gun before FN bought Browning in 1977. Manufactured in Japan, the Citori has

significant differences from the B25 in the locking, bolting, and ejection systems to reduce production costs.

By 1988, the continued soaring of costs in Belgium forced FN to build their Superposed, called the B325, totally at the Miroku plant. Unlike the B25 or B125, it has a fully removable forend. Finally, more recently in 1995, FN is marketing the B425, which is cheaper to build because the barrels use the monobloc system as opposed to the chopper lump barrels used on prior models. The B425 system uses chrome molybdenum steel and the barrels are brazed together and the rib added.

All of these models still offer the 410 in virtually any configuration. However, the classic B25 Superposed 410, apart from an eccentric Custom Shop order, has been consigned to the collector and historian. The total production run of Browning and FN Superposed from 1930 to 1977, minus 10 years due to World War II, was 411,017 guns in all bores.

Finally, Schwing reports a heretofore little known story about a 410 prototype made with a scaled-down action. Just before Browning sold to FN in 1977, Val Browning designed and Nicolai's FN team built a 410 with a dedicated 410-size frame. Evidently, only photos exist of this, what Val Browning called "a perfect jewel of a gun." What a find this would be and what a production run the B25 410 gun had for 25 years!

Ned Schwing has pointed out that both Val Browning and Winchester's John Olin were enthusiastic 410 shooters and both were compelled to build and produce their "baby." For Olin, it was the Model 21; for Val Browning it was the Superposed on a scaled-down and dedicated 410 frame. The latter never happened [8].

The Browning Superposed 410 References

1. Schwing, Ned, *The Browning Superposed*, 1996, Krause Publications, Iola, Wisconsin.
2. Browning, John and Curt Gentry, *John M. Browning, American Gunmaker*, Browning 1964.
3. Schwing, Ned, personal correspondence 1994, Fredricksburg, Texas.
4. Eastman, Max, *Browning Firearms, a Chronology 1924 to 1985*, Eastman Publisher, 1985.
5. Schwing, Ned, "Making Sense of the Superposed," *Shooting Sportsman*, May/June 1977.
6. Browning records historian, personal correspondence 1995, Morgan, Utah.
7. Jaqua, William, personal correspondence 1992.
8. Schwing, Ned, personal communication 2000.

CHAPTER SIX

ITHACA

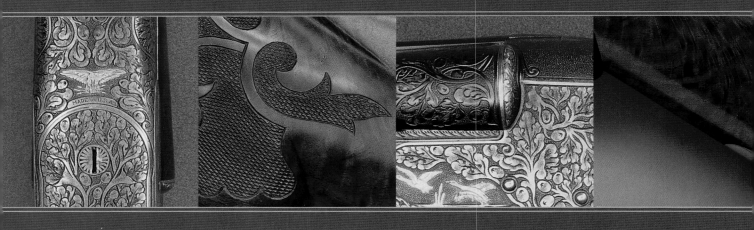

The Ithaca Gun Company ranks among the great American firearm firms of the first half of the 20th century. In particular, the New Ithaca Double (NID) series, begun in 1925, the product of a long evolutionary process, must be considered a classic and consummate example of the shotgun makers' art, beginning with the English Mantons of early 19th-century England.

Started in 1883, Ithaca issued the first recorded catalog in 1885. In 1893, they introduced the top-lever hammerless "V" spring boxlock, the Crass Model, designed by Fred Crass. It was bolted by an adjustable barrel underlug and a doll's head rib extension. It remained in production until 1901.

The Lewis Model followed from 1901 to 1906. It featured redesigned cocking levers and ejectors together with a bolted doll's head. The Miniér Model, from 1906 to 1908, converted the mainspring from "V" to coils and employed the rod and cam-cocking lever. The Flues Model lasted from 1908 to 1925. The lock system was more than twice as fast as any other American hammer.

Finally, the NID gun, Ithaca's premier product, a double side-by-side, was introduced in 1925-26. Ithaca made over 47,000, beginning with SN 425000, and it incorporated the Flues lock system. This lock achievement, introduced in 1908 at SN 175000, reduced the lock parts to three components: hammer, sear, and coiled mainspring with a rapid lock time of "1/625"

second, tested at Cornell University in 1910. Production of the NID continued from 1925 to 1948.

The NID gun used the Flues boxlock but changed the cocking system to a push rod pin to the hammer and a cocking cam in the forend. Furthermore, it eliminated the underlug, and the action locked to the barrels by a top bolt of a rotary toe hook design, locking the rib extension, similar to the L.C. Smith and A.H. Fox. Using this system left more steel in the frame, and after they more precisely machined the rotary bolt's radius, the gun was heralded for its strength of action and closure.

Ithaca offered this gun in grades "Field" through "Sousa" and stocked them with American walnut. They never used Circassian walnut, and the locks were less polished and regulated than those of its high-grade competitors. It was also less expensive in comparable grades. However, the checkering was superb and may have been without equal among the competition.

This then was the technical background which led to the introduction of the 410 bore in the 1926 catalog, in all grades including the "Sousa" in the NID model.

They weighed 5-3/4 pounds, initially with 2 3/8-, then 2 7/8- in 1931, and finally 3-inch chambers in 1935. They had a checkered pistol grip stock, and options available included automatic ejectors, single trigger, beavertail forend, and a ventilated rib. They all had fluid steel barrels from 26 to 32 inches in length. The incomparable Bob Edwards' Damascus barrels were phased out soon after the turn of the century, as smokeless powder required greater tensile strength. Nonetheless, the Edwards' barrel legacy lived on and the gun had a great reputation for its precision patterning.

The "Auto and Burglar" gun, introduced in 1922, continued in production until 1933, for a total run of 1240 guns. At that time, a shotgun pistol with less than 18-inch barrels became illegal. Most A&B guns were 10-inch double side-by-sides with a pistol gun handle and manufactured in both the Flues and NID models. According to John McMorrow, the now deceased Ithaca historian with whom I had several interviews in the late 1970s, the company made five NID 410s. These were made from 1928 to 1938. Snyder lists the serial numbers as follows: 452245 and 452246, both with 26-inch barrels, in 1928; 452251 and 452252 with 12 1/2- and 10-inch barrels in 1929; and 461194 with an 18 1/2-inch barrel in 1938 [1].

Ithaca purchased the Lefever Arms Company in 1915 and introduced an inexpensive boxlock double, the "New Lefever Nitro Special" in 1921. Following that, in 1929, they introduced the "Western Long Range Double," an even cheaper gun. Both models were available in the 410 with 26-inch barrels. These were extractor guns with double or single triggers. When "Nitro Special" production ceased in 1947, over 235,000 guns had been produced, of which approximately 1000 to 2000 were in the 410 bore. These were built with the Flues lock action and the NID cocking system without engraving or cocking indicators and with six-lines-to-the-inch checkering.

The "Western Long Range" gun had the same action and barrels as the "Nitro Special" but no checkering and the stock was of plainer wood. Less than 2 percent of the almost 66,000 produced were made in the 410 bore. The rationale for these two guns may have been to provide a low-cost but well-built gun out of existing Flues parts made obsolete by the NID series.

Ithaca introduced an "upgraded version" of the "Nitro Special" in 1935 and discontinued it in 1940. They made 2496 guns during the run, approximately 150 of which were in the 410 bore [2]. It was called the Lefever "A" grade. The rib was improved, the frame was color case hardened, there was some engraving, and the wood with a checkered pistol grip stock was of higher quality than in the "Nitro Special." Introduced as a "Skeet" model with 26-inch barrels, it was also offered with "Field" specifications. Options included automatic ejectors, a beavertail forend, and a single trigger. These "Field" options were standard in the "Skeet" model (Photo 1). Again, Ithaca used existing Flues lock components. However, the gun bolted only with a rib extension mating with two insertions from the standing breech. Like the NID, the barrel underbolt had been removed.

Existing Lefever "A"-grade 410s must be very rare indeed, as serial number 300619 is the only one I have ever seen. One other was sold at a 2001 American auction, number 300274. Most have probably vanished due to the triple evils of time, abuse, and neglect (see Chapter 10).

NID 410 Gauge

According to McMorrow, all NID guns, regardless of grade, had the same action and barrel metal quality. The differences were in the workmanship, wood, checkering, and engraving. Automatic ejectors were standard in grades "4E" through "7E," the "E" meaning ejector.

Photo 1: Ithaca 5E, SN 457527 (top); Ithaca 7E, SN 467672 (middle); and a Lefever "A" grade, SN 300619, "Skeet" Model (bottom).

G. Allan Brown photo ⌄

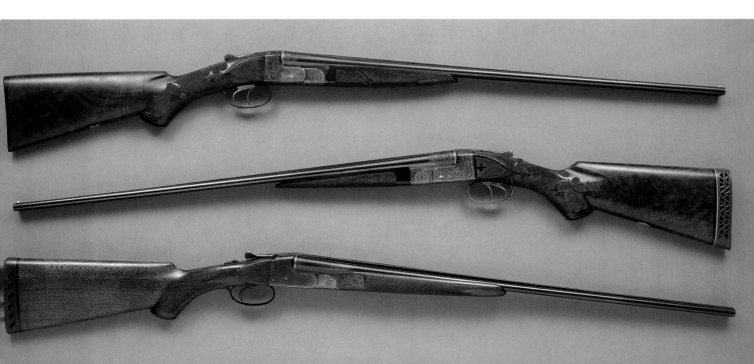

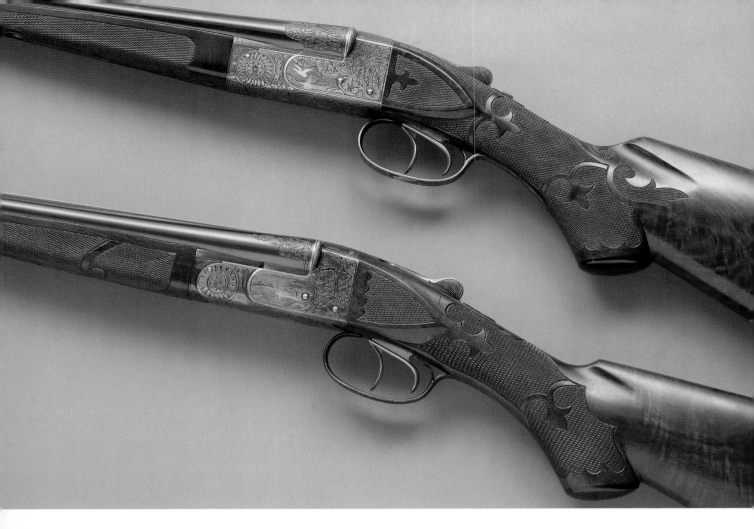

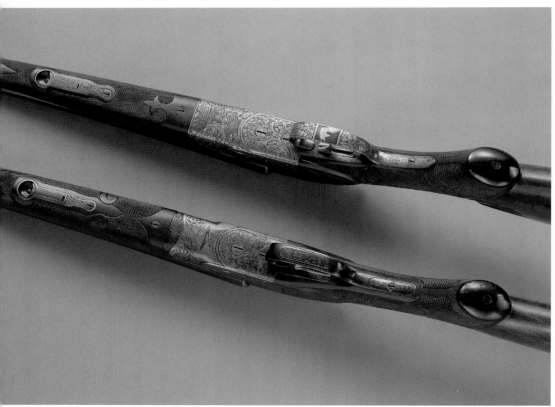

Photo 2: An Ithaca 7E, SN 467672 is pictured over an Ithaca 5E, SN 457527.

G. Allan Brown photo

Photo 6: Bottom views of SN 467672 and SN 457527.

G. Allan Brown photo

Photos 3 - 5: Close views of the McGraw engraving and Ithaca's unparalleled checkering of SN 467672.

Levasheff photos >

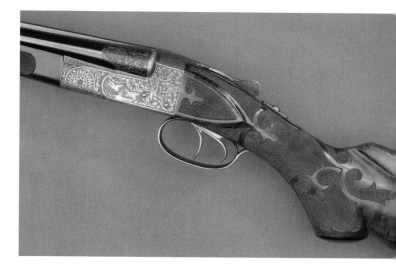

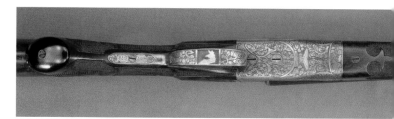

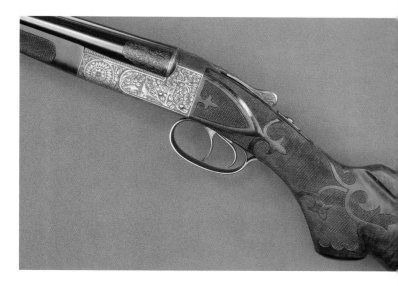

Based upon information contained in the "Fox and Crows" catalog, the "7E" model was introduced in approximately 1911 with a $400 price tag. It had Krupp or Whitworth fluid steel barrels and the locks were hand polished and damascened. A gold bird decorated the frame bottom, a gold inlaid pointer dog on one side and a setter on the opposite.

McMorrow reported that the highest grade 410 in the records was "7E," of which two were made. He related an unconfirmed story about two 410s made in the "Sousa" grade, commissioned by the Delaware DuPont family for their dog handlers to shoot over dogs. However, the numbers were not in the file. This is one of many interesting stories of high-grade guns often floating in the smoke of gun show gossip, eventually confirmed or becoming proverbial and passing into gun mythology.

One of the two "7E" models is in pristine condition. Serial number 467672 (Photos 2-6) is reported by Ithaca to have been engraved by William McGraw, a 20th-century master of his craft (Photo 7). The original hanging tags, a copy of the original bill of sale, and correspondence and pictures from the widow about the original owner, accompany the gun. The gun was a special order for a friend of the president of Ithaca with whom the owner shot on many occasions. These memorabilia provide fascinating history of the gun's first years in existence (Photos 8, 9). For many years this gun was in the care of Mr. and Mrs. Joseph Pelton, Ohio shotgun fanciers. Of particular interest to wild sheep hunters is the fact that this married couple may be the only husband and wife team to have each successfully hunted the North American Grand Slam in wild sheep in the 1950s.

The second "7E" 410 was stolen in 1928 and never recovered. Walter Snyder, in his comprehensive and definitive study, refers to an issue of *Sportsmen's Review*, May 5, 1928 [3]. The review tells of the theft of a "7E" 410, SN 448950, April 21, 1928, in Omaha, Nebraska, with a value of $400. It has a single trigger, gold inlays, and ivory sights. Hopefully, it may someday reappear.

According to McMorrow's records, a total of eight to 11 guns were made in "Sousa" grade in all bores save 410 and 22 were made in "7E" including two 410s and two 28 bores. Recently, however, a 1993 gun auction offered a "Sousa" 410, SN 457543, with a straight grip stock (almost all 410s were half pistol grip), game scene engraved with gold animal inlays, beavertail forend, gold single trigger, and "fleur-de-lis" checkering. According to Ithaca records, this gun left the factory as a 410 "Field"-grade gun.

During the SN 457543 search, at my request, the Ithaca employee claimed to surface another 410 entry, SN 456813, with 28-inch barrels, single trigger, beavertail forend, and a ventilated rib with a mermaid on the trigger guard. It was sold to John Boa in Chicago for $618 on January 9, 1930. This was the wholesale price of a "Sousa" grade gun, according to a 1929 price list. However, months later, Walter Snyder and Les Hovencamp of Ithaca could not confirm the existence of this gun. Number 456813 was a standard 10 bore. For this, I have no explanation, except for the possibility that the first researcher misread a 10 bore for a 410. This, however, does not explain the wholesale price!

During the 1993 Snyder-Hovencamp search, however, they did uncover a jewel, an apparently authentic "Sousa" grade 410 in the ledger book. Serial Number 454423 has a single trigger and ventilated rib on 26-inch barrels with ivory sights. The factory shipped the gun to John Boa of Chicago on January 5, 1929, and then reshipped to D.M. Frame on April 24, 1929. John Boa's name figures prominently as a purchaser of many high-grade Ithacas. Snyder reports that a former employee, Keith Houghtling also recalled this "Sousa"-grade 410. It is also reported that number 456800 is recorded as a "high grade" 410 with 28-inch barrels without further details.

More recently, in 2001, Sid Cleveland, current Ithaca Historian, reports a William McGraw gold inlay engraved 410, number 469715, grade not specified, with double triggers and 26-inch barrels and made in 1941.

According to McMorrow, six "5E" 410s were made, with three currently known to exist and are recorded. Number 457527 has double triggers and a raised solid rib, and is in mint condition (Photo 10). Number 467667, also mint, has double triggers, and a matted solid rib. Number 454029 has a single trigger, gold inlays in white, an elevated rib, with a replaced stock and forend. Two other "5Es" are recorded in the ledgers as shipped in 1930, both with single triggers, ventilated ribs, ivory sights, butt pads, and 26-inch barrels. Their serial numbers are 456885 and 456886. The sixth is unaccounted for, both in the records and in reality.

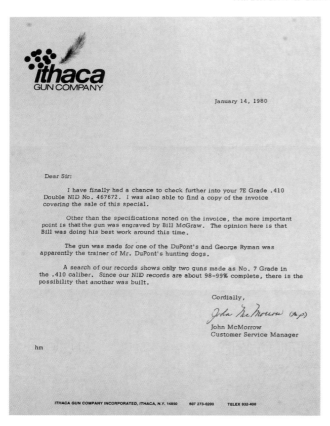

Photo 7: Letter from Ithaca regarding the McGraw-engraved 7E.

Glenn Campbell photo ∧

Photo 8: Original invoice and hanging tag of SN 467672.

Glenn Campbell photo ∨

Photo 9: Personal photo of the wife of the original owner, George Ryman, the 7E Ithaca, some of their setters, and harvested game in the snows of Pennsylvania.

∨ *Glenn Campbell photo*

McMorrow reported that 14 410s were made in the "4E" grade, seven in "3" grade, 40 in "2" grade, 64 in "1" grade, and 790 in "Field" grade. According to invoices, Ithaca produced only 30 410s from 1927 to 1933, with the large majority made after the chambers were converted to 3 inches in 1935. Most of the very high-grade 410s have serial numbers in the 450000 range and above, indicating manufacture after early 1928.

Interestingly, Allen recently reported that most of the 410 "Field"-grade guns he has seen were made by 1926 in the 430000 range and were of the "First Variation" [4]. Approximately 10,000 guns in all bores were made between 1925 and 1926. This first-generation 410 weighed 5-1/2 pounds and was chambered for 2 1/2-inch shells, according to the 1926 catalog. Characterizing the "First Variation" was a polished case-colored action, German-style top cocking indicators, American walnut stock, Flues model checkering, small grip, and a short forearm.

The 1926 catalog, listing for the first time the 410 bore, describes the top grade available as the "Sousa Special Ejector." It had a retail price of $750, compared to the $37.50 "Field"-grade 410. A single selective trigger made by the "Miller Single Trigger Manufacturing Co." was an additional $30.

By 1935, the "Field" grade sold for $39.75, and Ithaca had just introduced the "Skeet" 410 with 3-inch chambers, ejectors, beavertail forend, and recoil pad, selling for $86.20.

The NID 410 was a sturdy, dependable, and high-quality gun that has now become a classic and worthy of an owner's pride of possession. If you own a high-grade 410, enjoy its artistic splendor and its solid shooting characteristics.

Postscript

Ithaca Classic Doubles of Victor, New York, resurrected the classic NID double in 1998. Stephen Lamboy purchased the name, the original factory prints, and the manufacturing rights. Initially, Italy produced the component parts using CAD/CNC technology [5]. The new guns have chopper-lump barrels on actions made of Hi-Chrome nickel molybdenum steel. The rib extension is lengthened, and all gauges have properly scaled actions for the barrels. The 12 bore is proofed to 1700 BAR. Parts of old and new guns are not interchangeable.

The serial numbers began with 470,000. The stocks are black American walnut with the fleur-de-lis checkering pattern up to 32 lines per inch. Hand engraving by Creative Art modeled their patterns after original McGraw's. A scaled-down action 410 is available at 5-1/4 pounds in "Special Field," 4E, 7E, and "Sousa" grades.

Alas, in 2003, this new company went into receivership. Fortunately, it was bought by another vendor, Dakota Arms.

McIntosh reports that New Ithaca Doubles are finished at a "higher level of craftsmanship and quality than the original NID." He is also enthused about its handling and pointability [6].

Photo 10: The Ithaca 5E, SN 457527, over a Model 21 Winchester, a classic standard model of the 1950s—a comparison.

ᐯ *Levasheff photo*

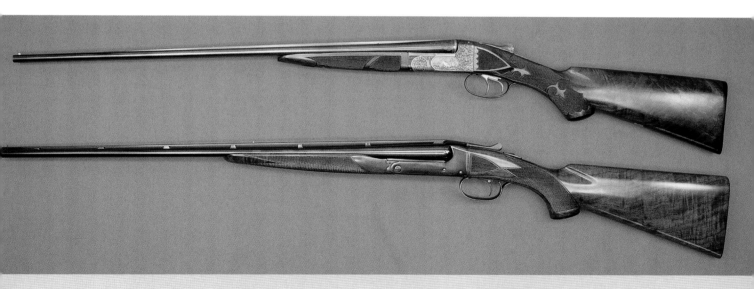

Ithaca References

1. Snyder, Walter, *The Ithaca Gun Company,* 1991 Wallsworth Publishing Co, Missouri.
2. Ackley, Linda, Ithaca historical correspondence, April 30, 1984.
3. *Sportsmen's Review,* May 5, 1928.
4. Allen, William R., "New Ithaca Double Field Grade," *The Double Gun,* Vol. 5, Issue 3, Autumn 1994.
5. Vic Venters, *Shooting Sportsman,* July/August 1998.
6. Michael McIntosh, *Shooting Sportsman,* Jan/Feb 2000.

CHAPTER SEVEN

PARKER BROTHERS

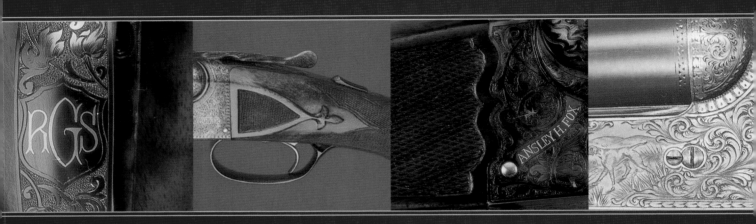

he story of the extraordinary success of the Parker shotgun has been told and retold on numerous occasions in magazine articles, chapters, and book-length dissertations, beginning in the 1950s. Many controversial questions about the Parker gun were definitively answered in 1998 and 2000, in a two-volume historical review of the actual existing Parker records [1].

To the extent that a recapitulation of this history serves to illuminate certain facets of the even more remarkable Parker 410-gauge story, this writer will risk trying the patience of the Parker aficionado. Indeed, the general history of Parker is reproducibly constant from narrative to narrative with only minor variations in the details, now corrected or fine-tuned by the two-volume history.

The story had remained incomplete until recently when Remington Arms allowed a historical search and compilation of existing Parker records. Hence, a large database of dates, serial numbers, grades, and production numbers is now available. The combined efforts of several writers and researchers have produced a monumental work of history. Now we know in detail the evolution of Parker technology and skill predating the 410 bore, and how this bore ultimately found a warm and comfortable home in the Parker inventory.

The information contained in this chapter is from five sources: 1) the written record of reliable Parker writers throughout the last 40 years; 2) the author's personal observations cataloged over 25 years; 3) anecdotal data supplied by Parker cognoscenti throughout the country including the highly reliable and respected William Jaqua, Otis Odom, Don Criswell, and Herschel Chadick; 4) recollections from the Parker family members; and 5) *The Parker Story* and its review of existing archives.

Originally written 10 years ago, this chapter has needed relatively little revision following the publication of *The Parker Story*. The changes are mainly related to production numbers and greater specificity regarding dates and serial numbers.

History

In 1888, the first hammerless boxlock was recorded as serial number 55295. The first quality small-bore gun by an American manufacturer, a 28-gauge, SN 94373, was introduced in 1899. In 1902, the perfected automatic ejector is first recorded on gun number 112920. In 1912, James P. Hayes proposed simplifying the cocking system, reducing the number of parts from 18 to four, but only some of his proposals were incorporated into production.

First announced in a flyer in 1922 was the single trigger. However, the "second single trigger," gun SN 196938, a DHE, was booked in 1921.

The beavertail forend was first noted in 1915, on SN 171598, an A1 Special (A1S) double. The ventilated rib was first offered in 1917 on the single-barrel trap gun and on the double in 1923, number 204548, an AHE gun.

The Parker 410, therefore, was introduced at a time when Parker Bros. had completed their technical evolution and was building their final and perfected product. Excluding the prototype by Charles Parker (see below), the first 410 recorded is SN 215833 in the 1926 dark green "Geese" catalog. This bore's production numbers, serial numbers, and grades will be discussed to the extent now known.

The last catalog listing the PH grade was in 1926. The last PH 410 recorded (of a total of three) was number 226186. The skeet-configured gun is first recorded in 1929, SN 232262. The first recorded skeet 410 was in 1931, SN 235933, with a single trigger, ejectors, and beavertail forend. The last recorded 410, number 241788, is a DHE gun. However, a later gun (SN 242387), a GH 410, was said to have been shipped in 1947 [2]. This gun remains unrecorded in the stock books (see Postscript).

Robert Rudolph Runge and son Robert Phoenix Runge were two engravers who moved with Parker from Meriden to Ilion. Their pictures are in the 1937 catalog and they are the premier artisans central to the Parker 410 upgrade story. Larry DelGrego, another Parker artisan, married the daughter of Herman Shura, and was a final assembler for Parker at both Meriden and Ilion. When he opened his own establishment in the early 1950s to service Parker shotgun owners, he teamed with Robert Rudolph Runge and eventually Runge's son to create one of the most complex and contentious stories in the history of American shotgun collecting, the Parker Upgrade.

The 410 Odyssey

The story of the 410 gauge is essentially the story of Charles Stewart Parker, the great-grandson of the founder, who I interviewed in 1978. His innovative drive led to the development of the single most exciting American shotgun ever built. Certainly, the 410 is the most beautiful and rarest of the important gauges manufactured by Parker Bros. in their history. However, little did Charles Parker realize in 1924, when he first began making the Parker 410 that his progeny would make and, in some cases, break the hearts of so many Parker lovers.

In 1978, four years before Charles Parker died, this writer, speaking with him, elicited a detailed history of the 410's embryogenesis. Louis C. Parker III subsequently and further elaborated upon the information, in a 1983 conversation about a year following the death of Charles Parker.

After graduating from Yale University, Charles Parker chose his family's gun company as his life's work. He apprenticed for 2 years in each shop, spending time with barrel making, stocking, and action development. His "report card" is available in the family archives, detailing his activity in each shop. He eventually

entered management, and by 1924, personally began to assemble the first 410 gauge.

He utilized an A1S 28-gauge stock from a gun that had been returned for restocking. He had a set of Lefever barrels sent to him by Ithaca. He changed the lug of the barrels from a Lefever to a Parker type in order to fit a 28-gauge Parker Vulcan frame, lightened to 000 by steel milling. Originally, the 28-gauge frame had been steel milled from the water table of a 0 size 20-gauge frame, resulting in a 00. This 00 frame was then further milled to 000. This made the 410 much lighter, but it still weighed over six pounds, heavy in comparison to a typical British 410 whose frame was scaled down in width and depth to match the small barrels. Charles wanted a "heavy" 410 so that the American man would accept it as a "serious" gun.

This newly fashioned VH Vulcan 000 frame, together with the Lefever barrels from Ithaca and the A1S 28-gauge stock, was assembled and finished with a splinter forend and double triggers. The assembly was completed in 1924-1925, and numbered 190767. This gun was eventually sold by Charles Parker to a famed Parker collector and metallurgist in Alabama, Warren C. Jeffery, who, in turn, resold it to a Parker collector in Pennsylvania. It now reposes in the National Rifle Association Museum in northern Virginia. Charles Parker wrote a detailed letter regarding its gestation when he sold the gun, but this letter has vanished.

Soon after the manufacturing of the prototype, Roy Wilcox, of the International Silver Company, ordered the first 410 in VHE grade. He may have been instrumental in persuading Charles Parker to assemble the prototype, and he "talked" Charles into a first order of six 410s. These guns apparently were manufactured and shipped during 1926 and 1927.

It was with great pride that Charles Parker recounted that he personally lightened the 28-gauge Vulcan frame and replaced the Lefever lug with a Parker lug. He personally undertook the assembly of the first gun. He was quick to say that the reason for this was that he was unable to coax any of the artisans in the various shops to undertake these specific tasks. Furthermore, he recalls that senior management had not taken this prototype seriously, and they did not intend to place this bore into production. This was prior to the first order by the Wilcox family.

In 1927, the gauge became publicly available. Charles estimated that from 1927 to 1931, less than 1 percent of Parker gun output was in the 410 gauge. He was close. According to the archives, Parker made 20,334 guns from 1926 to 1930, 304 of which were 410s, or approximately 1.5 percent [3]. He recalled no production figures but specifically stated that they made no P-grade guns in the 410. However, we now know there are three PH 410s recorded, numbers 218479, 223161, and 226186.

Louis Parker Jr. and son Louis C. Parker III had estimated that less than 5 percent of the total output from 1927 to 1939 was in 410 or 28 bore. Therefore, something less than 1250 guns in both bores were made from 1927 onwards, of which the distinct

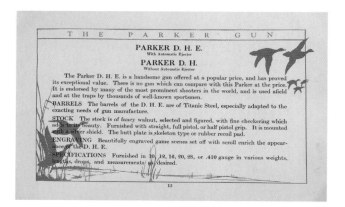

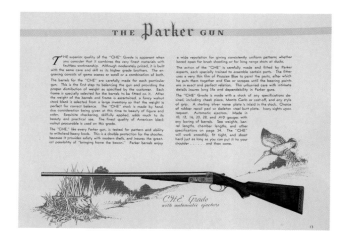

^ **Photo 1:** In a 1930 Parker catalog, the DHE was the highest grade offered in the 410.

Glenn Campbell photo

^ **Photo 2:** In a 1934 Parker catalog, the DHE was again the highest grade offered in the 410.

Glenn Campbell photo

^ **Photo 3:** In this 1937 Parker catalog, the 410 was offered in all grades.

Glenn Campbell photo

minority was the 410. We now know there are 506 recorded 410s. *The Parker Story*, because there are two missing stock books in the relevant timeframe for 410 production, estimates a higher number actually made, using the statistical sampling techniques. The most recent extrapolation recognizes 519 [3].

They calculated that the 410-bore records are 28 percent incomplete and used a "missing record allowance" to estimate a final production number. From November 1920, SN 192498, until the end of production, approximately 49,974 guns were produced. The stock books for 12,156 of these guns are missing. In the window of time relevant to 410 production, approximately 19,584 guns were produced and the stock books for 6078 of these guns are missing. These do not include missing IBM cards, if any, for guns after number 238934. With the country now deep into the depression, the stock books, beginning with SN 236537, reveal that approximately 199 were manufactured after Remington purchased Parker in 1934. This is at variance with more recent data from those records, which record a total of 519 guns built in 410. They built 304 from 1926 to 1930 (numbers 215400-235733); 171 from 1931 to 1935 (numbers 235734-238805); as well as 44 from 1937 to 1942 (numbers 238806-242487). The year 1936 is omitted from the data [3].

Charles Parker told me that the highest grade 410 made between 1927 and 1938 was a CHE. He told his heirs that the highest grade 410 up to 1937 was a DHE. This is consistent with 1930 and 1934 catalogs in which only the V, G, and D grades were offered (Photos 1, 2). In the 1937 catalog, the 410 was offered in all grades (Photo 3). This appeared to be a tribute to the gauge's increasing popularity in the 1930s, partly due to the influx of women and children into the sport of clay target shooting and partly due to the expert's desire for a greater challenge. Contrary to Charles Parker's recollection, the stock books on this point reveal one CHE 410 made in 1930 (SN 234906), one in 1935 (SN 237220), and one in 1936 (SN 239411), all before 1937 when it was first cataloged.

The 410 Production

The first Parker 410 is a VHE 26-inch pistol grip gun, SN 215833, once owned by Leon Kelly, the first and most prolific of the great Parker 410 collectors. The second 410, SN 216303, a VH gun, currently exists and has been authenticated by the stock books and is in my Parker 410 archive records of existing 410 guns. There are two earlier numbered guns, numbers 180178 and 175050, which were original 28-bore guns that had been returned to the factory for 410 barrel installation. Another currently existing early 410, SN 216624, a VH gun, appeared in the May 1974 *Arms Gazette*, and is not recorded.

Number 180178 is an A1S 28-gauge gun on a 00 frame manufactured in 1918 that was returned and fitted with 410 barrels in October 1937. These barrels were engraved by Robert Runge Sr. and Fredrick Anschutz and the gun re-checkered by

George Lane (Photos 4, 5, 5A). Previously, in 1935, this gun had been returned to the factory for a new set of 28-gauge barrels. This gun was donated to Duck's Unlimited in the mid-1980s and last offered publicly in 1992 for $185,000 by William Jaqua. It is now with a southern California collector.

The second existing very early 410, SN 175050, is recorded as a 24-inch barreled CHE gun, originally a 28 gauge. A third, a VH 410, SN 153763, is not recorded as either a 410 or a 28-gauge gun.

In my archives, the vast majority of the documented 410 guns were manufactured after 1931. These data categorizes 200 410 guns that have been detailed as to serial number, grade, and, in most cases, options and condition. In almost all cases, these guns were publicly traded among dealers and collectors and have been authenticated (specific information is available by inquiry).

In my archives, there are six guns recorded in the 217000 range, three in the 218000 range, and seven in the 219000 range. In the stock books, there are 20, 30, and 12 respectively. There is a missing stock book after number 219840.

Photos 4, 5: Two views of the famous A1S (SN 180178) 28/410-gauge gun auctioned by Ducks Unlimited in the late 1980s.

Ducks Unlimited photos ∨

Photo 5A: A posed view of ∧ SN 180178.

Jaqua photo

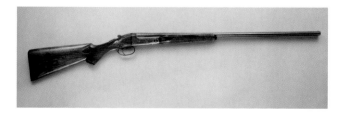

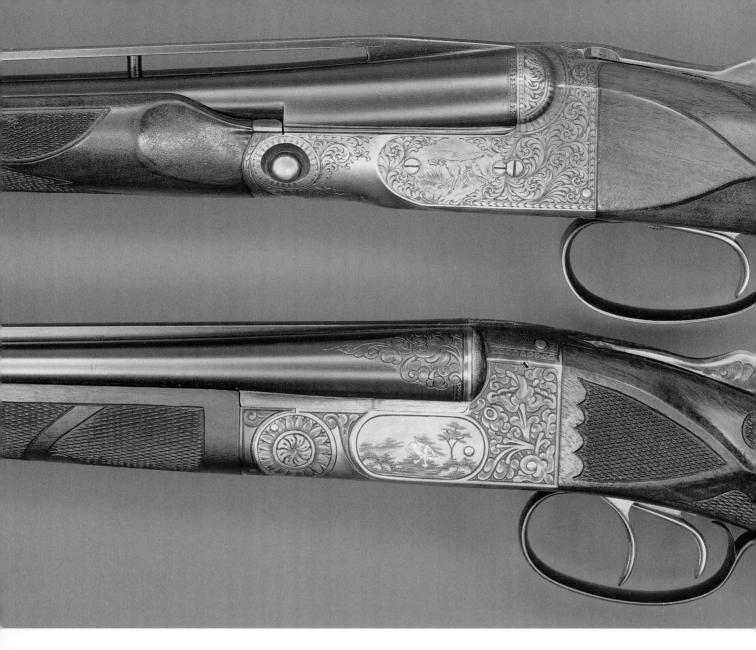

The ventilated rib option occurs in only seven 410 guns as recorded in the Parker records; one each in VHE and CHE, three in DHE, and two in the GHE grades. My archives record five ventilated rib 410s, but two are not found in the stock books—SN 221959, a BHE 410, and SN 242291, upgraded by Runge from a GHE to an A1S. The original CHE, number 241429, with a ventilated rib is pictured (Photo 6).

Virtually all original 410s were made on the 000 frame after 1928. Subsequently, however, a couple rare 410s appear to have been manufactured originally on the 00 frame including a VH, SN 237257, and a GHE, SN 231691. The latter gun's stock book is missing. There are a number of known 410 bores on a 00 frame. Rarely, an original buyer simply wanted a heavier-framed 410. Of other 00 frame 410s, some are recorded as original 28 bore and returned to the factory for a set of 410 barrels; in others, the 410 barrels were added after the factory ceased production by vendors such as Larry DelGrego.

Photo 6: A Parker CHE 410, SN 241429, is shown above an Ithaca 5E 410, SN 457527.

Levasheff photo

Thirty-one 28-inch, four 30-inch, and one 25-inch barreled 410s are recorded. The rest are 26-inch. According to the records, 149 410s have single triggers, the vast majority produced after number 235932 in 1930.

Up until 1930, the 410 was chambered for the 2 1/2-inch cartridge. Sometime after 1932, they converted to the popular 3-inch cartridge for the small wing and ground game shooter that emerged in increasing numbers in the 1930s. The records are silent on this point, but almost certainly, when Olin-Winchester developed the 3-inch cartridge, Parker elongated their chambers. Proof pressure for the 410 with 2 1/2-inch cartridges with 65 grains of powder and 273 grains of shot is 7.75 tons per square inch.

Parker made what appears to be 81 skeet-configured 410s (i.e. single trigger, beavertail forend, etc.): one CHE, eight DHEs, eight GHEs, and 64 VHEs.

In the 1937 to 1938 timeframe, when Remington moved the Parker Gun Company to Ilion, the 410 was then offered in all grades up through A1S. Therefore, a 410 in a grade higher than a DHE should have a serial number above approximately 240106, with the above-noted exceptions.

For a number of years, it was thought that a GHE, SN 242291, upgraded to A1S by Runge for Otis Odom[1] was the last 410 manufactured. Then, GHE number 242387 surfaced in the gun literature. To date neither gun is recorded in *The Parker Story*. The last 410 listed is SN 241788. The 410 was last cataloged in 1940. The last 410 is dated from 1939 to 1942 (see Postscript).

---

[1] Personal friend in frequent communication with author.

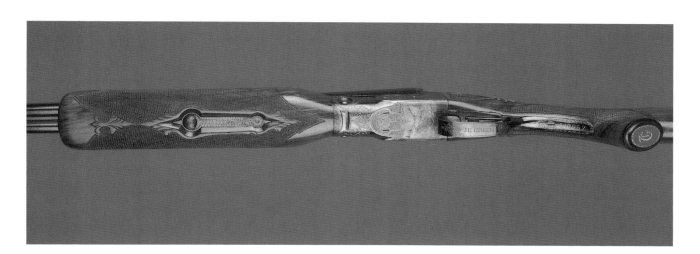

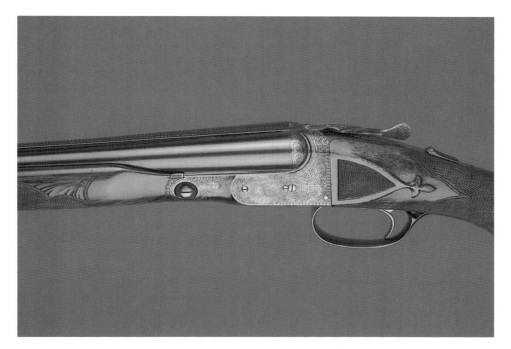

∧

Photo 7: Bottom view of SN 240657.

Chadick photo

Photo 8: Side view of SN 240657, a good example of superb upgrade artisan work to a BHE.

< *Chadick photo*

A large number of Parker 410s have either been upgraded or refinished. There are, however, a number of original guns in good to excellent condition. Unfortunately, their monetary value tends to preclude their use as a field gun. This is a great shame, as the Parker 410 is the finest balanced and pointing American gun made by human hands in the "classical" period of double gun making.

The Upgrade Imbroglio

The Parker shotgun, particularly the 410 gauge, has generated more controversy, ruptured more friendships, instigated more litigation, broken more hearts, and caused more personal vendettas and public squabbles—verbal and written—than any other shotgun in the history of this human tool. The reasons are twofold. First, the Parker 410 remains the preeminent American side-by-side double shotgun and its excellence is rarely equaled by other American manufacturers of the past. Second, the previous absence of reliable records subjected the potential buyer of the 410 to the whims of the marketplace and its many entrepreneurs of varying degrees of fastidiousness. Without factory-based authenticity, opinion often substituted for fact, and that opinion may have been prejudiced by economic self-interest.

Remington Arms Company, which purchased Parker Bros. in 1934, until recently had done a disservice to the Parker shotgun collecting and dealer fraternity by refusing access to the Parker records, in part or in whole, for verification purposes. Indeed, a September 1968 issue of *Guns & Ammo* quotes a Remington correspondent as having said, "The old Parker books stored in the factory's hall of records are really dusty old manuscripts. The material is not in any particular order, the writing is often difficult to read, and we, therefore, do not welcome requests for Parker information."

However, it is now known that Remington had preserved a significant number of Parker record books, particularly since 1920, in which only four of 16 books are missing. After 1935, SN 238934, IBM cards were used. They may have been unwilling to release the necessary documentation on each gun because of the problems inherent in what had become a minor industry: Parker Upgrading.

Photo 9: Full view of CHE 410, SN 241429, with a ventilated rib.

Levasheff photo

Photo 10 (bottom): The Parker CHE 410, SN 241429, is shown above a Parker DHE.

G. Allan Brown photo

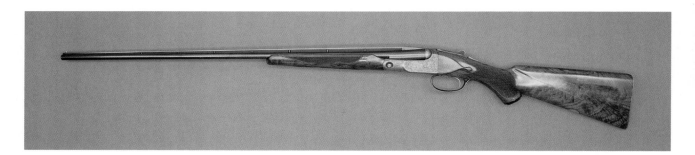

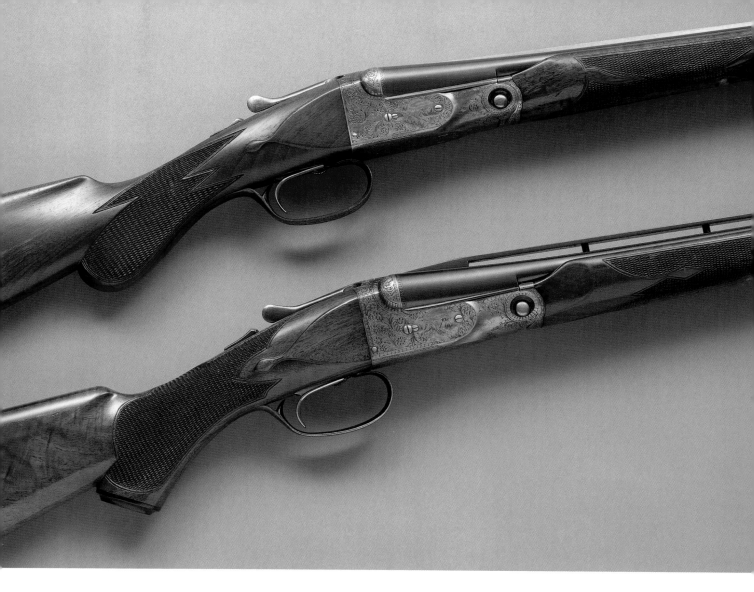

Upgrading began to occur when Remington ceased making Parkers and when a number of fine artisans such as the two Robert Runges and Larry DelGrego became independent gunsmiths and began servicing Parker customers.

Their frank and quite honest 410 upgrading, in most instances signed by the upgraders, utilized elaborate metal engravings, superior wood, and fine checkering. They also performed a complete change of markings, producing simulated high-grade Parkers from A1Ss to CHEs, and, at least in three cases, PH-grade guns. This was done certainly without any intent to misrepresent since the guns were signed as upgrades. Certain other upgrades such as those produced by Pachmayr are readily identifiable, again originally produced without intent to mislead. The signed upgrades by the Runges and DelGrego represent an elaborate and brilliant superimposition of high-grade work upon an originally lower-grade gun.

Many of these guns, however, have been exploited by others in the Parker resale market and have betrayed a number of unwary gun collectors and investors. Herein lies the problem. In addition, it is with great care and circumspection that the

Photo 12: A bottom view of the CHE, SN 241429, and the DHE (top).

G. Allan Brown photo ∨

Photo 11: A close up view of ∧ the CHE, SN 241429, and the DHE (top).

G. Allan Brown photo

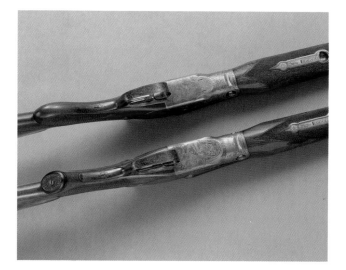

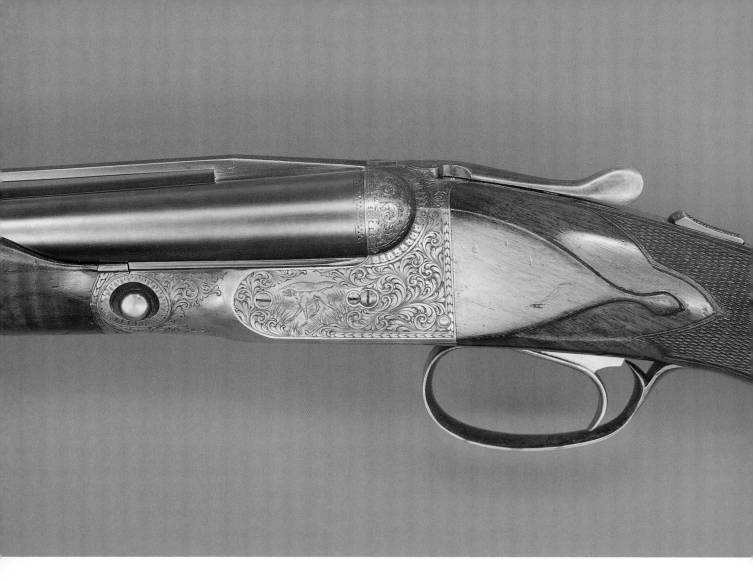

Photo 12A: A detailed view of the elegant engraving of a CHE.

G. Allan Brown photo

writer's appendix will be made available on request to the collector. If Remington had maintained and made the Parker records available in good repair from the beginning, the entire upgrade problem would have never occurred.

The very fact of Parker excellence in the absence of factory authentication has placed a premium on originality and condition. It has made the Parker market subject to the flamboyance of its most artful manipulators.

Fortunately, over the years there have been a number of very knowledgeable Parker shotgun cognoscenti, including William Jaqua, Otis Odom, John Kilgore, Don Criswell, Herschel Chadick, Leon Kelly, and Alan Phillips, among others, upon whose expertise and judgment the Parker aficionado can depend.

Finally and happily, Remington did the "right thing" for the shotgun collecting fraternity of America by allowing the cata-

loging of serial numbers, grades, and production data to the extent possible and appears to be willing to make this information generally available. Most, if not all of the records of the last 25 years of Parker's history, are salvageable. It is this vintage gun that was particularly susceptible to upgrading, and that most applies to the 410 bore.

For example, Leon Kelly[2] personally ordered seven upgrades to be made from original VHE or VH guns, five of which were done by both Robert Runges. Kelly, at one time, owned 30 410s and had personally inspected 10 additional guns. He was perhaps the first of the prolific collectors beginning in the 1950s. Of those that passed his purview, less than half were in their original condition. Of the over 200 410s in the author's archives, less than one-third are original and unrefinished. Otis Odom, of impeccable veracity and the greatest and most knowledgeable Parker collector in the last quarter of the 20th century, also affirms that a small minority of the Parkers he has examined remain in original condition.

---

2 Personal communication.

I know of only one article specifically devoted to the 410 Parker that reached the reading public. It appeared in *Arms Gazette* in May 1978. This article appears to be a minefield of mistaken data, primarily because a number of what appear to be upgraded Parker 410s were identified as originals. The data has not stood the test of critical scrutiny and record verification. However, the effect of the article has been salutary in that it has led to greater public awareness of what is or is not original. As the years flow by, this is assuming greater and greater importance as the high-grade original guns reach into the six-figure dollar range.

Existing 410s In My Archives

A1S

Based upon my archival data, all 410s above the BHE grade with one exception, an AHE number 241576, represent upgrades, most of which are clearly identified as such. This includes 10 A1Ss. An 11th is an A1S (SN 180178) that was originally, as detailed earlier, a 28-bore manufactured in 1918 and returned for a set of 410 barrels in 1937 (Photos 4 and 5). The Parker stock books have verified this.

AAHE and AHE

There are three known AAHE grades, numbers 236680, 239686, and 237187, which are acknowledged Runge or DelGrego upgrades. There are five known AHEs, four of which are upgrades, with one of them, SN 244245, far above the last known Parker number. Charles Parker's memory was not completely accurate, since SN 241576 is in the records as having been made in the narrow window of time between 1938 and World War II as an AHE with a single trigger and a large forend. This has not surfaced for public assessment.

BHE

There are nine archived BHE 410s, six of which are identifiable Runge or DelGrego upgrades. One was originally a VHE 28-bore gun, SN 240657, with added 24-inch 410 barrels. Manufactured on an original 00 frame, it represents an example of a bigger bore gun that returned for a smaller gauge set of barrels, a common occurrence. This gun has been upgraded and refinished in considerable detail (Photos 7 and 8).

Of the remaining three, one is the well-known "Linder gun," SN 241788, with double triggers, a splinter forend, and pistol grip stock. The stock book shows this to have been a non-ejector DH 410 with a large forend, the last 410 made. The last BHE made in any bore was SN 240957 in the Parker records.

The two additional BHE 410s, numbers 221960 and 221959, cannot be verified since the stock book for this sequence is missing. These are 1927 guns, long before Parker offered the 410 in any grade above DHE. Number 221960 has Acme steel barrels, which are seen on CH, BH, and AH guns, and the gun has been through the DelGrego operation. It was auctioned at Butterfield's in the late

1990s. Number 221959 has 32-inch barrels, a ventilated rib, Acme steel barrels, single trigger, and beavertail forend. It is pictured in *The Parker Story* and is called "A double trap."

A final 410 in the "style of" a BHE, SN 242189, was originally a VHE in the inventory of William Jaqua. This was also auctioned at Butterfield's in the late 1990s. The number postdates the last 410 from the Parker records, number 241788. The earlier noted upgraded BHE 28 gauge, SN 240657, on a 00 frame and later added 24-inch 410 barrels as a skeet ensemble, is part of a set of skeet guns featured in *The Parker Story*.

CHE

There is collected archived data on 13 existing CHE 410s. Five are confirmed as originals in *The Parker Story*. Number 241081 has 28-inch barrels and double triggers and came to auction in the late 1990s. Numbers 237220, 234906, and 239411 have 26-inch barrels and a single trigger. Number 241429 has 28-inch barrels, single trigger, beavertail forend, capped pistol grip, and a ventilated rib.

The latter gun is not only 100 percent original but also in mint condition. According to Bill Jaqua, this is probably the finest Parker 410 shotgun known to exist, considering all factors, including rarity, options, condition, and originality (Photos 9-12A).

Number 239411 was Robert W. Woodruff's gun, former President and Chairman of Coca Cola. We learn more about him in the M21 Winchester story.

Of the remaining eight, seven are upgrades, either signed by Joseph Runge/DelGrego, or confirmed from the Parker records. One was upgraded from a DHE, one from a VH, and the rest from VHEs. The eighth gun, number 175050, is a 28 gauge in the stock book with 24-inch barrels.

A 14th CHE 410, number 242153, does not appear in any appendix in *The Parker Story* but is mentioned in the narrative. This gun, along with a 28-gauge mate, number 242152, was said to have been given to General George S. Patton, the famed World War II commander. The 28 gauge is pictured but a "photo could not be obtained" of the 410.

In 1934, the CHE with a single trigger was priced at $267.30. The A1S was $825.

The Remaining Grades With The Parker Records Compared To This Writer's Archives Of Existing 410s

There are 24 known and numbered DHEs in the author's archives, none of which appear to represent an upgrade, but many of which have been refinished or refurbished to varying degrees. One of the 24, SN 241109, has a ventilated rib. This compares with 48 DHE 410s in *The Parker Story* records. One has 30-inch barrels, one 28-inch, and the rest have 26-inch barrels. Three DHEs in the Parker records have a ventilated rib, numbers 241109, 235813, and 235332. Illustrated is an original DHE with a beavertail forend and a single trigger (Photos 10-13).

There are six PHE or PH 410s, of which two, according to Leon Kelly, are acknowledged upgrades. Another is a "DelGrego New." The three remaining—PH SN 218479, PHE SN 223161, and PHE SN 226186—are verified by the records as original P-grade 410s.

There are 26 GHE or GH guns with one containing a ventilated rib, SN 242291, not booked and eventually converted to an A1S. This also includes a GHE 410 reported to be the last Parker shotgun made in 1947, SN 242387, also not booked (see Postscript). The Parker records list 28 GHE or GH 410s, two with a ventilated rib, numbers 239264 and 241206. One gun has 28-inch barrels, the rest 26-inch. In my archives, there are no GHEs upgraded from a lower grade, but most are refinished.

Photo 13: A Parker DHE 410 in original condition showing the characteristic subtle engraving of this grade.

Levasheff photo

Photo 14: The DHE 410 is shown above a VHE 410 with a round pistol grip and splinter forend seen in the typical field gun.

Levasheff photo ∨

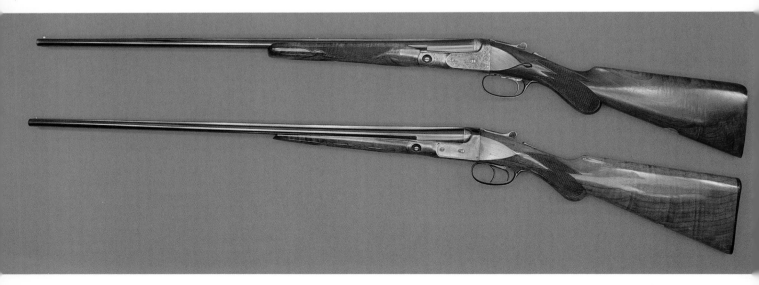

Sixty-nine VHEs and 39 VH 410s are author archived. One VHE has a ventilated rib, SN 238764. Many have been refinished or refurbished. Very few are completely original and in mint condition. An original double trigger, splinter forend VHE on a double 00 frame is illustrated here (Photo 14). Elegance in wood and metal!

The Volume II records list 421 VHEs and VHs, one with 30-inch barrels, two with 22-inch, five with 28-inch, and the rest with 26-inch barrels. Approximately 108 VHE and VH guns were made with a single trigger—all save one, SN 235927—beginning in 1931.

A Volume I table of *The Parker Story* numbers the VHE and VH 410 as 469, which includes statistical sampling due to the missing stock books.

Like the Winchester Model 21, the Purdey, and Holland & Holland 410 shotgun author archives, approximately 40 percent of the manufactured Parker 410s have been publicly identified and are in the archives. This was the case for the above makers prior to factory production confirmation.

This writer invites interested collectors, dealers, and investors to inquire regarding a particular serial number that may be in the archives. Whatever information is available will be readily provided to the inquirer. I do not, however, represent that all of the information is 100 percent accurate, nor do I guarantee the presence or absence of authenticity. I am stating my opinion, which, in general, includes the opinions of a number of 410 Parker specialists. Additionally, I invite readers to provide additional serial numbers and a comprehensive description of the gun that can be added to the database. The archives detail the current status (the last quarter of the 20th century) of a given 410, not necessarily how it left the factory.

Parker Reproduction Shotguns by Winchester

Imitation, being the ultimate form of flattery and admiration, led Tom Skeuse, one of the early Parker connoisseurs, to build a modern-day Parker using the Olin-Winchester facilities in Japan [4,5]. With the assistance of his son Jack of Reagent Chemicals and using precision computer technology and modern metallurgy, approximately 12,225 guns in 12, 20, 28, and 410 bore were built between 1984 and 1989, the regular production years. These guns were beautifully faithful to the original crafted Parker.

Jack Skeuse, who was in charge of this remarkable project, reported that approximately 133 410 shotguns had been in various stages of fabrication.[3] Twenty-five in the A1S grade and eight in the BHE or DHE grade were completed. All were made using a 0000 frame, a size in which the original Parker 410 was never manufactured. The company had all the tooling and components to complete the remaining 410s and had intended to do so on

special order. Additionally, they had made a combination 410/28 two-barrel set on the Parker 000 frame during the regular production years.

The final 410 tally including the post-production assembly years of the 1990s includes 11 DHEs, nine BHEs, and 16 A1S 28/410 gauge sets. The combination sets were made on a 000 frame.

A general consensus that the Parker reproduction series was functionally and artistically successful makes this gun very desirable, both as a wonderful tool in the field and as a collectable.

The Fox 410

Tony Galazan's Connecticut Shotgun Manufacturing Company, a gunmaker of the highest order, has done a similar *tour de force* with the Fox shotgun using computer technology and modern materials to produce a gun, in this case, better than the original! Additionally, although the original Fox was never made in the 410 bore, a modern Fox 410 is available on special order. One such 410, SN F205675, has recently been completed. The engraving was by T. George utilizing a dense brocade style with a gold woodcock on the foreplate. The effect is striking (Photos 15-17).

Conclusion

The evolution of the Parker 410 is, in one important way, analogous to the quality 410s manufactured by other great gunmakers including Winchester, L.C. Smith, Ithaca, Purdey, Holland & Holland, Westley Richards, Boss, and Purdey. That is to say, the 410, for the most part, was produced after these companies had reached the final stage in the development of their shotgun fabrication.

The Parker Bros. brought to their final perfection the 410 bore with its unsurpassed balancing and pointing qualities and its handcrafted manufacturing and ornamentation. They produced an instrument of unparalleled utility and aesthetic pleasure.

Postscript

It now appears that the 410 Parker saga was not completed with the two-volume *The Parker Story*, and it may never be finalized.

In 2000, Ronald Kirby, Executive Director, and colleagues of the Parker Gun Collectors Association unearthed additional Parker records generated during the Remington stewardship. I will list the documents and then attempt to explain their significance with respect to the 410 bore.

Exhibit one, two pages, is titled "Parker guns on hand that can be reconditioned." This memo is not dated but was produced at least after gun SN 241937, a 16-gauge DHE, and therefore after 1941. In this memo is a single trigger VHE 410, SN 239707, a 26-inch skeet gun with a "straight grip," which is recorded in *The Parker Story*.

Exhibit two, dated "4-21-42," is titled "Warehouse stock April 18th of items ordered but not released." The highest numbered gun is SN 242385, with no 410s recorded.

---

3 Personal communication.

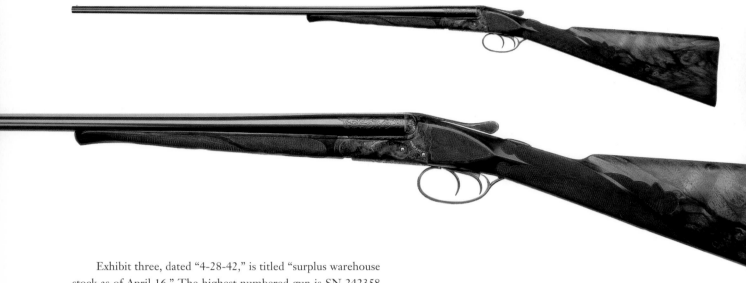

Exhibit three, dated "4-28-42," is titled "surplus warehouse stock as of April 16." The highest numbered gun is SN 242358 and included are four 410s, three of which are listed in *The Parker Story*. Three are DHEs, numbers 237188, 238226, and 239761. The first two are skeet guns, the third is modified and full. All three have 26-inch barrels and a single trigger.

The fourth 410, number 238476, is a VHE gun with 26-inch barrels, choked modified and full, with a single trigger. This is not listed in *The Parker Story*.

"Exhibit III" is titled "completed guns on hand" and dated "12-9-42." This includes guns in the warehouse available for

Photos 15-17: Various views of an A.H. Fox, SN F205675, illustrating the engraving, wood, conformation, and gold woodcock in flight.

Paul Goodwin photos

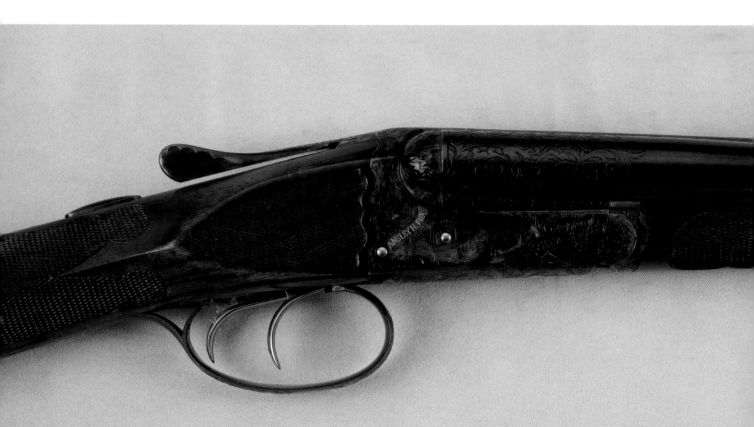

shipment with the highest number, SN 242344, and which lists no 410s. It also includes a memo titled "guns being reconditioned" "as new guns" and "should be finished by January 1, 1943." This memo lists three VHE 410s, all skeet guns with 26-inch barrels, numbers 237214, 239252, and 241215. *The Parker Story* catalogs all these guns.

A third part of this exhibit is described as "miscellaneous guns (samples)" in "showcase at Ilion" which "could be reconditioned for sale as new guns." The highest gun is number 239896. None are 410s.

"Exhibit IV" is yet another document dated "12-9-42," whose highest serialized gun is number 241017 with no 410s listed.

Additional resurrected and authentic Parker documents in the Remington "Archives" include data that solve a few 410 mysteries.

A document titled "Expected reconditioned cost" lists one DHE and four VHE 410s. VHE number 242406 is a single trigger action without barrels, stock, or forend. DHE number 241109 has 26-inch barrels. The final three VHE 410s have 26-inch barrels and are "field" guns, numbers 242386, 242387, and 242434. One of these guns, SN 242434, surfaced explosively in the 1980s on the gun show circuit as an A1S upgrade, beautifully done by European-American craftsmen. Another, SN 242387, has surfaced in the public literature as a GHE 410 and as the

"Last Parker 410." This latter gun may have been upgraded at the factory or somewhere else sometime in the aftermarket.

The above four VHE 410s in the 242,000 range are not cataloged in *The Parker Story.*

The fact that there are two additional unrecorded 410s, number 242291, upgraded to an A1S, and number 242054, upgraded by Otis Odom to an AHE, should not be surprising. A number of 410s in the 242,000 range are now documented as having been original Parker VHE 410s. More may come to light.

The latest numbered gun in these documents is SN 242435. A tragic note refers to the "need to purchase forging" of the forend lock lever, since the "forge shop is devoted exclusively to military work."

Four of the above now-documented 410s, are not listed in *The Parker Story* and their existence brings into fuller relief the remarkable story of the Parker 410, a melodrama surely not ended.

Parker Brothers References

1. *The Parker Story*, 2 Volumes, 1998 and 2000, R.W. Gunther, W.L. Mullins, L.C. Parker III, C.E. Price, D.P. Côté.*
2. McIntosh, Michael, *Best Guns*, 1989
3. Price, Charlie, "Parker Gun Gauges Over The Years," *The Double Gun Journal*, Vol. 13, Issue 3, August 2002.
4. Skeuse, Jack, telephone interview June 13, 1996.
5. Sisley, Nick, "Reproductions," *Shotgun Sports*, Jan.-Feb. 1996.

The Parker Story Joint Venture Group, Knoxville, Tenn.

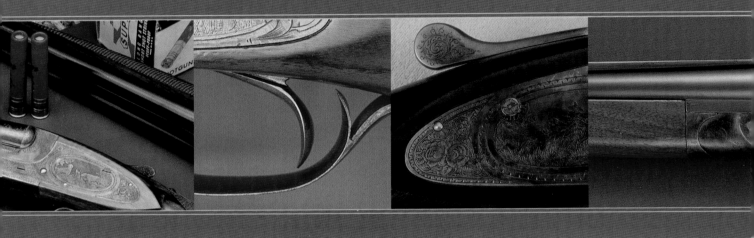

CHAPTER EIGHT

L.C. SMITH

According to William Brophy's comprehensive and magisterial book on the L.C. Smith, the company manufactured approximately 2665 410s beginning in 1926 [1,2]. Reportedly, they shipped the first 410 on October 9, 1926. Catalog information on the 410, however, did not become available until 1927. At that time, the 410 was offered in every grade through the Monogram. Specifically, it was not offered in the Premier and Deluxe grades.

A close survey of the records indicates that L.C. Smith manufactured 2375 guns in Field grade, 220 in Ideal, 29 in Skeet Special, two in Trap, 33 in Specialty, and six in Crown grade. Guns have been reported privately in Eagle, Monogram, Premier, and Deluxe grades, but these reports have not been confirmed by factory records and, for that reason, are unlikely to exist as original high-grade 410s (Photo 1).

The last high-grade 410, a Crown grade, was shipped in 1950, Serial Number 55982 (Photos 2, 3, 4). The plant shipped the gun to the Kerr Sport Shop, a Beverly Hills, California retail store owned by Alex Kerr (Photo 5). Kerr was a member of the family that made the Mason-Kerr jar used by every American mother of the first half of the 20th century to preserve "canned" foods. Kerr was a California clay target champion and hobnobbed with Hollywood swells to whom he sold many expensive guns.

His post-World War II gunroom manager was Jerry Knight who was, to all that knew him, a prince of a man. Jerry was at the counter one day in the 1950s helping Elvis Presley select a shotgun. A nearby man was admiring another smoothbore within Elvis' hearing. Elvis turned to him and asked him if he planned to buy it. The man said, "I would love to, but I could never afford it. I am a grade school teacher." Elvis turned to Jerry and said, "Put his gun on my bill, and give it to this teacher; with his work he deserves it."

Photo 3: Bottom view of the Crown 410, SN 55982.

∨ *Levasheff photo*

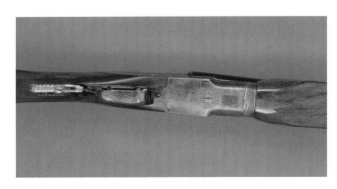

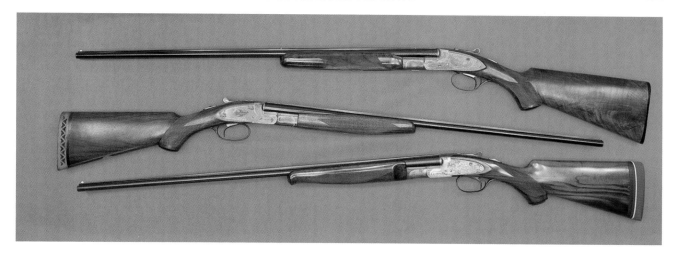

Kerr sold the Crown 410 to the Helms family. They owned the Helms Bakery that sold baked goods, by home delivery, to almost every family in southern California before and after World War II, including mine. Helms was also a strong material supporter of Amateur Athletics in the middle third of the 20th century in America.

This is a 26-inch barrel gun with a single trigger and is in unfired mint condition. This gun represents perhaps the most complete expression of the L.C. Smith 410 in its engineering marvels and its aesthetic embellishments. These include the featherweight frame, which they offered from the beginning of the 410 era, a single-sighting plane rib, a single selective trigger, beavertail forend and automatic ejectors. Of the six Crown-grade 410s documented in factory records, four are known to exist and have been authenticated by various reliable observers. Like the Parker, the L.C. Smith 410 benefited from the most advanced technology available, first at the Hunter Arms Company and then at the L.C. Smith Gun Company.

Smith manufactured two Trap-grade 410s, SN 178570 and SN 171963. The former, made on a featherweight frame, is in wonderful condition and features a selective single trigger and beavertail forend with 28-inch barrels. It left the factory in

Photo 4: Top view of the Crown 410, SN 55982, showing the distinctive "Crown" at the fulcrum of the top lever.

Levasheff photo

Photo 1: Three Smith 410s: Crown grade, SN 55982 (top); Skeet Special grade, SN 194925 (middle); and Trap grade, SN 178570 (bottom).

Levasheff photo

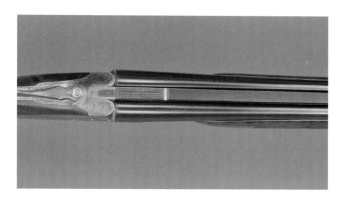

Photo 2: A Crown 410, SN 55982, original and virtually unfired with full case colors.

G. Allan Brown photo

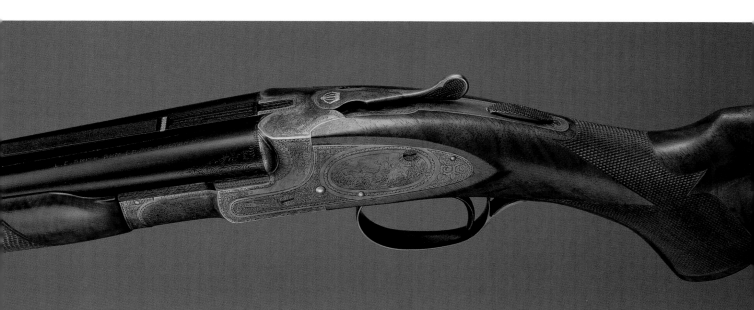

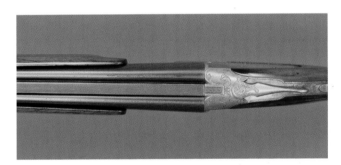

September of 1939 (Photos 6 and 7). The latter, with skeet chokes, has a ventilated rib, a Hunter-One single selective trigger, and a beavertail forend. The barrels are 25 inches, an unusual length. It was offered for sale in 1997 with a refinished stock (Photo 8).[1]

In 1926, when the 410 became available, the company offered both the featherweight as well as the regular frame. It is a tribute to the company that it built every gauge on a frame proportionate to the size and weight of the cartridge. The weight of the 410 varied from 5 to 5-1/2 pounds, depending upon barrel length. Similarly, a scaled-down frame for small-bore shotguns was the rule in British guns and for some of the classic American

---

1 A "Trap"-grade 410, FWE 141717, was offered for public sale in 1999 with 26-inch barrels, double triggers, and pistol grip. It is "100% new in box." This gun is not confirmed in the factory records.

Photo 7: Top view of the Trap 410, SN 178570.

∨   *Levasheff photo*

Photo 5: The original ledger for the Crown 410, SN 55982.

Glenn Campbell photo

Photo 6: Side view of a Trap 410, SN 178570, with the unusual engraving of shooters.

Levasheff photo   ∨

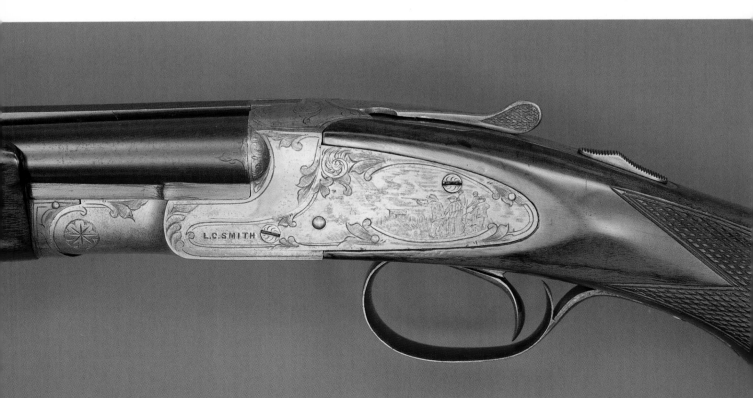

Photo 8: The original ledger for the Trap 410, SN 178570.

Glenn Campbell photo

Elmer Keith described the Smith version as consisting of two fingers on the rotary bolt, one wide, operating through a cut in the extended rib, and a narrower one that hooked over the extreme top protrusion of the extended rib.

Brown, when he created the hammerless L.C. Smith in 1886, cocked the internal hammers by torque rather than the conventional push rod or lifter, so common in contemporary doubles. This was another display of Brown's mechanical ingenuity, unique but effective. He modernized the L.C. Smith by engineering a new cocking and bolting system and applying it to the back-action hammerless sidelock. Prior to the turn of the century, the back-action locks housed both hammer as well as hammerless guns.

The L.C. Smith is justly famous for its very advanced back-action lock, and, in the higher grades, the insides of the lockplates were damascened and the internal parts were highly polished.

There was an interesting interlude from 1895 to 1901 when the Smith sidelock was characterized by a bar-action sidelock in which the mainspring was in front of the trigger and its apex pointed forward, running along the side of the extended bar of the action frame. The Brophy book pictures an early bar-action hammer gun and reports that approximately 10,907 of 82,499 hammer guns were made with the bar action. The remaining were back-action guns. No hammerless guns are known to have been made in the bar action.

After 1901, Smith made all its guns with the back-action sidelock in which the mainspring rests behind the trigger with its apex pointing backward towards the shooter.

The back action's disadvantage, in comparison to the bar action, is a less crisp trigger pull. The bar-action sidelock gives the best sear/tumbler engagement angle, resulting in a very clean trigger pull. The back action's striking advantage is that deep inletting along the action bar is not required; therefore, the frame strength is not reduced, as it necessarily is when the mainspring is forward as it is in the bar action.

To compensate for this weakness in the bar action, the manufacturers devised a top bolt, such as the Greener crossbolt, the Purdey third fastener, or the Westley Richards doll's head, to counteract the inherent weakness of the bar-action sidelock.

Before 1895, it is presumed that all L.C. Smiths were manufactured with the back action, both hammer and hammerless. After 1901, all L.C. Smiths were manufactured in the back action, hammer or hammerless, and it is certainly true that all hammerless Smiths were of the back-action type.

The Smith sidelock, whether bar- or back-action, was far superior to the Baker sidelock, the only other American sidelock ever manufactured. It should be noted that the original Lefever guns were, in fact, boxlock-action guns with sideplates for engraving. The sidelock gun tends to be vulnerable near the receiver. The forces of recoil cause the stock to split at the tang and at the rear of the sideplates because of the necessary amount of wood removed to fit the sidelocks; hence reducing the bearing

doubles such as the Parker and the Ithaca. Such was not the case for the Winchester Model 21 though. Winchester built its sub-gauges on a 20-gauge frame.

Historical Survey

The modern L.C. Smith gun first took form in 1883 when Alexander T. Brown redesigned the Smith as a "top-action, double crossbolted, and breech-loading gun." The locking system and the rib extension, which was essentially a rotary locking bolt, remained unchanged throughout the course of the gun's history. McIntosh, in describing the rotary bolt, likened it to the early hammerless Ithaca and the new Lefever, the final design of Dan Lefever [3].

In 1886, Brown developed the hammerless L.C. Smith. Shotgun writers considered the bolting system with the characteristic rib extension, patterned on the modification of the Greener crossbolt, as the strongest system ever devised. Elmer Keith has written, "I have never known an L.C. Smith to open up on firing but have had both Fox and Ithacas kick open" [4].

The final design of the Ithaca NID shotgun incorporated the rotary bolt in 1926, and all 410s manufactured by Ithaca benefited from this final locking design.

surface between the receiver and stock. There was occasional stock breakage with low-grade L.C. Smiths, particularly when stocked in American walnut, despite high-quality manufacture and its unique bolting system.

The first safety was installed in 1886. By 1888, Smith made the first hammerless guns available, all in back-action. By 1895, the barrels were of Whitworth fluid compressed steel, and in the high grades, the stock was of the finest Circassian walnut. In the high grades, the locks were hand-made with the interiors beautifully damascened.

According to Brophy, the bridles of the locks of all higher-grade L.C. Smiths were "delicately filigreed," and the internal mechanisms polished to a "mirror-like finish." They developed their first automatic ejector in 1895, later modified by the Lewis patent in 1901. In 1904, the Hunter-One trigger became available, and in 1907, they added the 20 gauge. In 1909, they advertised a featherweight frame to complement the regular frame.

In 1913, Smith changed the grading system from a numerical to a nominal one, according to available catalogs. The Crown grade replaced #5, the Monogram remained unchanged, and the Premier grade replaced the A3. The Deluxe became a new and highest grade. In 1915, they introduced the Fulton boxlock shotgun, and in 1925, the beavertail forend and ventilated rib became available.

By 1905, only Whitworth barrels were available in the high-grade guns with the Krupp steel barrels discontinued. The #5 gun in the pre-1913 grading system, the fourth highest grade, which eventually became the Crown grade post-1913, was available in either Damascus or Nitro steel barrels. Considering the price and quality of this particular gun, Brophy called it the "best buy."

Hunter Arms Company in Fulton, New York, made 842 Crown-grade guns between 1913 and 1945, and the L.C. Smith Gun Company made another 48 Crown-grade guns through 1950. The gold crown inlay on the top lever was standard for decades. Not until 1937, however, did the catalog narrative mention the gold inlay crown on the top lever.

Photo 10: A Skeet Special with its characteristic beavertail forend, SN 194925.

∨   *G. Allan Brown photo*

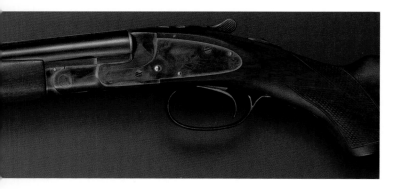

Introduced in 1913, the next grade down, the Specialty, was available with either Nitro steel or Damascus barrels. It was available with only steel barrels from 1917 until the gun's discontinuation in 1939.

Smith offered the 410 in all grades up through the Monogram but there are no factory records confirming that a 410 was manufactured in the Monogram, Eagle, or Olympic grade. In 1992, an L.C. Smith 410 in Monogram grade, serial number 27641, surfaced. It has automatic ejectors, single trigger, beavertail forend, and a checkered butt stock. It has a raised single-sighting plane rib and a gold bar at the breech end of the rib. The gold bar is dented, the barrels re-blued, and the stock cleaned up or replaced. Factory records show it as a Specialty grade when it left the factory.

More recently, an Eagle-grade 410 has emerged, number FWE114216, with 28-inch barrels, a capped pistol grip, and a 24-karat gold presentation shield in the stock. Reportedly, it left the plant ledger book as a Field-grade gun. However, it is described as a "Lunch Box" production and a plaque supposedly exists that says it was "Custom Made" for the head of the case color department. Why no Monogram guns, and few high-grade 410s, were ever made is a reflection of the pre-World War II demographics and of the economy at the time. Specifically, the 410 was at that time considered a kid or woman's gun and this, together with the fact that the bulk of the 410's production years were during the 1930's depression, amply explains the lack of high-grade guns. This also explains the few original Parker 410s above the DH grade (see Parker chapter).

It is interesting that of the three types of rib that L.C. Smith offered, I have only seen a single ventilated rib 410 in Crown grade (SN 138075) and one single-sighting plane rib, first introduced in 1939, on a Crown 410 (SN 55982). The third type of rib is the wide-matted concave or flat-surfaced rib that was standard in all L.C. Smith guns by 1925, the year of the introduction of the ventilated rib. Smith discontinued the ventilated rib in 1945 when the Hunter Arms Company became the L.C. Smith Gun Company. After 1945, only the solid and the single-sighting plane ribs were available.

The 410

By 1926, the company was able to incorporate its highest level of technology into the 410, which remained unchanged until the company's end. In 1937, Smith introduced the Hunter Special model, including the 410 gauge, and in 1938, the 410 became available in the Fulton model as well. Both were boxlock guns (Photo 9).

In 1939, the single-sighting plane rib became available and the company incorporated it into a number of 410s, one of which was the very last Crown shipped in 1950. In 1939, the Skeet Special grade became available but not catalog listed until 1941. One example is unfired and pristine in its original case (Photos 10 and 11).

In 1945, Smith dropped the Fulton and Hunter Special

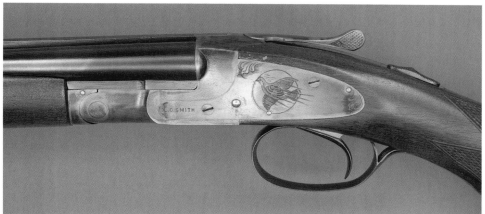

Photo 9: A Hunter Special ∧
410 (well built but inexpensive
for a "double") shown above a
Fulton 410.

G. Allan Brown photo

Photo 11: A Skeet Special, SN
194925, and its unique engraving pattern.

Levasheff photo

<

models and it is interesting they manufactured the 410 in these
two models for only approximately 7 years. Unfortunately, the
production numbers are entirely unknown. They also dropped
the Skeet Special in 1945, and it appears that during the 6-year
production period, they manufactured approximately 29 Skeet
Special 410s.

By the time manufacturing commenced on the 410s, the
barrel steel was graded as follows: Armour steel for Field grade,
London steel for Ideal and Skeet Special grades, Crown steel for
Trap grade, Nitro steel for Crown, Eagle, and Specialty grades,
and Whitworth steel for grades above Crown. What these steel
grades mean concerning their metallurgic properties is obscure.

When the beavertail forend was introduced on the double-

barrel Trap in 1920, it required a recoil rod. This was due to the
greater weight and mass in the front end of the forend, which
secured the tip to the forend iron. This recoil rod was not installed
in the Skeet Special or in any standard beavertail forend on guns
made by the L.C. Smith Company. Initially, the forend did not
have a Schnabel configuration. Subsequently though, the Schnabel
became a feature and is seen in some of the Smith 410s pictured.

In the early years, the Jacob Glahn family engraved the
high-grade Smiths and their work was cruder than engraving
subsequently seen. Thereafter, Albert E. Kraus began engraving
most of the highest-grade L.C. Smiths and his work aesthetically and technically ranks with the greatest of English and
American engravers during the 20th century. High or bold relief,
with or without gold inlays, characterized his exquisite work.

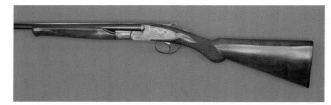

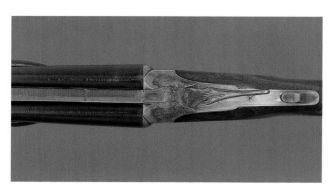

Photos 12-14: Various views of a Specialty grade 410.

Levasheff photos

<

Photo 15: The two-barrel Crown 410.

Lewis Drake photo ∧

According to Brophy, he remained with the company until 1945 when his understudy, Charles Jarred, succeeded him.

Regarding the serial numbers of the 410s in existence, in 1917 the Hunter Arms Company, which included the L.C. Smith, Hunter, and Fulton guns, began a new series of numbers ranging from 101 to 202,967. Therefore, all 410s made before 1945 were in that series. In 1945, with the formation of the L.C. Smith Gun Company, serial numbers ranged from FWS 1 through FWS 56796. According to the records, a number of Field 410s, at least three Ideal, and one known Crown, had serial numbers in the latter series of numbers.

After 1926, the company cataloged 410s in various grades through Monogram. Both 26- and 28-inch barrels were available as well as full or half pistol grip, or straight stock. Above the Crown grade, they used only Whitworth steel barrels, and in all grades, a ventilated rib, Hunter-One trigger, beavertail forend, single-sighting plane rib, and featherweight or regular frame were available.

The Skeet Special 410 barrels were choked Skeet I and II and all guns included a streamlined beavertail forend and automatic ejectors. The checkered butt was characteristic. In addition, the Skeet Special had a single-sighting plane rib and utilized London steel barrels at 26-, 27-, and 28-inch lengths. Of the 770 manufactured and sold in all gauges, 29 were 410s. The company also produced 33 Specialty grade 410s (Photos 12-14, 16).

An interesting story involves one of the six Crown 410s, SN 138075 [5]. It was shipped to C.W. Kress on September 2, 1933, with a single set of 28-inch barrels, a ventilated rib, and a featherweight frame. A second set of barrels was added later and marked "2," although there is no factory confirmation that the company actually made the barrels. The trigger guard has gold initials and was, at some point, re-blued (Photo 15).

There are two catalogs dealing specifically with the 410. One is the "L.C. Smith 410 Caliber Gun," which states that it was available in "all grades with or without automatic ejector and Hunter-One trigger." The second catalog, titled "The L.C. Smith 410 Gauge Gun," is pictured in Brophy's book. The dates of these catalogs are unknown.

There is a noteworthy book produced by Bob Brownell of Montezuma, Iowa, called the *L.C. Smith Plan of Specification.* That book contains a drawing of a featherweight 410 barrel [2].

Finally, it is notable that the company produced a single 28-gauge prototype, which remains in the possession of family heirs. It was grade 00, with a serial number of 100.

The Smith 410 elicited a wide variety of opinions. On the one hand, Jack O'Connor announced that the 410 gauge was "never made" [6]. On the other hand, and more recently, McIntosh, who, admitting that he is "not much of a 410 fan," went on to say that a Smith 410 is a "thing to behold." He described it as a "strikingly sleek little gun" "that handled like a rapier" [3].

The 410 manufactured by L.C. Smith represents another great American example of our infatuation with functional instruments used for recreational pastimes. As America's only 410 sidelock gun, the L.C. Smith will forever remain a splendid illustration of this indulgence.

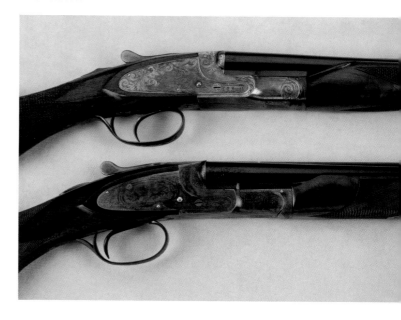

Photo 17: A Skeet Special 410 shown above a Trap-grade 410 in order to compare the engraving.

Paul Goodwin photo ∨

Photo 16: A Specialty-grade 410 ∧ shown above a Crown 410. Compare the engraving.

Paul Goodwin photo

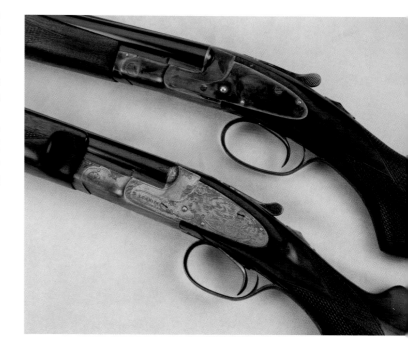

L.C. Smith References

1. Brophy, Lt. Col. William S., *L.C. Smith Shotguns*, Beinfeld Pub., 1977.
2. Brophy, Lt. Col. (Ret.) William S., *Plans & Specifications of the L.C. Smith Shotgun*, F. Brownell & Sons, Montezuma, IA, 1982.
3. McIntosh, Michael, "Another Look at Elsie", *Shooting Sportsman*, Jan/Feb 1994.
4. Keith, Elmer, *Shotguns by Keith*, Bonanza Books, N.Y. 1967.
5. Headrick, William, *Double Gun Journal*, Vol. 5, Issue 3, 1994, pg. 112.
6. O'Connor, Jack, *The Shotgun Book*, Alfred A. Knopf, N.Y. 1965.

CHAPTER NINE

WINCHESTER, THE MODEL 21

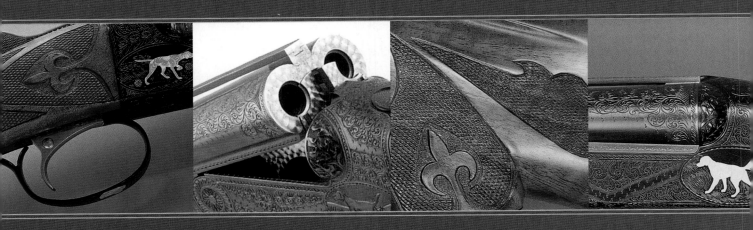

P arker Bros., L.C. Smith, and Ithaca Gun Company began producing their doubles in the 410 bore by the late 1920s. Winchester, which had produced two single-barrel models in the 410 bore in the first quarter of the 20th century (Model 20 and Model 37), did not produce the Model 21, their great side-by-side double, in the 410 until after 1950. This was almost 20 years after they introduced Model 21, the strongest of all American classic double shotguns (Photos 1, 2).

John Olin told this writer that the success of the Model 42, introduced in 1933, sufficiently satisfied the customer's need or desire for the 410 bore. However, after World War II, interest in a 410 Model 21 was ignited by a hybrid prototype [1].

The Progeny

According to several sources, including John Olin as well as Ned Schwing in his comprehensive *Winchester's Finest, the Model 21*, Ernie Simmons Sr. had produced by 1950 what appeared to be the forerunner of the Model 21 410 [2]. He attached two Model 37 410 barrels to a Model 21 20-gauge frame. A competitor used this gun at a national skeet tournament in Dallas, Texas, in 1950.

Factory management saw the gun and was seduced by its possibilities. They went back to their Connecticut factory to construct a side-by-side 410 using Model 21 components. They took

a 20-gauge frame and milled away the arrow-shaped side panels, then customary on the Model 21 action. Savings in weight were minimal, all of 2 ounces; however, the surface lines of the frame were cleaner and easier to engrave. In fact, by 1960, Winchester removed the teardrop or arrow-shaped side panels from all Model 21 actions after they discovered the extra metal was not needed to strengthen the action at the angle of the frame. Additionally, they skeletonized this frame by machining out horizontal slots from the floor or water table of the action body.

They bored to 410 gauge a set of Model 21 20-gauge barrels. They then tapered or profiled two-thirds of the muzzle end, leaving the one-third breech end in 20-gauge size and configuration to match the 20-gauge frame. They also skeletonized the barrel flats, like the action floor. The forend iron was 20-gauge size but with the wood tapered to match the profiled barrels.

The resulting gun was shown to John Olin in 1950, who, exerting executive privilege, made it his own. In fact, Olin had five sets of 410 barrels in different lengths and chokes made to match this action [3]. This resulted in the original 410 Model 21, SN 25087.

The Fabrication

The 410 was always a special order "Custom Built" grade, unlike other gauges before 1960. Prior to this time, most Model 21s

Photo 1: A 20-gauge Grand American Model 21, circa 1978 (top) and a custom Model 21 28 gauge with the pre-1960 "teardrop" frame.

Levasheff photo

Photo 2: A Parker CHE 20 gauge, 2-barrel set (above) and a 20-gauge Grand American Model 21, 2-barrel set, engraved by Nick Kusmit (right).

Paul Goodwin photos

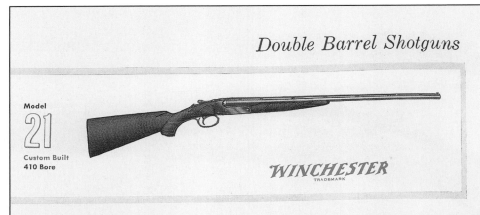

Double Barrel Shotguns

Model 21 Custom Built 410 Bore

WINCHESTER TRADEMARK

THE exquisite beauty, grace, and refinement of this jewel among sporting guns has an irresistible appeal to the firearms connoisseur.

Its raciness, perfect balance, and the way it "comes alive" in the hands, tempt and challenge the skill of veterans searching for new thrills in their quest of quail, woodcock and other upland game.

Score-conscious small-bore skeet shooters will shoot this loveliest of all 410 Bores with confidence increased by pride of ownership and the knowledge that incomparably it is the very best in performance and reliability.

Like all 410 bores, youngsters and the ladies will appreciate its pleasant lack of recoil; nevertheless the Custom Built 410 Bore is distinctly a *man's* gun, made for the discriminating and for the expert.

The Custom Built 410 Bore is made only on special order to exactly the same specifications as other Custom Built Model 21 shotguns except that the frame is smaller and lighter, and it is available only in 26″ Ventilated Rib Barrels — any chokes.

Barrels and frame are carefully polished and "browned" a rich blue-black satin finish. Finest selection of Full Fancy American Walnut is used for the slim beavertail forearm and hand-made stock shaped to individual requirements. Fancy hand-checkering attractively done on grip and forearm. Black plastic insert on forearm tip and a steel cap on pistol grip add further touches of refinement.

All action parts are hand-smoothed to further ease of operation. Bright surfaces are highly polished and engine-turned for added beauty. Panel on top rib near breech hand-engraved "Custom Built by Winchester."

Pistol grip or straight grip stocks; composition butt plate or checkered wood butt are optional.

Stocks with Monte Carlo, cheek piece or cast-off may be had at a nominal extra charge.

Extra fancy stock carving, simple or elaborate engraving, silver, gold or platinum inlays limited only by desires of the purchaser.

66

<

Photo 3: Page 66 from a red and yellow Winchester catalog, the first catalog reference to the Model 21 410 gauge.

Paul Goodwin photo

were standard grades and relatively few were "Custom." When the Custom Shop opened in 1960, all Model 21s became Custom Built.

The 410 made its first appearance in the yellow and red, 8-1/2 by 11-inch, 1955 Winchester catalog. It remained a cataloged item until 1959. The 410 offering in the catalog targeted women and the young. However, it is described as "a man's gun" for the "discriminating and for the expert." Standard features included 26-inch barrels, ventilated rib, polished and engine-turned action, American walnut pistol- or straight-grip stock, slim beavertail forend and 3-inch chambers (Photo 3).

The 410 barrels weighed 3 pounds, 6 ounces in contrast to 2 pounds, 12 ounces for the 20-gauge barrels. All 410s had automatic ejectors and a single trigger. The company dropped plain extractors from the Model 21 in 1941 and abandoned double

triggers in 1944. Checkering was 24 to 26 lines to the inch and all machine markings were polished out.

The Model 21 410 was chamber tested to 7.5 tons, certifying it as a most powerful ensemble. The 12 gauge underwent a similar proof test using 2000 proof loads just before the first introduction of the model in 1931.

The locking system uses a large underbolt located so far from the angle of the frame that the angle experiences little stresses and there is less downward thrust to the barrel. Using this very long frame negates the requirement for a top bolt such as a Doll's head or rotary bolt [4].

The Model 21 boxlock action made of 4140 chrome vanadium steel uses a coil spring rather than the "V" spring seen in the typical Anson & Deeley (A&D) action. The firing pins are structurally integrated with the hammers.

The barrels, made of heat-treated 4140 chrome molybdenum steel, have vertical dovetail interlocks soldered and not brazed; hence, they retain both temper and strength. The tensile strength of this steel was over 90 tons per square inch and the blued frame is nearly twice as strong as casehardened actions [5]. The single trigger has an inertia-type mechanism that "cannot be doubled," according to catalog literature. A factory-published "Parts Legend" lists 87 components.

After 1959, there were no further catalog offerings of the 410. John Olin exercised strict control of the production of this bore, mainly for Olin's business and personal friends or for promotional reasons. Supposedly, this was due to the limited number of small-bore barrels. Schwing argues that the 410 was nothing more than John Olin's pet project, an aftermarket gun cobbled together with 20-gauge components, and therefore not a serious innovation.

Photo 4: One of two unique ∧ Pigeon-grade 410s (SN W32672), circa 1976-77, with 21-6 engraving, 21-B carving and checkering. Built by Winchester as a "Tool and Process Tryout Sample, Process Verification Sample."

J.C. Devine Auction photo

Interestingly, the 28 bore, introduced in 1936, had never been a catalog offering and no price lists were available to the public. Winchester made approximately 32,478 Model 21 frames between 1930 and 1955 and no more were to be forthcoming. They produced almost 29,000 guns by 1959. This fact becomes important in assessing the originality of a specific 410 bore for which the factory may have no record.

Production Data

From 1952 to 1959, Schwing reports that Winchester manufactured an estimated 44 guns as original 410 bores, all Custom Built. This excludes all multi-gauge sets. Data has been retrieved on 37 of the 44 guns built in this timeframe. Thirty-three had 26-inch barrels and four had 28-inch barrels. Twenty-seven guns had a pistol grip stock and the remaining 10 had a straight stock.

Photos 5-7: Three views of the Grand American 410 Model 21, the "Sahara Gun," SN W32667.

G. Allan Brown photos

Nineteen guns had a Winchester buttplate, while 14 had a checkered butt. Chokes were skeet and skeet in 19, modified and full in 13.

Eight guns had an extra set of 410 barrels. All had ventilated ribs except one that was probably not original. Five had 22 lines per inch of checkering and four had 21-A stock carving. There were two matched sets with consecutive serial numbers.

Between 1951 and 1959, of the 37 410 guns with available data, 26 had no engraving. Five had gold only including the "Fin & Feather" gun, SN31314, manufactured in 1955. This gun has 26-inch barrels, a ventilated rib, skeet chokes, and has no checkering or scroll engraving. For decades, this gun belonged to Bill Harlan, a Whittier, California, man of infinite courtesy and immense shotgun knowledge. He once critiqued a 410 L.C. Smith, thought to be original, down to the lock plates, screws, rib supports, checkering pattern vintage, wood finish, barrel flats, and action water table, like I had never seen before or since. He was one of the impressive personality types on the gun show circuit. Now 90 years old, he came to California in 1932 with his father, who was a Christian minister on Alvarado Street in Los Angeles. For 40 years, he ran the E.B. Manning & Sons, a major

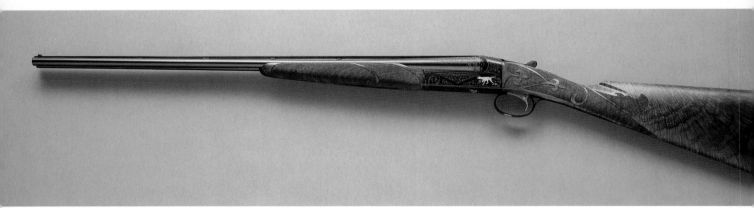

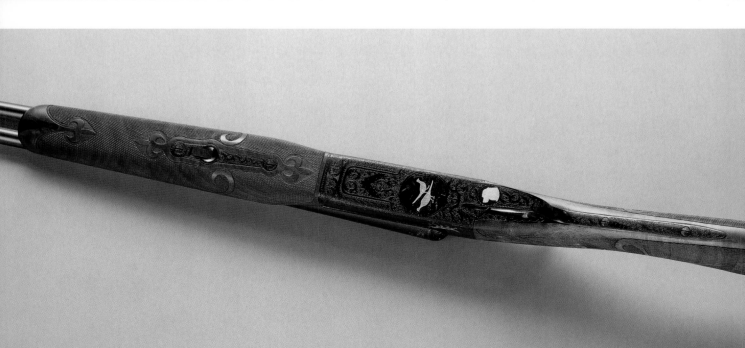

U.S. beef company. At one time, he was the major collector of Model 21 410s, including the "Fin & Feather" 410.

Two guns have the 21-6 engraving pattern with gold, two have 21-3 engraving, and one has 21-1 engraving. One was engraved outside of the factory.

Again, excluding multi-barrel sets, the Custom Shop produced five more original Custom 410s from 1960 to 1981-82, when the shop closed under Winchester aegis. One of the five manufactured is SN 32666, shipped in 1971, with 26-inch barrels, ventilated rib, full chokes, and 21-5 engraving. Two were in the Pigeon grade and their location had been unknown. One recently surfaced and sold at auction in 2002. It has 28-inch barrels with Pigeon-grade engraving. It was finished in 1977, serial number 32672, a number higher than those found in the standard record book for the 410 bore. However, its originality appears authentic (Photo 4).

Winchester made two more guns with consecutive serial numbers in the Grand American grade. Of these two, Winchester auctioned the first for charity at the Sahara Gun Show in 1978 and eventually it resold for over $100,000 (Photos 5-8). The other Grand American is on display in the Cody Firearms Museum under Winchester aegis. Nick Kusmit engraved The Sahara Gun and Jasper Salerno—protégé of the great Model 21 engravers, Nick and John Kusmit—engraved the Cody gun. The latter four guns were "promotional" tools elegantly called "Process Verification Samples" [2].

Over 32,000 Model 21s came out of the Winchester factory, but only 229 were in the Grand American grade. They were produced during the Custom years from 1960 until 1982. During this period, they made a combined total of 1014 Custom, Pigeon, and Grand American Model 21s.

According to a senior executive in 1977, one of the curators[1] of the Custom Shop stated at the time that all 410s were made with the Winchester Model 21 name and gauge stamped or inscribed somewhere on the barrels [6]. Furthermore, he related that all 410s had the water table of the frame "milled out" (skeletonized). However, the experienced Winchester collector, Alan Phillips, showed a 410 gauge (SN 24086) that had three unique features for this gauge: a non-skeletonized frame, a solid rib, and a teardrop frame. This gun, now called the "Hazelwood Gun," was shipped in 1965 to Ted E. Hazelwood, a former director of worldwide marketing for Winchester. This may have been a Model 21 20 bore with added 410 barrels; however, the presence of a factory letter appears to certify its existence as an original 410.

---

1 Robert Parcella also held the title of curator of the Model 21 records.

Photo 8: The *American Rifleman* magazine display of the "Sahara Gun."

Glenn Campbell photo

It is noteworthy that 24 authentic 410s, confirmed in the original factory records, surfaced publicly before the records were opened for historical research. This represents over half of all 410s made. A further 14 were retrieved from the records by a Custom Shop employee by 1985. Therefore, 38 410s were authenticated before Schwing's definitive book was published in 1990, when he reported the presence of 49 guns having been manufactured as original 410s. This may have some relevance to the Parker 410 story in terms of known existing 410s vs. original production numbers, based upon this writer's Parker archives of existing 410s.

It should be noted that at least 14 410s are floating around that were not in the original factory records. Two of these were "added" to the records, and a factory letter and a statement by John Olin authenticated two more; namely SN 24086, the Hazelwood gun, and SN 32560, the 410-28 Grand American ensemble. Winchester built the latter gun for Arden Daniels, a Whittier, California, man who helped Richard Nixon in his early political career. A California skeet champion, a crack dove shot, and a long-time friend of my dad's, Daniels was the Goodyear Tire dealer for the western United States for decades.

Additional existing guns include an after-market, gold-inlaid 410 (SN 32564); an after-market, Ken-Hunt-engraved 410 covered in gold (SN 10506); and a W. Kolouch after-market-engraved 410 with 28-inch barrels with many gold inlays (SN 32675). Also in existence is a post-factory closure, a 3-barrel set that includes a 410 barrel (SN 32566), and a 410 that came out of the factory-closure inventory sale in the white with a 30 1/4-inch barrel. Eventually, Nick Kusmit completed this long-barreled gun with Pigeon-style engraving (SN 31849). Their pedigrees can be evaluated through the Winchester records.

Another interesting 410 story is one told by Nick Kusmit to Edward Ulrich [7]. John Olin wanted a M21 410 made even lighter than was customary, and he suggested drilling a series of 1/8-inch holes equally spaced at the breech end of the barrels. That this proved to be safe and functional was a testament to the M21's strength.

There is a curious 410 gun, SN 36372, that is a number far beyond the last reported Model 21 serial number, approximately 32478. Two additional 410s, not authenticated by factory records, have the affixed "W." Therefore, they were made after 1969, conforming to the Federal Gun Control Act of 1968.

The Model 21 shop closed in 1981. In 1989, the U.S. Repeating Arms Company purchased the Model 21 and Custom Shop and manufactured at least five to 10 more 410s in all grades, each as part of a set of gauges. Most such sets were made for a western American who, at the time, had one of the greatest collections of M21s in the world. They ceased production in 1990. These guns have inscribed on the barrel rib "Custom Built Winchester." This distinguishes these guns from the original custom Winchester guns that say "Custom Built by Winchester."

Before 1960, the Model 21 was a production gun and did not have such a top rib marking on any gauge. All original skeet 410s were marked "Skeet & Skeet," wherein the larger skeet bores are marked "W1" and "W2."

Subsequently, in the mid-1990s, Edward Ulrich bought the Winchester Custom Shop and Tony Galazan's Connecticut Shotgun Mfg. Co. bought the M21 operation. This included all parts, machinery, and inventory including a few 410 barrels. Galazan then built five multi-barrel "Grand Royales" M21s for the U.S. Repeating Arms Co. with 410/28- or 410/28/20-gauge ensembles. This grade differed from the Grand American in that it sported more gold, higher finish, better wood, and a bust of John Olin on a side panel [3].

Today, 2003, Tony Galazan's Connecticut Shotgun Mfg. Co., with the production rights to the Model 21, will build any gauge in any grade, including the 410, in a scaled-down action body [9].

Winchester built a number of 410 barrels that were for 20-gauge guns and these multi-barrel sets occasionally appear for public consumption. In fact, Hazelwood and Dave Carlson, both long-time Winchester employees, have estimated they made approximately 70 to 80 410 barrels before the shutdown of the Custom Shop in 1981.

A long-time senior Winchester representative has estimated that a number of complete or incomplete 410 guns left the factory without becoming part of the written record, such as gifts from John Olin to friends [8]. How this could have happened without violating Federal Firearms laws of that era remains unexplained.

A final M21 small-bore story was reported recently [10]. In the mid-1950s, Winchester built two 32-bore guns, uniquely numbered 32-1 and 32-2, for Robert Woodruff, the President of Coca Cola. They had 26-inch barrels, straight stocks, and beavertail forends. These "one offs"[2] were at the direction of John Olin, to whom Woodruff was a close friend and hunting partner.

Then, more recently, Edward Ulrich found a set of 32-gauge barrels and had a complete 32-gauge gun made, number 32-3. This gauge was never built for the public by the great American double gunmakers; however, most of the British gunmakers produced the rare 32 gauge, especially before 1900. In Europe, it was far more common as 32-gauge cartridges are in plentiful supply.

Conclusion

Like all great American 410s, Winchester made the Model 21 at the end of an evolutionary process. They built the only with ejectors and a single trigger—extractors and double triggers having been discarded from this model by the early 1940s. All, save possibly one, had a ventilated rib. It appears that of all the original 410 guns, only three were original Grand American models, the Sahara (SN 32667), the Cody (SN 32668), and the Daniels 410-28 ensemble (SN 32560).

The 410 was never a production-line gun, even in the 1950s before the Custom Shop took over the Model 21 fabrication. Checkering was 24 to 26 lines per inch, and all lock and trigger components were highly polished with the barrel flats and water tables engine turned.

A number of 410 barrels and even entire guns were smuggled out of the Custom Shop, the so-called "lunch pail" guns and re-appeared later on the collector market. On inspection, they appear to be either authentic Model 21s for which there are no original factory records, or they represent multi-barrel guns on non-skeletonized 20-gauge frames. Some were returned to the factory for upgrading and then entered into the records. Other Model 21 guns were added to the records when they returned for 410 barrels.

It is interesting that Winchester's first and only prior top-lever, breech-opener, hammerless 410 gun was the Model 20, a well-made single-barrel 410 manufactured from 1919 to 1924 (see Early American 410 chapter).

It is evident that the Model 21 410, like almost all other classic double 410s, represented the culmination in the technical and artistic development of the Model 21. "The 21" was probably the "strongest, most rugged, and most trouble free double ever made" [11]. "Dollar for dollar, it was perhaps the best double gun ever built" [6]. The Model 21 occupies a firm position in the hierarchy of great shotguns of the world.

The Model 21 was John Olin's symbolic paramour in that she created the 410 bore which, in turn, gave birth to a second generation Model 21 after 1959, one of the most desired guns in shotgun history. Sadly, despite its mechanical strength and aesthetic ingenuity, the 410's rarity and, hence, cost makes it impractical for rough shooting.

The Model 21 410 bore, an outstanding example of beauty, pleasure, and strength is, at once, the powerful symbol and exquisite result of the gunmaker's craft.

---

2 Headless construction in grammatical terms.

Winchester, The Model 21 References

1. Olin, John, Personal Interview, 1977.
2. Schwing, Ned, *Winchester's Finest, the Model 21,* Krause Publications, 1990.
3. Ulrich, Edward, *Double Gun Journal,* Summer, 1999.
4. Zutz, Don, *The Double Shotgun,* Revised, Winchester Press, 1985.
5. Schwing, Ned, "Winchester's Model 21," *Shooting Sportsman,* Jan/Feb 1998.
6. Hummel, Carl, Telephone Interview, 1977.
7. Ulrich, Edward, *Double Gun Journal,* Winter, 2000.
8. Ulrich, Edward, Personal Interview, 2000.
9. Venters, Vic, *Shooting Sportsman,* Jan/Feb 2003
10. Ulrich, Edward, *Double Gun Journal,* Autumn, 2000.
11. O'Connor, Jack, *The Shotgun Book,* P. 62, Alfred A. Knopf, New York, 1965.

CHAPTER TEN

INTERESTING EARLY 20TH-CENTURY AMERICAN 410 SHOTGUNS

It is unlikely that a future historian will uncover the beginnings of the American smoothbore 410, principally because unlike Great Britain and Europe, there has not been a central Proof House in America through which all guns must pass. Therefore, there is no localized repository of data to determine when the 410-bore shotgun was first manufactured in America. Its origin in America appears to have been well after the turn of the century and consequently long after the British 410 became available for the average shooter or collector.

The classical double 410s—Parkers, Ithacas, and L.C. Smiths—made their appearance in the second half of the 1920s, a time of financial prosperity and social license. The Winchester Model 21 410 appeared in the early 1950s, a time of conservatism, a time of the "silent" university generation, my generation.

However, US Industry invented and produced many other types of smoothbore 410s in all configurations for the American market, long before these classic doubles. In the 20th century, American manufacturers produced 410 shotguns in five different action types: the classic top-lever breech opener, the pump, the semiautomatic, the bolt, and the lever action.

Iver Johnson 410s

Perhaps the first American 410 of consequence was the Iver Johnson Champion Model 36 or Model 39 ("the lightweight 36 smallbore"), according to the Johnson catalog of the time. It was the first American-made shotgun to have barrel and lug forged as one piece rather than brazed together. It was also the first single-barrel top-lever breech opener with the exposed hammer set in the center of the flame tang. Iver Johnson introduced the model in 1908. The 410-gauge Model 39 came out in 1916 and continued in production until 1957. It weighed 5-3/4 pounds with a 26-inch barrel. A matted top rib, introduced in 1913, was available. The frame was color case-hardened.

A classic 410-gauge example, SN 69395C, was manufactured in 1938 with all available options (Photo 1). It has a 36-inch barrel, raised matted rib, checkered black walnut Schnabel-type forend and stock (indicating a deluxe version), automatic ejector, and sling swivels. The case-colored frame is bold and rich. Supposedly, an owl's head on the buttplate was a Masonic emblem of the era. The single barrel says "Smokeless Powder," indicating a post-World War I gun. This gun, because it is deluxe with a 36-inch barrel, is unique in the records. The gun's reliability was legendary, and it was known as the "farmer's friend."

A second 410 offering in 1924 by Iver Johnson was the side-by-side hammerless boxlock Hercules with automatic ejectors

∧ **Photo 1:** A Deluxe Iver Johnson Champion Model 39 410,
SN 69395C.

G. Allan Brown photo

and a single selective trigger as options. The Skeeter Model 410, begun in 1933, was identical to the Hercules except for a more expensive walnut stock and beavertail forend, designed for the increasing number of skeet shooters in the 1930s. This model stayed in production until 1946. Interestingly, the names Hercules and Skeeter did not appear in the original catalog offerings. Production numbers of all three models in the 410 are unknown, but existing 410 guns must be few in number as they seldom show up in advertisements or at gun shows.

Winchester 410s

Model 20

As unique and well made as the Champion was, the Winchester Model 20 410, made from 1919 to 1924, may have been as well made as any mass-production gun in history. Winchester made approximately 23,616 of the model. This was a 26-inch, full-choke, single-barrel, ejector, top-lever, breech-opener, hammer, boxlock gun made only in the 410 bore with 2 1/2-inch chambers and weighing 6 pounds. The stock was well-finished black walnut with a pistol grip. The 1920 catalog claimed an "effective range of 30 yards" for "small game hunting." According to Stadt, this well-proportioned gun was the first Winchester top-lever breech opener and the first Winchester 410 (Photo 2) [1].

The gun was available in a "Junior Trap Shooting Outfit." This included the gun, a midget hand trap, 150 loaded 410 cartridges, 100 clay targets, and a variety of gun maintenance accessories and brochures, packed in an attractive case. The whole "Outfit" weighed 40 pounds. Although manufacturing ceased in 1924, the last guns were not sold until 1931. Interestingly, the 1919 price was $30, reduced to $16.50 by 1922 [1]. According to Madis, the company assembled 12,358 Model 20s for export between 1927 and 1935 [2]. Manton & Co., an Asian-Indian retail gun seller, listed this model in their 1926-27 catalog and described it as a "naturalist's" shotgun and priced at 90 rupees.

Model 41

A second Winchester 410 appeared in 1920, the Model 41. This was a two-piece takedown, 24-inch, single-barrel, single-shot, bolt-action gun weighing 4-1/2 pounds. It had a black walnut pistol-grip stock. In 1933, Winchester lengthened the chamber to accommodate the 3-inch cartridge, and in 1934 it was discontinued after they made approximately 22,146 guns. Madis reports that the company assembled almost 1200 additional guns from 1934 to 1941 from existing components. It was not serial numbered. This model was the first bolt-action 410 built in America. Both the Model 20 and the Model 41 were well made but overpriced for the demand and never achieved the anticipated sales volume.

∧ **Photo 2:** Model 20 Winchester 410.

G. Allan Brown photo

Photo 3: Model 42 Winchester ∧ 410, SN 122382.

G. Allan Brown photo

Model 42

First manufactured in 1933, a third Winchester 410 remained in production for 30 years with an approximate production of 159,353 guns [3]. This was the incomparable Model 42, a hand-machined and hand-assembled gun.

It was a slide-action ("pump" in the vernacular) hammerless repeating shotgun with a tubular magazine holding six 2 1/2-inch shells or five 3-inch shells. It was the first repeating pump 410 ever made. The Presidential Proclamation of 1935 limited all semiautomatic or pump repeating shotguns to three cartridges, forcing Winchester to plug the magazine.

This gun followed the apparent format and basic mechanics of the Model 12, except all components of the Model 42 were not only miniaturized, but also specifically designed and built for the 410 cartridge. For example, the right side of the Model 42 receiver has a detachable plate held by two screws for lock access. The Model 12 is solid on both sides. It is credited as the first American 410 built for the 3-inch 3/4-ounce cartridge, making the 410 ballistics, with double the usual 410 charge, more usable for birds and small game. At the same time, it accommodated the 2 1/2-inch cartridge requirement for skeet shooters. The assertion is that the Model 42 quickly drove the Marlin 410 lever-action repeating shotgun into oblivion, as it could take only 2 1/2-inch cartridges. Winchester seemed to concur in this assertion in a sales manual of the time. This is a surprising statement because Marlin discontinued the 410 model in 1932, a year before the Model 42 came out.

This truly beautiful gun of the past is seldom seen today in its original form in the field for game or on the skeet range. It was available in a bewildering assortment of style, barrel, choke, chamber, stock, and slide handle options, and is mostly seen today on a collector's table at gun shows or read about in gun advertisements. Elmer Keith, a man who was infatuated with the big bore, called it a "very fine Roman candle," the nicest thing he had ever said about any 410 gauge.

Barrels ranged from 26 to 28 inches and were available with no rib, with a raised solid matted rib, or with a ventilated rib. The slide-handle wood had circular grooves in the Standard Grade and fancy checkering in the higher grades. The weight varied in the Standard grade from 5-7/8 pounds to 6 pounds, depending upon barrel length. In the Skeet grade, weight varied from 6 to 6-1/2 pounds.

A 1934 Winchester catalog describes two grades, Standard and Skeet. A 1940 Winchester catalog describes the Trap grade with "Special" walnut stock and checkering. Schwing, however, reports that the Trap grade was available only from 1934 to 1939 with approximately 231 guns made in that grade [4]. The Trap grade had deluxe wood with the double diamond-checkering pattern and a solid raised rib. It was never originally built with a ventilated rib, for reasons noted below.

The Deluxe grade was a special order gun from the Custom Shop, first seen after World War II in a 1950 Winchester retail price list. By this time, the Trap grade had disappeared from the catalog. The Deluxe stayed in production until 1963.

A fifth grade appeared from 1947 to 1952 called the Pigeon grade, a deluxe gun with a pigeon engraved on the receiver extension. The Pigeon grade never appeared in a catalog. A Pigeon-grade Model 12 did and Schwing proposes that those wanting a matching Model 42 requested the pigeon engraving. Winchester obliged those aficionados, though the grade was never formally and publicly offered. Although no factory records exist for this grade, Schwing estimates that Winchester produced less than 100 Pigeon Model 42s. From 1953 to 1961, of 46,624 guns made, 1117 were Skeet grade and 524 were special order, which included the Pigeon-grade guns.

Several controversies exist about the Model 42 [4,5]. The first relates to the ventilated rib, as some collectors doubt its originality. If the originality is authentic, the Winchester Proof Mark is offset to the left on the barrel and chamber portion of the receiver and, therefore, fully exposed. A non-original or added post-factory rib would obscure the Proof Mark.

The solid raised matted rib became available by late 1933 but the ventilated rib did not show up until 1954. According to the Winchester 1955 catalog, it was initially available only in the Skeet or Deluxe grades. The first ventilated rib had "doughnut" posts in which the diameter of the base of the post was larger than the diameter of the post itself, giving a two-tiered circular appearance. Reportedly, this configuration began around SN 125000 in the September 1953 timeframe. However, pictured is SN 122382, a Skeet-grade 28-inch full-choke gun with 3-inch chambers and a pistol-grip stock. This gun, manufactured in May 1953, has the classic "doughnut" post with the fully exposed Winchester Proof Mark on the barrel, confirming its originality. This illustrates the considerable overlap or variability in the manufacture of options and full gun assembly (Photo 3).

Schwing describes a second variation of the round post, without the larger diameter base, used from mid-1956 to mid-1958, from approximately SN 141000 to SN 149000.

A third and final ventilated rib appeared in 1958 with much larger oval or rectangular posts beginning, approximately, with SN 150000. The side of the rib contained a stamping with two different "Simmons" brands. The first said "Simmons Patented." The second, beginning around SN 160000, said "Simmons Gun Specialty, Inc., Kansas City, Mo."

Winchester manufactured and assembled the first two variations of the ventilated rib in their New Haven plant. Simmons provided the third and final variation on a subcontract from Winchester [4]. According to Schwing, Simmons designed all the ribs and allowed Winchester to use the basic design. However, at some point either Winchester or Simmons decided to make the posts oval or rectangular rather than round. Simmons installed the third variation of the ventilated rib on the barrel in the white after Winchester had provided the Winchester Proof Mark. None of the three variations were aftermarket ribs.

Regardless of the ventilated rib variations, if the Model 42 exhibits the correct offset location of the Winchester Proof Mark on both barrel and receiver, then the gun is almost certainly factory original [5]. It is of note, according to the existing records from 1954 to 1961 of over 36,000 guns made, that probably less than 1000 had a ventilated rib.

A second controversy relates to the actual as opposed to the assumed designer or inventor of the Model 42. A strong case can be made for William Roemer, whose name is signed as the "inventor" below a number of the patent illustrations. These illuminate the details of the Model 42 mechanism. This evidence, plus his position in the firm as a chief draftsman by 1918 to chief gun designer and head of gun service engineering before retirement in 1951, supports this position. Schwing suggests that Edwin Pugsley, head of development, probably handed Roemer the "assignment" to design a 410 Model 12. Thomas C. Johnson may have acted as an advisor and counselor. It is a fact that Roemer invented the M-1 carbine. Further

tangential support for Roemer is that in 1951, as he was nearing retirement, Winchester presented him with a Model 42 with the serial number 0.

Conversely, some say that Thomas C. Johnson, the designer of the Model 12, is the actual designer of the Model 42 [5]. They base this assertion on two facts: That Johnson invented the Model 12 and that there are many similarities with the Model 42 and the fact that Roemer was, at one time, a "younger subordinate" of Johnson. The hypothesis is that the Model 42 patents were "assigned" to Roemer; there is no explanation of a reason for this assignment. Both positions have some merit, but the former has direct evidence for Roemer as the inventor, while the latter position is based upon circumstantial evidence alone.

A factory-engraved Model 42, considering the total model production, is very rare indeed. No factory records of engraving are available from 1933 to 1948; however, from 1948 to 1963, at least 41 were engraved, based upon the personal records of John and Nick Kusmit [4]. Undoubtedly several more were originally

∧ **Photo 4:** Model 42 Winchester 410, #2 Skeet grade.

G. Allan Brown photo

Marlin

New .410 Gauge Repeating Shotgun

Our Very Latest Model and A Great Winner
22 or 26-inch barrel, 6 shots   **Price $30.80**

A light weight, nicely balanced repeater using the scatter load and the round ball. A gun that will take the place of both your shotgun and rifle for many purposes. For the boy not old enough to handle a heavy gauge and a pleasant companion for your wife or daughter. Effective for brush and field shooting and at the gun club for skeet. An ideal gun on the farm for shooting pests and other small animals and with the round ball for deer at short range. Carefully made with Marlin accuracy.

The Marlin Firearms Co.
NEW HAVEN, CONN.

1931

Photo 5: Model 37 Winchester 410. ∧

G. Allan Brown photo

Photo 6: Marlin Model 410 catalog material, circa 1931.

Glenn Campbell photo

‹

engraved. A number of guns were returned to the factory after 1963 and up through 1978 for refinishing and engraving.

Winchester rarely made the Model 42 with multiple barrels. A factory letter in 1980 confirmed the originality of a three-barrel set, SN 93296, in the hands of a happy collector. It is a "special skeet" grade with 3-inch full, 3-inch modified, and 2 1/2-inch skeet barrels and chambers. Winchester produced less than "a dozen" three-barrel sets.

Production numbers are not precise and varied from Watrous' 159,353 to Schwing's estimate of 160,000. Apparently,

Winchester produced 164,801 receivers and sent 158,800 assembled guns to the warehouse before shipping.

An American love affair, an American original she was. Alas, she is now an important part of American gun history, a seductress who first beguiled a generation of shooters and now a generation of collectors. Pictured is a collector's dream. The second built Model 42 has surfaced. Made in 1933, it is a Skeet-grade 26-inch barrel gun in pristine condition with a "Fancy" checkered walnut forend and stock (Photo 4). It was made before a rib was available and when only Standard and Skeet models were manufactured.

Model 37

A fourth Winchester smoothbore 410 was the Model 37. This was a single-shot "steel bilt" gun available in gauges 12 through 410. It was introduced in 1936. It was a top-lever breech opener with an automatic ejector and a "semi-hammerless action." According to the 1936 sales catalog, it was constructed entirely of steel without castings, unique for guns of this price category. The 1938 sales manual says the 410 has its own "special" miniature frame, and the barrels, with a forged lug, ranged from 26 to 28 inches with a 3-inch chamber. The pistol grip stock dimensions were the same as those of the Model 42 and Model 21, and the forend was full, providing a superb grip. It was available as the Model 37-A Youth (Photo 5).

∧ **Photo 7:** Marlin Model 410 "Deluxe", SN 6607, circa 1930.

G. Allan Brown photo

Photo 8: Marlin brochure from 1930 regarding the stock offering.

Glenn Campbell photo ∨

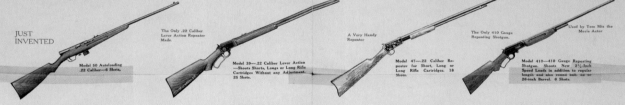

The company made 1,015,554 guns from 1936 to 1963, and none had a serial number. This was perhaps the best-built non-serial-numbered gun ever made. Production numbers for the 410 are unknown, but factory representatives estimate it was less than 5 percent of the production. Model 37 410s made before 1948 had the depressed Winchester logo painted red under the receiver (i.e. the "Red Letter 37s"). The 410 was said to have been "custom built" in promotional literature. In the 1947 Stoeger's *Shooter's Bible*, it was priced at $14.55. The Model 24, by comparison, cost $47.95.

Stadt reports that John Olin had 24 to 30 Model 37 410s cut to 18-inch barrels, legal-length pistols, and sawed off at the pistol grip. His crew used them for snake protection at his Nilo Farms in Georgia.

Marlin 410s

Model 410

No one that has shot the Model 410 will ever understand why the gun was discontinued in 1932, after only 4 years, and a total production of less than 10,000 guns [6,7]. It was and remains a rip-roaring six-shot 2 1/2-inch cartridge lever-action smooth-bore that is a throwback to 19th-century gunning. It was and remains a delight to shoot from the hip or to throw up to the shoulder for a quick reflex shot.

First introduced in 1929, this gun may never have been a marketing idea. Rather, an engineer may have looked at a large surplus of old 1894 lever 44/40-caliber rifle actions and decided a 410 smoothbore, given the gauge's burgeoning popularity in the late 1920s, was just the solution. Indeed, the Model 410 was designed to shoot both scattershot and round ball as promotional material illustrates (Photo 6).

Assuming this hypothesis is correct, once Marlin used up the old actions, the model was dropped. Subsequent and more modern lever-action rifles such as the Marlin Model 93 and 95 were never available in the 44/40 caliber, according to Marlin catalogs of the 1930s'. This, together with the depression, would explain the Model 410 discontinuation.

The explanation that the 3-inch cartridge made the Model 410 obsolete will not stand scrutiny because manufacturing stopped 1 to 2 years before the emergence of the 3-inch shell. Similarly, the development of the Winchester Model 42, which did not appear until at least after the Model 410 production ceased, had nothing to do with the Marlin's demise.

The gun has a solid frame made with a 22- or 26-inch barrel, although William Brophy had never seen a 22-inch gun. The action has a partially exposed hammer and a side ejector. The

black walnut stock has an "S" pistol grip and a hard rubber buttplate. It is lightweight for the times, 6 pounds, and shoots six 2 1/2-inch cartridges—shotshell or round ball.

Marlin also produced a "Deluxe" model according to Brophy, although it was not cataloged or price listed [6]. The forearm and pistol grip were checkered with the "F"-quality double-diamond pattern, 18 lines to the inch. These have proven to be very rare (Photo 7).

Marlin targeted the farmer, the skeet shooter, and the wife and child with the Model 410. It was given also as a free bonus in 1930 to any buyer who bought four "preferred" shares of the Marlin Company for $100, according to an original pamphlet of the time. This was an effort to further capitalize the company in the early years of the depression. The gun itself retailed for $30.80 in 1930 [7] (Photo 8).

It was the first and only repeating 410 at that time. Additionally, it was the first lever-action 410 and the second lever-action shotgun ever made. The first was the John Browning-invented Winchester 1887, made for 10 and 12 gauge only. Up until 2001, when Winchester introduced its "New Model 9410," no other lever-action 410, or shotgun for that matter, was manufactured except for one in the 1930s and two shortly following World War II. These included the Kessler Levermatic, made from 1951 to 1953, and never made in 410. The Ithaca Model 66 was made from 1963 to 1978 in 12, 20, and 410 gauge. According to the Stoeger catalog of 1922, the Savage Model 99 takedown rifle was offered for a short time in the early 1930s with an interchangeable 24-inch, 2-pound 410 barrel.

Serial numbers reveal two kinds of series: A no prefix range from 54 to 8435 and a "U" letter prefix range from U535 to U2174. Unfortunately, systematic records were not kept. William Brophy has documented or verified 184 Model 410s still in existence, comprising the above serial number range. He had confirmed, before his death, two guns with "deluxe" wood and "F"-quality checkering on the stock with typical Marlin double-diamond checkering of that era. These are SN 6623 and SN 6607. The latter is in mint condition [6,7] (Photo 7).

Model 90

Marlin invented this over/under shotgun in 1936 [7,8]. Brophy reports that for many years it was the only over/under shotgun made in America after the discontinuation of the Remington Model 32 between 1942 and 1947. The Browning Superposed gun was Belgium made. The Model 90 was made for Sears Roebuck & Co., who marketed the gun as the "Ranger" before World War II and as "J.C. Higgins" after the war. The Sears production was characterized by the prefix number "103." Marlin also sold the same gun under their name with their own serial number system.

The 410 was offered for 13 years from 1939 to 1952 in the boxlock action with 26-inch barrels and 3-inch chambers with

---

1 Brophy describes the stock and receiver as identical with the Model 93 rifle, including the side ejector, square bolt, and lever. The true pedigree of this 410 remains obscure and is probably forever lost in the mist of time past.

extractors. Although the single trigger was listed as available as early as 1949, it was not until 1954 that a non-selective inertia block single trigger was inventoried for the Model 90! Since the 410 ceased production in 1952, it is unlikely that there is a Model 90 410 in existence with a single trigger!

A change in the barrel configuration occurred after 1950. Up to this time, the space between the two barrels was closed by a steel plate brazed or welded horizontally on both sides of the barrels. After 1950, the space was open. An open-space barrel must be very rare since none has appeared on the resale market, and factory records on this point are nonexistent.

At the time of the 410 introduction in 1939, they offered a 410 smoothbore small-caliber rifle/barrel ensemble. They also offered to the discriminating target shooter the "Skeet King" Model 90 410 with a hand-engraved frame and black American walnut wood (Photo 9).

Brophy notes that, despite the absence of records, under either the Sears or Marlin aegis, they made approximately 15,000 guns in all gauges through 1942. Marlin made an additional 19,000 plus guns from 1952-53 to 1963 in all gauges with either single or double triggers, discontinuing the double-trigger model

in 1957. Two 28-gauge guns were made in 1953. The Marlin Co. historian has seen or heard of only three Model 90 410s in his 28 years at the factory—a very rare gauge indeed. It is notable that the Model 90 410 was priced at $51.55 in the 1945 Stoeger's, 10 percent more expensive than the Hunter Special.

Other Interesting 410s of the First Two-Thirds of the 20th Century

By the 1920s, the 410 had become a popular bore for the clay pigeon shooter and small game hunter. Naturally, the free market tooled up to provide the product in volume and cheaply. Hence, the huge New York City jobber, H. & D. Folsom Arms Company, which had been importing cheaply made Belgian guns since the 1880s, began to make the 410 bore available by the 1920s. McIntosh reports that Folsom used over 200 trade names for these guns [9].

Other hardware and mail order companies did the same [10]. According to Jack O'Connor, the Crescent Firearms Company of Norwich, Connecticut, a manufacturing subsidiary of first Folsom and later Stevens Arms, made tens of thousands of cheap guns that were jobbed out by Folsom under their many different

Photo 9: Marlin Model 90 410 ∧ with frame engraving of a dog on point, a "Skeet King" model.

G. Allan Brown photo

trade names, and occasionally under Crescent's own label as well [11]. After World War I, Crescent made a few of these in the 410 bore.

In the 1920s and '30s, Crescent made the rare 410 double gun under their own label. They were inexpensive but well made side-by-sides with or without ejectors, using the Anson & Deeley boxlock or the back-action sidelock, the latter in their Quail model (Photo 10).

Most such 410s have vanished with use and time. However, occasionally one will surface at a gun show as a Crescent or under a private label of a now non-existent retail or wholesale gun company such as the American Gun Company, etc. [12]. The imports had Belgian or Spanish proof marks [13]. The American-built guns, by Crescent for example, had no proof marks. The depression eventually shut down Crescent and other American sources of these "contract guns."

Sources for contract guns were some of the great gunmakers of Europe. Stoeger had retailed, under the brand name of "Zephyr," a line of double shotguns from the "Field"-grade Anson & Deeley boxlock, priced in 1945 at $125, to the "Royal" -grade sidelock gun at $415. These were available, but rarely, if ever, built in the 410 bore. The Stoeger line was made by German and Belgian companies including J.P. Sauer, Fabrique Nationale, and later by Spanish and Italian firms, such as Beretta. In 1932, their side-by-side ranged from the Model 400 at $92.50 to the Deluxe No. 219 at $600. Intermediate grades included two bar-action sidelocks, the Model 410 and No. 218.

Their over/under line with the A&D boxlock and Krupp or Boehler steel barrels included the Greener cross bolt and barrel underlugs and sideplates in the two highest grades. These ranged from Model No. 228 at $175 in 1932 to the Paragon 236E at $1150.

By 1956, Stoeger offered the side-by-side Model 4E and 4EDS in 410 with a Holland & Holland action priced from $144 to $198. These appeared to have been Spanish built. A single trigger and ventilated rib were the options. By 1965, their only offered 410 was an A&D boxlock side-by-side with double triggers and extractors, priced at $118. The 410 was available in both barrel configurations but only one has ever surfaced in modern times (Photo 11). Depending upon price, configuration, and maker, the Stoeger guns were of highly variable quality.[2]

Many American firms such as Savage, Stevens, Marlin, Springfield, Harrington & Richardson, Remington, Mossberg, Ithaca, and Hunter Arms Company built inexpensive but sturdy 410s from the 1930s to, in some cases, the present time. These were made in various action and barrel configurations.

Side-by-side double 410s of this class included the Fulton, priced in 1945 at $38.60, and the Hunter Special at $45.35, both

made by the Hunter Arms Company, especially before World War II (see Photo 9 in L.C. Smith chapter). These were similar in price to Iver Johnson's double Hercules at $44.50. These guns could be had with a single trigger and automatic ejectors. Similarly, the Savage Arms-made Fox Model B at $33.70 in 1945 was a side-by-side with extractors and double triggers. This was available through the 1980s.

Other 410 side-by-sides in this category of guns included the Savage Arms Company-made Stevens Model 530 boxlock priced at $29.25 in 1945, which became the Model 311 by 1956, and available through the 1980s. My aunt owned a single-shot, single-barrel Savage-made Stevens Model 94F 410 with a 3-inch chamber and an exposed hammer. I had the use of this gun before my adolescence and, accompanying my dad, shot a lot of game with it.

The Stevens Firearm 410 story may go back to 1912-1915 when the then independent J. Stevens Arms Co. made a single-shot, exposed-hammer, under-lever breech-opener gun with a 26-inch barrel for "ball or shellshot" in the "44 gauge," the Model 101 [14]. Although the .410 caliber is actually a 67 gauge, the Model 101 comfortably fires a 410 cartridge! Stevens made the 410 bore in a number of subsequent Stevens models. These include the No. 35 "Off-hand" Auto-Shot shotgun pistol for shellshot with an 8- or 12.5-inch barrel, made from 1931-1935; the No. 107 and 105 hammer top-lever single shot; the No. 240 over/under 410 smoothbore/22 caliber rifle; and the No. 330 and 311 (see above) side-by-side made until 1989.

Apart from the Marlin 410, lever-action shotguns in the 410 bore were rare. Ithaca built a Model 66 from 1963 to 1978, available in 12, 20, and 410, with a rebounding partially exposed hammer, described as a "Super Single." The only other vintage lever-action 410 known to me is the Savage Model 99 lever-action rifle that has an auxiliary 24-inch 410-shotgun barrel with a 2 1/2-inch chamber. This gun was available with all rifle calibers and cataloged from 1932 to 1945. In 2001, Winchester introduced its own version of a lever action 410, the "New Model 9410." This smoothbore is a "direct descendent" of the Winchester Model 94. It is available with 20- or 24-inch barrels and, oddly, only chambered for the 2 1/2-inch cartridge.

Few companies made a pump or slide-action 410 and none remotely approached the Winchester Model 42 in quality or popularity. The Remington Model 31 slide action, built from 1931 to 1949, was never available in the 410 bore. Likewise, the well-made Ithaca Model 37 pump, introduced in 1937 and reintroduced as the Model 87 in 1987, was never made in the 410.

The Stevens Model 620 pump became available by 1965 as a 410, then called the Model 77, and manufactured for several years. The Mossberg Model 500 pump was not available in the 410 until the late 1960s and remains in stock today with a period in the early 1980s when it was called the Model 600.

The Remington Model 870 was not cataloged in 410 until after 1969, although a 410 was available through the Custom Shop from 1950.

2 Another 410 Stoeger "RE Sidelock" double, 110113, with Spanish proof marks surfaced at a 2001 American auction. It is a double trigger gun with ejectors, weighing a heavy 6 pounds 9 ounces.

Photo 10: A Crescent Quail model 410 back-action sidelock with a full array of case colors.

G. Allan Brown photo

Photo 11: A Stoeger A&D boxlock ∧ 410 with German proof marks.

G. Allan Brown photo

Almost every shotgun manufacturer made bolt-action, single-barrel hammer or hammerless breech openers, and semi-automatic 410 guns at some point. The bolt 410 was made on the Webley & Scott action as a single-barrel breech opener. The semi-automatics were given birth by John Browning, the greatest gun inventor in world history.

There is an unusual category of gun recently well documented [15]. These are the smoothbore shot pistols, most of which were made for the 410-gauge 2 1/2-inch cartridge. The National Firearms Act of 1934 essentially outlawed these guns. The barrel was either 8 or 12 inches long or longer, and the gun was used for small game or pests such as rodents and snakes.

Makers included the prolific Harrington & Richardson Arms Co. who made approximately 54,000 of these "Handy-Guns" in three models from 1921 to 1934, most in 410 gauge. Other companies included a Crescent-made 410 scatter shot single- or double-barrel pistol from 1932 to 1934. Less than 4000 appear to have been made. The Stevens No. 35 "Off-Hand" (1923-1929) and "Auto-Shot" (1929-1934) were available in 410 bore. Both models appear to have had production runs of only a few thousand.

Another Harrington & Richardson Arms Co. (H-R) story surfaced in 2000 and deserves brief recounting here [16,17]. An H-R top-lever, centerfire hammer gun, a "410-44 Cal" smoothbore with British proof marks (SN A14414), was "attributed" to Annie Oakley's use on one of her pre-1903 British tours. A patent date of February 2, 1900, is stamped on the gun, making it a post-1900 fabrication. The attribution is based upon provenance, both indirect and remote, and a "series of dents and scratches on the right side but no visible inscription" on the stock [17]. A recent owner made a case, using powdered chalk, that the scratches on the stock could be read as "P," "M," "Z." Annie's real name was Phoebe Mozee.

An equally interesting point is that this appears to be a smoothbore through which shot or ball can be discharged, made in America by H-R and exported to Britain where it was proofed

and sold [16]. As was earlier recounted, before 1900, American firms such as Colt and H-R made guns—including 410 smoothbore canes, pistols, and long guns—for export to Britain where they were proofed in London or Birmingham and sold by retail gun dealers to the public.

This tale has proved sufficiently interesting to result in the gun having been offered for sale at a five-figure request in 2002!

The Ithaca "Auto & Burglar" gun was made in the 410 bore and very few left the factory (see Ithaca chapter). A 410 in any of the above models would be collectible; however, a ruling letter from the BATF is required to avoid a potential fine of $10,000 and 10 years in federal prison. And, all this for a gun with virtually no use to a criminal! Eric Larson, a world authority on the gun, has testified before Congress on multiple occasions on this and other matters in an effort to bring some sense out of this governmental nonsense.

Many of these interesting 410s were inexpensive and, therefore, were relatively common through the 1920s, '30s, and '40s. Unfortunately, farmers, clay target shooters, and youngsters heavily used most and few are seen today either in use or at gun shows. Most were destroyed by hard use, abuse, and neglect.

Interesting Early 20th Century American 410 Shotguns References

1. Stadt, Ronald W., *Winchester Shotguns and Shotshells*, Armory Publication, 1984.
2. Madis, George, *The Winchester Handbook*, George Madis, Brownsboro, TX, Art and Reference House, 1981.
3. Watrous, George R., *The History of Winchester Firearms, 1866 to 1975*, Winchester Press, 4th Ed., 1975.
4. Schwing, Ned, *The Winchester Model 42*, Krause Publication, 1990.
5. Brown, Gary M., "A Short History of the Model 42 Winchester," *CADA Gun Journal*, November 1992.
6. Brophy, William, Personal correspondence.
7. Brophy, William, *Marlin Firearms, A History*, Stackpole Books, 1989.
8. Goldshinsky, Edmund, Marlin Co. factory historian—personal correspondence 1994.
9. McIntosh, Michael, *Best Guns*, Country Sport Press, 1989.
10. Zutz, Don, "American Sporting Shotguns," *Shotgun Sports*, April 1998.
11. O'Connor, Jack, *The Shotgun Book*, Alfred A. Knopf, 1965.
12. *CADA Gun Journal*, page 77. November 1995.
13. Stoeger, *The Shooter's Bible*, 1945, No. 36, page 85.
14. Purington, Bill, Father and son collection of Stevens Firearms, personal correspondence.
15. Larson, Eric, *CADA Gun Journal*, August, September, and October 1994; May 1996; March 1998.
16. Smith, Guy N., *Shooting Sportsman*, January/February 2000.
17. Butterfields Auction, June 11-12, 2002.

CHAPTER ELEVEN

ATKIN, GRANT & LANG

welve Bore Two-Inch C

h solves the problem of building a thoroughly effect
bre 2-in. paper cartridge, with a ¾ oz. shot charge, ;
s of game at the usual sporting distances.
under, and in side-lock qualities just over, 5½ ll
in all qualities.

adies' and Boys' Guns

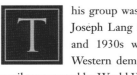

This group was the result of a Stephen Grant and Joseph Lang take-over splurge in the late 1920s and 1930s when the economies of the great Western democracies were sinking into oblivion until resurrected by World War II. They joined with Harrison & Hussey in 1930, Lancaster in 1932, Watson Brothers in 1935, and Beesley in 1939. In 1960, they joined with Henry Atkin & Son to form Atkin, Grant & Lang located at 7 Bury Street, London. Four years earlier, Atkin & Son had purchased Charles Hellis & Sons [1]. In 1971, Churchill bought Atkin, Grant & Lang, Ltd. and in 1976, this consortium moved to 61 Pall Mall, London.

In 1980, the firm ceased to exist, only to be resurrected by Cyril Adams of Texas in 1984 as Atkin, Grant & Lang, Ltd., making 36 "Best" London guns [2,3]. However, in 1997, Lord Masserene offered this firm's name and inventory for sale for a quarter million pounds [4]. Eventually, a group led by Ken Duglan of Broomhills Shooting Grounds in England bought the firm and now has resumed "Best" gun production. In the meantime, the Churchill name and records had been reestablished as a freestanding firm, and, following an ownership dispute in 1997, now settled, the company appears to be prospering (see Churchill chapter).

Stephen Grant, who had worked for Boss & Co., began his gun business in 1866 at 67A St. James's, London. In 1889, his sons joined him, and in 1920, the firm moved to 7 Bury St. before joining Lang in 1923-25.

In a brown-colored Stephen Grant & Joseph Lang, Ltd. catalog (post-World War II, after the Beesley absorption in 1939 and before the Atkin incorporation in 1960), a "high-grade small-bore ... 410 offered for ladies and boys," was made under the Watson name (Photo 1). This double weighed 4-1/2 pounds, and a single barrel version, 3-1/2 pounds. The Watson 410 A&D boxlock double occasionally surfaces on the resale market. Having joined Grant & Lang in 1935 under terms of necessity, Watson today has reemerged as an independent and continues to specialize in the smaller-bore, high-quality, round-bodied, and self-opening sidelock and boxlock shotguns (see Watson chapter).

Thanks to the courtesies extended by Ken Duglan, existing record books of these various firms were examined in 2000 for the details of their 410 smoothbore productions.

1. "Atkin Book"

The Atkin records contained in the Atkin book encompass Serial Number 101 in 1881 to SN 3601, 30 October 1976.

The first 410 was a hammer gun, SN 783, sent to "Lord Howard." The next was a top-lever hammer, SN 886, sent to the "Earl of Harewood." The manufacturing dates are not specific but are after 1885 and before 1895.

From that era, not specified in the records, to 1902, from SN 926 to SN 1556, they built or had built seven more hammer 410 guns—one a top-lever and the rest side-lever openers. The next 10 years recorded no 410s.

Beginning in 1912 with SN 2034, until 1927, SN 2827, ten Anson & Deeley (A&D) hammerless 410s are recorded. All were non-ejectors except SN 2826 and SN 2827, a consecutive pair recorded in October 1927. Three of these A&D 410s were made by "Osborne," a high-quality gunmaker to the trade.

Starting in 1927 with SN 2857, a single-barrel folding gun, their 410 production included six A&D hammerless doubles, three with ejectors; four single-barrel folding guns; seven single-barrel hammerless guns; two double-barrel hammers; and one single-barrel hammer 410. The last one, SN 3466, is undated and not characterized but was made sometime after 1942.

One of the A&D ejector guns, SN 2889, was sent to "Captain Fry" in 1928, and an A&D non-ejector, SN 3446, was sent to a "colonel" in 1943.

Atkin joined Grant & Lang in 1960, never having made or recorded a sidelock hammerless 410, with the peerless Atkin spring-opener action. G.T. Garwood (Gough Thomas), one of the most knowledgeable and influential gun writers of the 20th

Photo 1: Page from a Grant & Lang brown post-World War II catalog advertising a Watson Bros. 410.

∨   *Glenn Campbell photo*

The Twelve Bore Two-Inch Gun

This is one of our latest productions, which solves the problem of building a thoroughly effective weapon to enable users to shoot all day without fatigue. It fires the 12 bore 2-in. paper cartridge, with a ⅞ oz. shot charge, giving the required velocity, spread and penetration necessary to kill all kinds of game at the usual sporting distances.
The weight in box-lock qualities is just under, and in side-lock qualities just over, 5½ lbs., and the balance, handling and results are all that can be desired. Built in all qualities.

Ladies' and Boys' Guns

WATSON BROS. always made a speciality of high-grade small bore guns for ladies and boys, and these are continued as before.

"TEACHING THE YOUNG IDEA"
.410 and 28 Bore Shot-Guns
Specially Designed for Young People

At our Shooting Grounds special attention is given to fitting guns for the use of ladies, so that they may secure the confidence so necessary for becoming a good shot. In designing and constructing the guns the need for lightness, comfort and ease of handling is kept well in mind. The designs are based on the models illustrated and described in the preceding pages and the same prices apply.

The .410 is generally recognised as the ideal gun for the boy of eight or ten starting to learn shooting. Its light weight enables him to carry it without undue fatigue, and at the same time the heavier cartridge gives a pattern which he will find really useful in his early attempts on fur and feather. Weight about 4½ lbs. for double barrel guns and 3½ lbs. for singles.
28 bores are equally suitable for boys two or three years older, who by then are able to handle the slightly heavier gun and cartridges. Weight about 5 lbs.

11

^ **Photo 2:** A "Best" Grant double-rifle 410 conversion, SN 3981.

Paul Goodwin photo

Photo 3: The offset stock of SN 3981. The "Duke" was right-handed with only a left eye.

∨ *Paul Goodwin photo*

century, chose Atkin & Son to build his 12-bore shotgun using the spring-opening action in which he described the "smoothness" of opening and "uniformity of effort" to close it. The only Atkin 410 that has surfaced publicly in the past 30 years is SN 1447, recorded as a "top-lever hammer" in 1901. It is a back-action 28-inch double with 2 1/2-inch chambers. This is the sixth earliest Atkin 410 recorded.

2. "Grant Book"

The existing Grant records extend from 21 February 1867, SN 2480, to 1933, SN 8196, and not a single 410 is listed in this number sequence. However, in this book, there are recorded five 410s in a serial number range of 15000. SN 15065 is an A&D boxlock

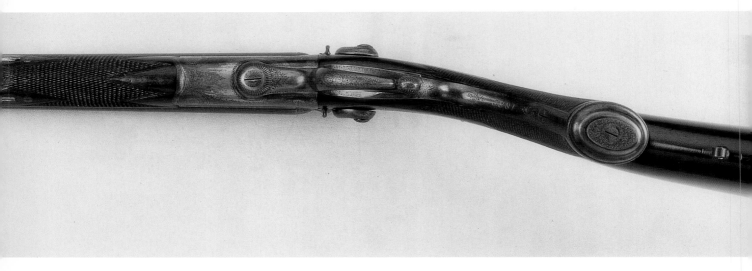

recorded in 1912. SN 15075 is a hammer gun with 28-inch barrels sent to "Lord Dalkeith" in 1916 that now resides in an
American collection. SN 15093 is a "stick" gun sent to "Sir
Alexander Gibb" in 1920. SN 15098 is an A&D boxlock with 26-
inch steel barrels and recorded in 1927 for 13 pounds, 13 shillings.

Finally and tellingly, SN 15099 was a back-action rebounding hammer gun with 26-inch steel barrels selling for 4 pounds
and "destroyed by enemy action." Although the date is not registered, it was probably during World War II.

There exists a "Best" Stephen Grant 360-caliber double
rifle made in 1876 for H.G. Leigh, SN 3981, which is an object
of splendor. It is a "breech-loader centre-fire" hammer back
action with gold-plated strikers and full scroll engraving with a
duke's crest. It is now a 410 conversion (Photos 2 and 3). It was
once owned by an English psychologist who gave it up in order
to "eternally possess it," a thought from George Santayana, a
Spanish philosopher. A rare early Grant back-action hammer gun
can be a beauty as the "Best" rifle/410 conversion illustrates.

Another 410 conversion is a beautiful single-barrel breech-
loading 577-caliber "Best" rifle, SN 6302, made in 1891 for a
"Count Wagner."

3. "Lang Books"

The original Joseph Lang firm, 1817-1875, was briefly reviewed
by a recently deceased descendent. He stated an earlier heir had
destroyed the family papers in 1935 [5].

The "Lang #1" book, beginning in 1859 with SN 2085 and
ending in 1892, records no 410 smoothbores.

The "Lang #2" book begins in 1893 with SN 10105 and lists
two 410s built in 1898, numbers 13172 and 13173, described as
Anson & Deeley boxlocks with 28-inch barrels. The latter gun,
made by "Ellis," a quality outworker for the trade, was sent to
"Hon. Beresford." With a separate numbering system, they list,
from SN 3000 to SN 3010, a series of 410 "Ball & Shot Pistols"
with a "side-lever ejector." Dated from 1892 to 1895, SN 3003
had an "extra barrel," 3009 an extra 300-bore barrel, and 3010 an
extra 750-bore barrel. Examples from this series of guns have
appeared on the auction market in Great Britain.

The "Lang #3" book begins with SN 7465 in 1890 and ends
in 1923 with SN 16547. For reasons unknown, this book's dates
and numbering system overlap both Book #1 and Book #2.

Book #3 records three single-barrel, side-lever hammer
guns made in 1895, SN 7950 to SN 7952; four double-barrel

> **Photo 4:** A Lang 410, SN
> 17192, made by "J. Saunders"
> "complete."
>
> *Paul Goodwin photo*

Photo 5: A rare Harrison & ∧
Hussey 410, SN 3336.

Paul Goodwin photo

boxlocks; a single-barrel (SN 8595) made by "Osborne" in 1898; and a double-barrel hammer (SN 29116) made in 1900. Lang made additional 410 guns after the "Grant & Lang" union of their recording system in 1923.

4. "Grant & Lang Book"

Although the merger was reported in 1925, the unified records began in 1923 with SN 16548 and a significant number of 410s are listed. The first is SN 16578, recorded in 1924, a bar-action sidelock with rebounding hammers and 28-inch barrels and sent to "Capt. Phelps" for 5 pounds, 15 shillings. It is a "Le Per Socine," referring to the maker. This appears to be the only bar-action sidelock made by or for "Grant & Lang."

They recorded under the "Grant & Lang" name four A&D 410s between 1926 and 1928—one by "James Carr" and three by "Rogers," both high-quality makers. The "James Carr" A&D went to "Sir Thomas Roydon" in 1926.

They then record seven A&D guns under the "Lang" name from 1928 to 1931. "Rogers" made two, "Harper" made one (he made virtually all of the Robertson 410s by Boss), and "J. Saunders" made two. The latter two are paired, SN 17192 (Photo 4) and SN 17193, and recorded in July 1931. Lang described them as "3rd-quality" ejector guns with 27-inch barrels.

From 1925 to 1935, they listed approximately 28 single-barrel folding guns, made by "L. Le Personnie," a Belgium firm, and retailed by "Ward & Son," "Ward Bros.," or "Salter & Varge" in England. One, in 1925, SN 16660, has the "Jeffrey Co." name attached and SN 16674 has the "Charles Osborne" name juxtaposed in the records. Approximately 13 have the "Lang" name attached to each serial number.

From 1935 until 1960, the "Grant & Lang" book recorded three A&D non-ejector 410s in 1934-35 by "Saunders," numbers 17405, 06 and 07. A hammerless "repeating" was listed in 1935, SN 17428. This may have been an American import for a special customer. The same year they recorded a "Winchester Repeating" M42, SN 17509, the great single-barrel pump 410 bore that dominated the American market for over four decades.

In 1934, they recorded a "Best" "Lang" 410, SN 17430, an A&D ejector for 56 pounds, which was double the cost of their typical A&D ejector for the times. From 1935 to 1937, they listed an additional 14 A&D guns by "Saunders"—four ejectors, and 10 non-ejectors, numbers 17586-93 and 17701-06. The initials "GL" stand next to each 410. This may mean the "Grant & Lang" name is on the gun.

From 1937 to 1949, they recorded an additional 15 A&D boxlock doubles—four ejectors, and 11 non-ejectors. All of these were "Watson Bros," numbers 18004-11, 18705-10, and 18825, the last A&D 410 in the "Grant & Lang" book.

In this same window of time in 1937, "Ward & Son" retailed 44 single-barrel, Belgium-made folding hammerless 410s, numbers 17721-44. In 1942, eight side-lever single-barrel guns were noted and renamed "Watson Bros" guns. These were numbers 18564-72, excepting 18566, which was a sidelock under-lever single-barrel 410. From 1946 to 1949, a group of probable Belgian-made "folding" 410s, numbers 18745 to 18794, were "manufactured" for Ward & Sons and "renamed" "Watson Bros." An additional 410 production run in this book was numbered 19090-101, all single-barrel folding guns for "Watson." Many 410 folding guns through 1960 were by or for "Ward & Son."

Additional permutations involving family or business associates deserve notice.

5. Lang & Hussey, Ltd.

The existence of an engraved "Lang & Hussey, Ltd." non-ejector boxlock A&D double 410, whose vintage can be determined by the 102 New Bond Street, London, address on the rib, occasions a brief comment about an interesting pedigree of firms.

James Lang, the son of Joseph, began his own firm in 1887. In 1895, he joined Henry J. Hussey, an assistant manager and gunmaker at Holland & Holland, to form "Lang & Hussey" at 102 New Bond St. This lasted until 1898 when they merged with the original Joseph Lang firm [6]. The result was "Lang & Hussey, Ltd.," which existed from 1898 until 1901, at which time Hussey resigned and the firm again became "Joseph Lang & Son." In 1925, Stephen Grant & Sons bought the Lang firm, forming "Stephen Grant & Joseph Lang, Ltd."; however, the union of its record book, the "Grant & Lang" book, began in 1923.

According to the "Lang #2" record book, the above-noted hammerless 410 (SN 13172) has 28-inch barrels with full-coverage engraving and was made in 1898. The A&D action was made by "Ellis." They made an identical 410, SN 13173, at the same time. Wouldn't these make a nice pair? The record book does not record what, in fact, is on the rib: "Lang & Hussey, Ltd."

6. Harrison & Hussey, Ltd. [7]

To further complicate the gunmakers' pedigrees, this firm existed from 1919 to 1930, according to factory records and letters. They built guns from components supplied by outside artisans. H.H. Hussey was the son of H.J. Hussey, who had left Lang in 1901. By 1927, according to correspondence, Claud E. Harrison, originally of Cogswell & Harrison, was the managing director, and Hussey was not listed as a director.

Two catalogs, a small blue one from 1925 and a later but undated larger orange one, both list the 41 Albemarle Street, London, address. Neither lists the 410 bore as available; however, the records speak otherwise.

They sold four double-barrel A&D boxlock 410s, one with ejectors, from 1919 to 1927—numbers 1074, 75, and 76 in 1919-1920, and SN 3336 in 1927 (Photo 5). They also sold three single-barrel folding hammerless guns in 1929.

Conclusion

These consortia of London firms prided themselves on the high-quality "Best" smoothbore, effectively competing with London's famous firms for periods of time, but ultimately succumbing to lack of public acceptance and the economies of socialism. The resurrection of many of these firms is a tribute to the re-capitalization of England begun with the Thatcher revolution.

Atkin, Grant & Lang References

1. Boothroyd, Geoffrey, S.T.C.M., March 9-15, 1995.
2. Wieland, Terry, Shooting Sportsman, March/April 1995.
3. Tate, D. and V. Venters, Shooting Sportsman, March/April 2001.
4. Personal correspondence.
5. Lang, Bill, S.T.C.M., July 13, 2000.
6. Akehurst, Richard, Game Guns & Rifles, C. Bell & Sons, Ltd., 1969.
7. Original records provided by Harris & Sheldon Group.

CHAPTER TWELVE

BOSS

T homas Boss, a masterful London gunmaker, appears to have started as a free-standing gunmaker at Edgware Road, London, in 1833. He had served his apprenticeship and journeymanship under the aegis of Joseph Manton and had enjoyed the patronage of James Purdey before establishing his independence.

He eventually settled in the St. James Street address where he remained until his death in 1857. In 1891, John Robertson purchased a partnership and became the full owner in 1903. Robertson resuscitated the firm, then in serious decline, by the quality of his "Best" guns and by nurturing two innovative patents that maintained Boss in front rank technically as well as artistically.

They moved to 13 Dover Street in 1908 and remained there until 1930. They then moved to 41 Albemarle Street where they remained until 1960. They then relocated to 13-14 Cork Street. In 1982, they returned to 13 Dover Street where they continued until 2000, at which time they were sold.

It was at the Cork Street address in 1976 that I first encountered this elegant gunmaker. As I prowled around the ancient, cracked gun racks housing the rare guns, furtively watched by a sleepy-eyed, lethargic, and polite but non-communicative custodian, I was persuaded that this firm was moribund. How wrong! Behind this somnolent exterior were several exquisite artisan gunmakers.

The firm was and remains a highest quality, low-volume maker, still producing one of the great guns of the world. In the past two decades, they have averaged approximately six to 10 guns a year. Based upon serial numbers through 1998, approximately 10,030 guns Boss guns left the shop.

The Robertson Era

Robertson's single trigger of 1893, based upon the three-pull system, was an immediate success. This three-pull system compensates for a "second trigger pull" made unknowingly by the shooter due to recoil forces. Robertson used a revolving capstan that turned with the second involuntary pull to bolt the second

>

Photos 1-4 (opposite page): Four views of a matched pair of 410 Boss smoothbores now used in Texas to shoot bobwhite, scaled quail and rabbit, SNs 8745 and 8746.

Perry Bass photos

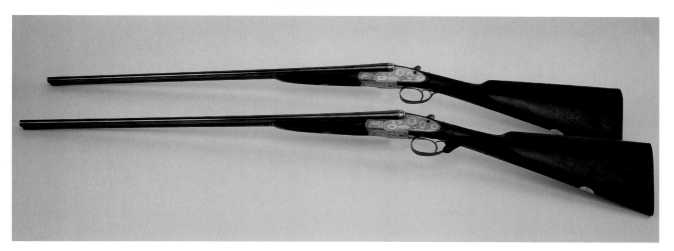

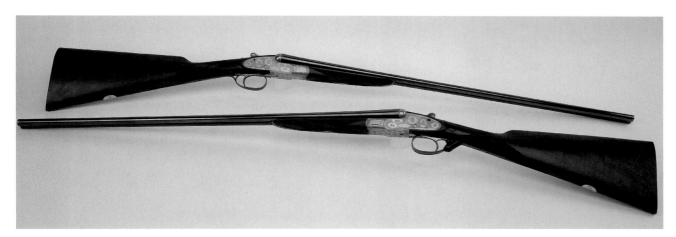

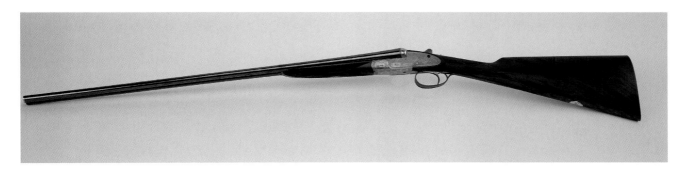

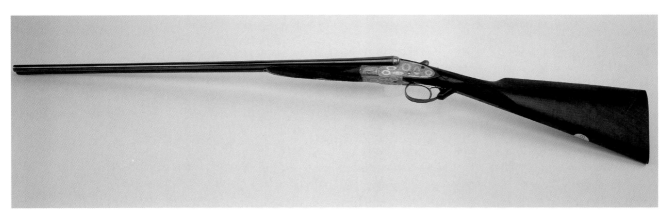

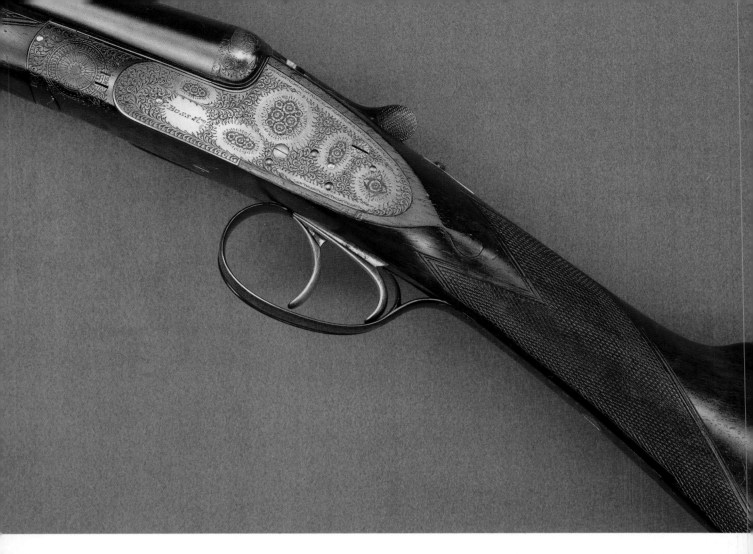

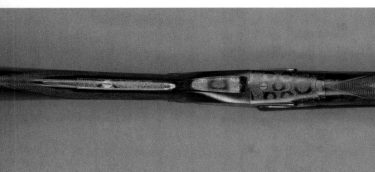
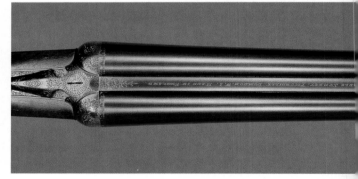

lock, thus preventing "doubling."

The second innovation was a low profile over/under shotgun of 1909, credited to a Scottish craftsman in the Boss factory. This over/under did not use under bolts and, thus, was similar to the Woodward over/under developed from 1908 through 1913, the later Holland & Holland, the modern Beretta, and the Remington 32 of the 1930s. They machined lugs into the posterior aspect of the barrels. The standing breech projected bolts to mate with bites on both sides of the lower barrel. This bifurcated lump locking system created a low silhouette by reducing the height of the action. Both of Robertson's innovations were mile-

∧ **Photos 5-7:** Three views of SN 8745A made for George Baker, a quiet but powerful American financier of the first half of the 20th century, who, according to his son, never used the gun.

Levasheff photos

stones in the perfection of the British shotgun.

The Boss bar-action sidelock, exquisitely machined and hand finished, is either masculinely square or sleekly rounded (not to be confused with a Dickson "round" or Blitz "trigger plate" action) in configuration. The latter's geometry is somewhat more elegant; however, both body types are a joy to behold.

The 410 Boss Side-by-Side

In a conversation in 1982 with Boss's ancient and retired barrel maker, Jack Rennie, he told me that the firm had made "perhaps" 13 410s—10 side-by-sides with double triggers, and "three or four" over/under 410s with single triggers.

The first 410 Boss manufactured appears to have been shipped in 1936. It is a bar-action double-triggered side-by-side, SN 8393.

Two of the side-by-sides are a matched pair, SN 8745 and SN 8746. They have 26-inch barrels with 2 1/2-inch chambers. They had double triggers and are self-opening, bar-action sidelocks. Made for an Englishman, Mr. Turner, and shipped in July

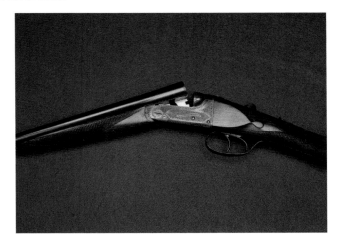

Photo 9: The "Sir J. Ball" 410, SN 8294, is a Robertson 410.

Glenn Campbell photo

Photo 8: The third produced Robertson 410 (SN 7871), the "Captain Burn" 410, is one of a matched pair.

Glenn Campbell photo

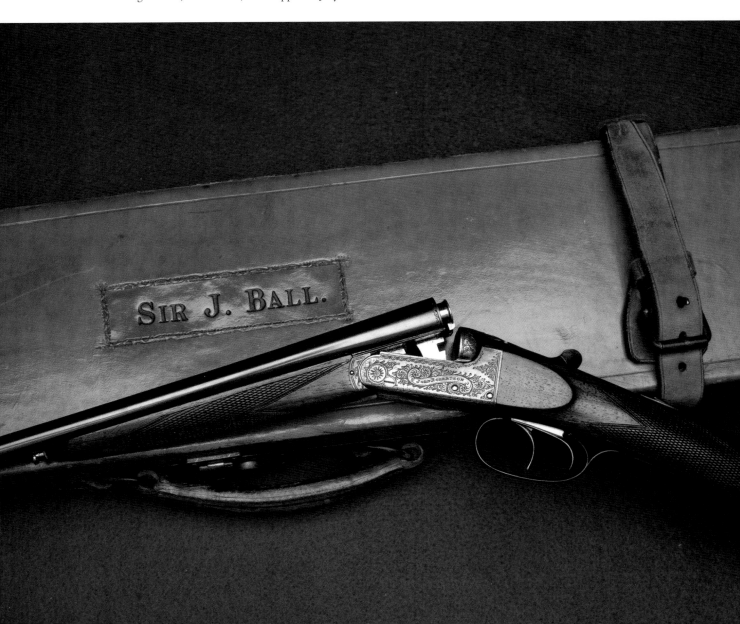

1947, each weighed 4 pounds, 4 ounces. Holland & Holland auctioned the pair in 1966 with an estimated price of 1500 pounds (Photos 1-4). Later the guns were re-stocked, converted to single triggers, and resold by Bill Jaqua to their current owner in 1982. They are in active use today in quail shooting in Texas.

According to factory records, Boss manufactured a second pair, incredibly numbered 8745A and 8746A, in 1948 (Photos 5-7). They made one for a Mr. George Baker and one for a Mr. Cushing, both Americans [2]. Both guns have square-configuration actions with 26-inch barrels, double triggers, splinter forends, and straight stocks. They feature checkered stock butts and the stock bottom of 8745A has a monogram inlay of gold with the initials E.B. This gun sold at a Sotheby auction in 1978 for $12,000.

Abercrombie & Fitch had another side-by-side 410 made in 1967, SN 9374. In 1974, they shipped a square-framed 28-inch side-by-side 410, SN 9935. This gun has a single trigger, splinter forend, straight stock, and a checkered butt stock with "13 Dover Street" on the barrels. Boss also made a 410 set of side-by-side barrels, SN 9280, for an existing gun, probably a 28 bore. Apparently, all side-by-sides except SN 9935 have double triggers.

After 1974, they refused to make any further 410s until persuaded in the late 1980s to make another bar-action side-by-side pair for "an American dealer," SN 10001 and SN 10002. The first gun has a square frame, and the other is rounded. Both have 26-inch barrels and single triggers.

The 410 Boss Over/Under

Boss shipped SN 8619, the first known over/under 410, in 1938, on the eve of World War II. The customer was the President of Coca Cola, Canada, who ordered for a friend. This gun weighed

Photo 10: The "Richards" 410, ∧ SN 8869, is a Robertson 410.

Glenn Campbell photo

4 pounds, 12 ounces, had 26-inch barrels and a 14 1/8-inch pull. It has a single trigger with a straight stock and a splinter forend. It recently sold at a Christie's auction for $112,000 in less than pristine condition.

They built yet another over/under 410 in 1948, SN 8787. It passed through the hands of Bill Jaqua who commented that, unlike the typical American over/under such as the Browning B25 or the Winchester 101, the gun sat very low in the shooter's leading palm, "resulting in both barrels being more directly in line with the shooter's extended hand."

Still another Boss over/under, SN 8855, shipped in 1949. A fourth over/under 410, SN 8879, completed in approximately 1950, briefly appeared at Christie's in 1998. It had 26-inch barrels, bouquet and scroll engraving, and a replacement 15 3/4-inch stock. Evidently, it did not sell. Finally, they more recently completed, in 1991, a fifth over/under 410, SN 10000, for the highly respected American dealer who commissioned numbers 10001 and 10002. Like the four earlier over/under guns, this one has a single trigger, 26-inch barrels, and a ventilated rib. You may wager that SN 10000 is handsomely appointed and will fetch a queen's ransom when sold. Ken Hunt engraved all three of the new 410s with a very intricate bouquet and scroll design.

Boss, in 1994, once again said they would not build any further 410s because they were not cost effective. However, a recent purchase by a group of investors, ending the Robertson's family involvement, promises to resuscitate the 410 bore as of the turn of the 21st century.

The 410 Robertson Boxlock Side-by-Side [3]

This story is untold in Donald Dallas' classic, *Boss & Co*; yet, the company did sponsor, had built by the best A&D boxlock makers, and sold under the name of "John Robertson," a matchless "Best" A&D boxlock gun for their selective clientele. The guns are 12, 20, 28, and 410 bores and the company integrated the serial numbers of these guns with the Boss numbers. The 410s were actioned by Mr. John Harper who also jointed barrels to action. All had 26-inch barrels and double triggers, ejectors, and they were London proofed.

I reviewed the then one existing "Robertson Record Book," on November 7, 1995, courtesy of Tony Lokatis, the office manager. Supposedly, this book recorded all "John Robertson" guns from 1930 to post-World War II, which apparently includes the entire production run.

There were 12 410s made. They produced four in 1930, numbers 7827 and 28, as well as 7871 and 72. Number 7871 was a Harper-made gun that shipped to Captain Pelham Burn in 1931 (Photo 8). Numbers 8033 and 34 were shipped in 1932, and SNs 8199 and 8200 were recorded in 1934. Number 8294 shipped to a knight in 1935. In 1936, numbers 8352 and 53 were shipped, and, in 1951, SN 8869 was sent to a jockey.

A fascinating footnote to the 410 story at Boss is an apparent trio of boxlock A&D action side-by-sides that passed through Boss in the 1950s. They were guns "made for John Robertson." They are recorded in the Boss records as numbers 9065, 9066, and 9067 and are very high grade in quality. (A caveat here since the record custodian first reported it to me, then denied it a year later.) They appear to have been made for a younger generation of the Robertson family, the sire of which did so much to bring Boss intact into the 20th century.

Besides the "Captain Burn's" 410 in the late 1990s, three more have appeared publicly. Number 8294 was shipped in 1935 in an oak and leather case to "Sir Ball" (Photo 9) and remains mint. In 1936, SNs 8352 and 53 were shipped. The latter gun went originally to Australia and now is in the United States.

This appeared to be the end of the Robertson 410 story until SN 8869, made for and sent to the great English jockey, Sir Gordon Richards, in 1951. It is remarkable for its 12 1/2-inch stock. This gun was recorded in the "Boss" records post World War II as "The Robertson Record Book" ended at the end of World War II (Photo 10).

Hence, there may have been another Robertson 410 made after World War II. In any event, these A&D boxlock guns made by John Harper represent the finest in an A&D boxlock, mechanically and aesthetically.

An added footnote is that in 1994, two exquisitely made 19th-century Boss rifles that had subsequently been converted to 410 smoothbore turned up (see Chapter 26).

Given the recent spurt in productivity and the moneyed shooter's return to high quality doubles, the firm will continue to be a discriminating force in British gunmaking in their new location at Bruton Street, London.

Boss References

1. Dallas, Donald, *Boss & Co.*, Quiller Press, London, 1995.
2. Boss letter and personal correspondence with Tony Lokatis at Boss, 1992.
3. Author's review of Robertson's records at Boss in 1994-95.

CHAPTER THIRTEEN

E.J. CHURCHILL, LTD.

E dwin John Churchill was not a classic British gun-maker in the sense of a skilled artisan-inventor turned executive. Rather he was a game and pigeon-shooting champion with an entrepreneur-ial instinct that found a haven in the gun business. He began his gun trade at 8 Agar Street, London, in 1890-91 [1]. He built his reputation upon his guns, very successfully used in live pigeon shooting in the 1890s. He also introduced, in that era, faster and lighter cartridges, helping to consolidate his name for his suc-cessful live pigeon ensemble of gun and cartridge [2].

Robert Churchill, a nephew who joined the firm in 1900, assumed control of a failing gun firm in 1910 upon the death of E.J. He slowly nursed it back to health through the Great War years of the second decade. So much so, that after the war, he was able to introduce a new concept of shooting, or at least give new energy to an old way of shooting, and with it a new gun. A May 1922 orange catalog at 8 Agar Street announced the introduction of the 25-inch barrel game gun.

This gun, a typical sidelock or Anson & Deeley (A&D) boxlock rebalanced with 25-inch barrels, was called the XXV gun. Both the shooting method and the short-barrel gun revolution-ized target and game shooting for the rest of the 20th century.

Today the "Churchill method" or its modification, popular-ized by Norman Clarke and Ken Davies of the Holland & Holland shooting grounds, is now extolled by a bevy of shooting writers in America for game and targets.

To this untutored shotgunner, it is nothing more than the reflexive or snapshooting I did as a kid with my single-shot ham-mer 410. For the game of my youth—California quail, mourning dove, and rabbit—it was "see, mount, and squeeze, all in one motion, without thought or calculation," as the 1922 Churchill catalog explains. I don't remember ever missing in those inno-cent days. The past sees only perfection.

The XXV was not for "slow and deliberate shooting" but rather for the "Churchill method" where the man "throws up his gun and looses it off without thought or calculation." Robert Churchill's 1955 book, *Game Shooting*, explains that behind his rationale was the fact that smokeless powders did not require long barrels for full combustion.

Implicit was another physiological fact underlying this shooting method. Namely, that two eyes are far more reliable in tracking a moving object than "calculation." The visual modality is best utilized "instinctively." Hence, a new appreciation of

---

1 "Instinctive" behavior is not a magical phenomenon appearing suddenly from an unknown deep reservoir. Rather it is a learned behavior deeply embedded in experience.

visual-motor coordination as a fluid symphony of movement whereby the hands become one with the eyes.

The 26 to 28-inch barrels have grown out of the XXV for this method of shooting primarily because men today are on average 5 inches taller and 25 pounds heavier than the men of the 1920s.

The 1922 Churchill catalog lists the Premier best sidelock, the Hercules A&D best boxlock, the Monte Carlo external hammer non-ejector sidelock, the Field sidelock, the Utility A&D, and an Under/Over boxlock. These were available in the 12 and the "small bores" of 16 and 20. All were available with the option of 25-inch barrels with the XXV gold inlayed on the barrels and action. The firm moved to Leicester Square in 1925, and at some point in the second half of the 1920s, the Crown-grade A&D boxlock was introduced as a grade just below the Utility.

The Original Record Books [1]

According to the "Workshop Book, Volume 1," Churchill's first gun, SN 156, is a 12-gauge smoothbore built in 1891. Earlier pages from the volume may be missing, as the number is a peculiar starting point. The first 410 smoothbore, SN 201, also built in 1891,[2] was a top-lever, hammer back-action double gun sent to "W.B. Bingham, Esq."

In 1997, an E.J. Churchill 410 A&D boxlock ejector with 2 1/2-inch chambers and 28-inch barrels surfaced in the London auction market with "8 Agar" on the rib. There was full coverage scroll engraving on the action. The serial number on the action is #426, and on the barrel #993. In the "workshop book," #426 is recorded as a 12-gauge rebounding hammer back-action gun with a rotatory under lever. However, D.A. Masters, in 1997, uncovered a "bench record" that recorded number 426 as having been made as a 410 double A&D boxlock ejector in 1893 for "Bingham," a family in business with Churchill and for whom he built the first 410, SN 201. The gun is beautiful and now resides with a fortunate collector (Photo 1).

The second 410 smoothbore in the "workshop book," SN 454, built in 1893, was a side lever, probably single-barrel gun. The next, SN 564, built in 1894, was a top-lever hammer back-action double, like the first. The next 410 is not numbered, but is listed next to 566, in 1895, as a double-barrel top-lever hammer gun for "T. Bostock, Esq."

It is noteworthy that the first 28 smoothbore, SN 445, built in 1893, was a top-lever gun with the Rogers hammerless bar action patented by W.C. Scott and had Southgate ejectors. This was a high quality gun meant for game or target shooting, and, unlike the 410, not meant for pest control or "collecting" of small wing and ground game.

Subsequently, Churchill began a long history of 410 shotgun production, and by 1905 had manufactured 20 410

smoothbores. Ten were single-barrel "collector" guns, eight were hammer back-action doubles, and two were A&D hammerless boxlock guns with the Baker ejector system, numbers 1181 and 1182, made as a pair in 1900.

The last 410 in this sequence, built in 1905, was a double-barrel hammer back action, SN 1508. During this period, Churchill made a number of 32-bore guns on hammer back actions or hammerless A&D actions.

Thereafter, a steady stream of 410s appeared under the Churchill name. From SN 2202 in 1914 to the 3400 range in 1934, they built 21 410s. All but the first, SN 2202, are hammerless A&D action doubles. The last three built in this era, SN 3485, 86 and 87, were Crown ejector guns. The latter two were sent to an "Earl" and "Viscount" respectively in 1933 and 1934. Number 3485, started in 1926 and finished in 1930, was sold to an American diplomat in Vienna, Austria, for 35 pounds. It had 25-inch barrels, 2 1/2-inch chambers, and a straight grip stock. This American had purchased a number of Churchill guns between the two wars. During this period, several of the A&D boxlocks were "Furnished by Harper," John Harper being a "best" maker to the trade.

During this era, barrel lengths ranged from 24 inches to 27 inches. Eight were shipped with 25-inch barrels, popularized by Churchill in the 1920s for reasons still accepted by the modern shooter. However, the 24-inch or 25-inch 410 was whippy and more precariously balanced than the longer barrels, even for the youth.

Number 3493, a Crown 410, was made in 1928 and thus out of time sequence, illustrating that the manufacturing process did not rigorously match serial number to year.

A 1922 orange catalog does not mention the Crown grade, yet this grade appears during that era, probably after the move to Leicester Square. Of the 20 410s of the period beginning in 1927, eight were designated Crown grade and all were built on the A&D action. One curiosity is an unnumbered gun designated with a "C" that was sent to Abercrombie & Fitch in New York in 1929 as a Field-grade 410. This grade was a boxlock between Crown and Utility and below Hercules, equivalent to the later Regal grade.

Often, during this era, gauges were built in sequence. For example, in 1924, eight 410s were made, SN 2222 to SN 2229, and then finished over several years as the buyers demanded. Another sequence was numbers 3481 and 3483 to 3487, finished from 1927 to 1934.

The next era, from 1930 to the eve of World War II, encompassed 410 production in the 4000 and 5000 serial number range. Beginning with SN 4613 and ending with SN 5999, all were A&D boxlocks, virtually all with ejectors. John Harper made many of them. They made 10 in the 4000 SN range, all Crown grade. Numbers 4613 to 4620 were A&D boxlock Crowns with 25-inch barrels and 3-inch chambers. These were allocated in July 1931, then finished and sold through 1936.

2 "Built" or "sold" will be used interchangeably; recognizing that many name makers had some of their guns built by the outside "trade."

THE FINEST
NEVARUST
CLEANER
ANTIRUST
&
LUBRICANT
FOR
GUNS, RIFLES, REVOLVERS
ETC.

LIGHTWOOD
& SON LTD.
Britannia Road
Banbury
Oxfordshire OX1 68TB

<

Photo 1: This Churchill 410, SN 426, is a very early intricately engraved ejector gun in its oak case.

Bonham photo

In the 5000 range, they made 25, nine in Crown grade, usually in paired serial numbers. Five were in the higher grade Utility, and 11 are described as "Plain" or ungraded. There is a trio of Utilities, SN 5242, 43 and 44, all with 22-inch barrels, shipped in 1935. Priced at 45 pounds each, they were up to 50 percent higher than a Crown grade. The other two Utilities, SNs 5593 and 5594, shipped in 1936 with 26-inch barrels, were similarly priced.

Many of the 410s during this time were also in sequence. For example, numbers 5237 to 5244, 5593 to 5596, and 5996 to 5999, were all 25-inch ungraded ejector guns, recorded in 1937 and 1938.

Four of the "Plain" 410s (all A&D ejectors)—numbers 5595 and 96, plus 5674 and 75—had 26-inch barrels and cost 20 pounds each in 1936. Clearly engraving and wood quality dictated much of the cost since many of the A&D actions and barrels came ready-made from Webley & Scott, one of the best ensembles ever seen in gun production.

The company recorded number 5262, a Crown ejector, in 1935. It had 3-inch chambers with 26-inch nitro-proofed barrels and recently appeared on the resale market, one of the few that appear to have survived the rigors of time, use, and mercury salts.

Another Crown pair, numbers 5299 and 5300, with "full" engraving and 25-inch barrels, was sent to a New Yorker at the then swank address "E. 64th St." It would be wonderful to unearth some of these guns and trace their history during this desperate time. Were they used as garden guns by the young and old? For clay pigeon shooting by skeet shooters? Or, as in the case of the 22-inch guns, by young aviators preparing for the next war and eventually doomed to a fiery Hurricane or Spitfire death high in the air during the "Battle of Britain"?

The 6000 range includes SN 6000, SN 6098, and SN 6176, all Crown grade shipped prior to World War II. Two more, SN 6184 and SN 6439, both Crown grades, began production during World War II, and shipped in 1945. One went to the Rigby Company, the great London rifle makers. The first three shipped pre-war cost from 25 to 42 pounds. The latter two immediately post-war were 75 pounds, reflecting the inflationary effects of the war.

The catalogs of the Leicester Square era, 1925 through 1967, list the Premiere (spelling changed by the firm) and Imperial as the first- and second-grade sidelocks and the Hercules, Regal, and Crown as the first-, second-, and third-grade boxlocks. The Crown was just below the Utility model in the earlier grading system. The latter was replaced by the Regal grade at some point just before or after World War II in the catalog. Surprisingly, there was never a catalog listing smaller than the 20 bore despite the number of 410s the company made in the 1920s and 1930s.

Post-World War II

The 7000 range spanned the years of 1953 through 1958. Six were manufactured, all in Regal grade, which replaced Utility grade, the second highest boxlock in Churchill's hierarchy of guns. The Regal grade, an A&D boxlock with ejectors, makes its first appearance at this tine, and a pair, SN 7251 and 52, were sent to an "Emir" in the Middle East in 1957. They were 28-inch guns, priced at 133 pounds. One of the six, SN 7337, had a single trigger and sold for 162 pounds. A second pair, numbers 7281 and 82, shipped in 1958.

The 8000 range marked the end of Churchill's shotgun production as an independent company. The last shotgun of any bore, a 28-gauge Regal boxlock, SN 8776, shipped in 1974. Sixteen 410 guns were made in this serial number range from 1965 to 1974. All were Regal-grade guns with one exception, SN 8700, the last 410 by serial number Churchill built as an independent company. It was the only Hercules ever built in the 410 bore. This was the highest grade A&D boxlock ejector gun with an "easy opening" action. It was supervised by D.A. Masters, then works director, and now a director of the resurrected firm E.J. Churchill, circa 2000 [4].

This Hercules 410 has double triggers, 26-inch barrels, and went to America in 1972.

Churchill made 16 410s in its last 10 years as an independent company in this serial number range, beginning with SN 8093 in 1965 and ending with SN 8699 in 1974. (SN 8700 was shipped 2 years earlier.) The retail price of the first, in 1965, was 232 pounds, and the last, in 1974, 1250 pounds. All were A&D boxlocks with barrels ranging from 25 to 28 inches with ejectors and double triggers. A tangential workbook, however, lists three of these 16 as non-ejector guns.

SN 8167 to SN 8172 were identical 26-inch-barreled, double-triggered A&D ejector 410s with Belgian-made barrels and actions made by the famous actioner, S.J. Carr. These guns were all "engraved." A separate workbook listed SN 8167, 68 and 70 as non-ejector guns.

These seven consecutive guns, numbers 8167 to 8172, shipped between 1965 and 1966. Their "cost" was listed at 52 pounds and their selling price ranged from 140 to 190 pounds, with a singular exception of SN 8171, which has a beavertail forend and sold for 485 pounds! This may have also reflected extra engraving, checkering, and wood quality.

Serial number 8093 and a pair of guns, numbers 8218 and 19, went to Dublin in 1965 and 1966. SN 8153 went to Abercrombie & Fitch in New York in 1965. This gun, along with numbers 8405 and 8406, which also went to Abercrombie & Fitch, had Webley & Scott-made barrels and actions. Numbers 8611 and 8612, 28-inch and 25-inch-barreled 410s respectively, shipped in 1972.

Number 8153, a post-World War II Leicester Square 410, is a Regal-grade gun with 28-inch barrels and 3-inch chambers, weighing 4 pounds, 10-1/2 ounces. It has a beautiful straight

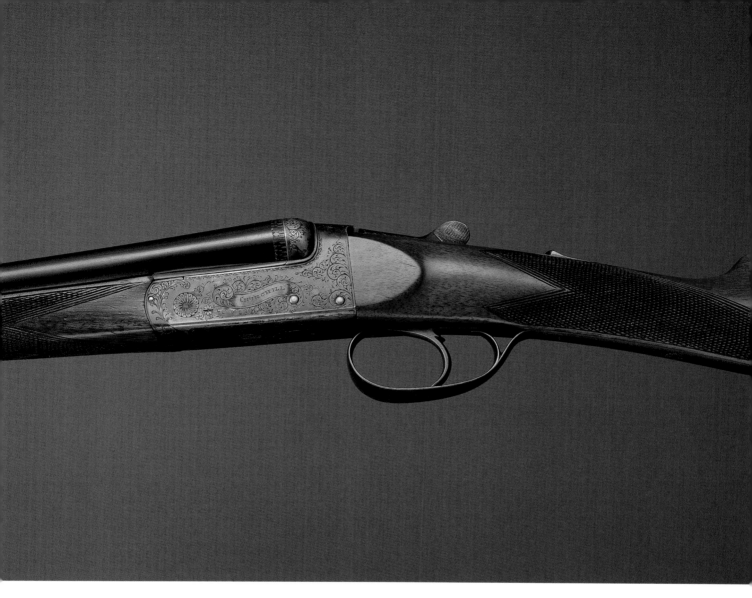

walnut stock, tight checkering, and typical rosette and scroll engraving on the action and other metal parts (Photo 2).

As an interesting side note, during this timeframe, Churchill built a trio of 28-bore guns in the Imperial grade, their second quality bar sidelock, the actions for which were supplied by A.A. Brown. Brown was and is one of the great actioners in British gun history. Numbers 8317, 18 and 19 shipped in 1967 to 1969, and SN 8318 had an extra set of barrels. These guns ranged from 600 to 710 pounds retail.

Although Churchill remained in Leicester Square until 1967, they apparently moved in 1934 to 32 Orange Street, geographically remaining within Leicester Square. In 1934, Robert Churchill opened a shooting school in Kent to capitalize on his reputation as a wizard of guns and ballistics. In 1958, Churchill died, and in 1964, after a brief marriage to Interarms Group in 1959, the firm "associated" with Atkin, Grant & Lang, Ltd [1].

A January 1966 white 9-inch by 11.5-inch Churchill catalog, with the 32 Orange Street, Leicester Square address, lists the

Photo 2: This Churchill 410, SN 8153, is a 1971 gun with almost full coverage rosette and scroll engraving.

G. Allan Brown photo

above models but notes that production of the Crown model, dropped after World War II, was resumed as a lightweight moderately priced 12 bore. Furthermore, their now revered XXV, changed in 1966 to "nickel steel" barrels with a French walnut stock in the Regal grade only. They describe the Hercules A&D boxlock, available in 12 and 20 bore only, as "similar" to the Premiere in workmanship. This catalog describes in detail the boxlock's three principal limbs: tumbler, sear, and cocking rod, as made by Webley & Scott.

The Regal and Crown grades were available in 12, 16, and 20 bore with or without ejectors. They built at least one non-ejector Regal 410 while at 32 Orange Street for it appears in an Orange Street (Churchill list No. 70) used gun list.

An October 1966 white two-page catalog and price list from Orange Street lists the Premiere at 800 pounds or $2,240, the Imperial at 600 pounds or $1,680, the Hercules at 400 pounds or $1,120, the Regal at 230 pounds or $644, and the Crown at 195 pounds or $546. A 410 bore was not listed.

In 1967, Churchill moved to 7 Bury Street, London, with Atkin, Grant & Lang, Ltd. The combined firm changed its name in 1971 to "Churchill & Atkin, Grant & Lang." This represented a fusion of several old and great gunmakers. The firm moved once more to 61 Pall Mall, London. To my knowledge, throughout this period to the present, the 410 bore has not been cataloged in Churchill literature.

Another fascinating aspect to the Churchill 410 story is the fact that although Churchill built many 410s prior to World War II, only five of these 410s have surfaced publicly in the last 20 years—numbers 3485, 4616, 5262, 5596, and 6184. How does one account for so few surfacing on the resale market during the last 20 years when we know that dozens were built in the late 1920s and 1930s? The Webley & Scott 410s of the same era presents an analogous situation. Webley built over 120 410 guns, but rarely does one see a Webley 410 boxlock for resale.

There appear to be three principal reasons. The first is the fact that many established shooting families bought a well-made 410 boxlock as a first gun for the young. These guns remain in families like heirlooms and are rarely sold. Second, many were sent to the colonies and did not survive hard use and nasty weather. Third, in England the 410 cartridge was the last gauge converted to a non-corrosive primer on a commercial basis. Non-corrosive cartridges were generally not available in the 410 bore until the 1960s. The result is that many pre-World War II 410s are "pitted beyond redemption" by mercury salts. This was due to the primers being composed of fulminate of mercury. Upon combustion, this substance was very corrosive to barrels.

The Merger

After the union in 1973, the numbering system of Churchill & Atkin, Grant & Lang was unified by putting the 20000 of Grant & Lang numbers in front of the Churchill factory "internal" numbering series, which was in the 3000 range. This resulted in a

final serial number in the 23000 series henceforth [3]. The original external numbering series of the Churchill ended in the 8700 range.

The 1981 Churchill & Atkin, Grant & Lang catalog from 61 Pall Mall listed the Churchill Premiere sidelock, the Hercules Easy Opener First Quality boxlock, and a Second Quality Regal boxlock as available only in the 12, 16, and 20 bore. They also advertised the Lancaster "Twelve-Twenty," the Atkin Spring Opener, and the Grant sidelock.

Notwithstanding the absence of the 410 bore in the multiple firms' advertising, they made a number of high quality Churchill 410 boxlocks in the 23000 range. The first was SN 23609, sent in 1974 to Leavenworth, Kansas. It was a Regal-grade 25-inch-barreled 410 with an A&D action, described as "Special." The meaning of this is unclear in the record book entry.

Thereafter, a whole series of 410s emerged from the factory until 1980, with the cessation of Churchill as a historical gunmaker. All 410s in the 23000 range were Regal grade. The 410 actions were apparently numbered in sequences. For example, 12 410s, numbers 23787 through 98, represent complete 410s with ejectors and XXV barrels shipped from 1979 to 1980, many to Abercrombie & Fitch in Houston, Texas, or Harrington & Richardson, a United States gunmaker. A smaller series, numbers 23815 through 17, were also shipped in 1980 as completed guns. These went to Christie's in the United States for auction, each at a 1979-80 cost of 2870 pounds. These guns had ejectors and XXV barrels.

An additional group of 410s—numbers 23665, 23666, 23690, 23718, and 23951—came out as full guns, some to consumer shows such as Euroarms in 1978 and the SHOT Show in the United States in 1979.

Twelve of these 410 guns, all Regal grades, sold at a remarkable Christie's auction in Dallas in 1981 in conjunction with the sponsorship of Abercrombie & Fitch. Ten were XXV guns, numbers 23791 through 98 and 23816-17. Two were not XXV guns, SN 23787 and SN 23951. Numbers 23813, 14 and 15 were a Regal XXV ensemble of three guns: 20, 28, and 410 respectively. The Regal name and XXV were gold inlayed.

In 1981, they also sent to America 10 "barreled-actions and parts" for ejector 410 3-inch chamber, 28-inch barrel guns of Regal type with unfinished wood and metal "in the white." These were numbers 23952 through 23961, and according to the 1981 Christie catalog, "They are unsigned and no right to use the Churchill name or model designations [on a subsequently completed gun] passes with their sale". These were made by "Gun Works" for Churchill when they were part of Atkin, Grant & Lang. The wholesale cost was 1000 pounds.

Despite the above caution, there is SN 23959, one of the "barreled-actions" now for sale as a "Premier" (the "e" is dropped) "Finest Quality Model" with sideplates, double triggers and the 61 Pall Mall address on the barrel rib. It is a beauty, but now you know the pedigree.

Although Churchill never cataloged the 410, there are dozens of 410s manufactured over the years in varying grades with most of the post-World War II guns in the United States and very few pre-World War II guns having survived.

The longtime director of E.J. Churchill, Ltd., Mr. D.A. Masters, provided an interesting note to the 410 Churchill story. He personally supervised the building of the only known Hercules A&D boxlock 410 from October 1969 to 1975 [4]. Additionally, a reliable gamekeeper told him there is in existence a heavily pitted 410 Premiere sidelock somewhere in the garden of England. Such stories enrich the lore of the quest.

In the Churchill records are two Lang 410s: SN 17724, a single barrel dated 1978, and SN 23674, an A&D boxlock ejector with double triggers and 25-inch barrels. The latter gun was sent to Nepal in 1973.

The Churchills described themselves as "practical gunmakers." This they certainly were, but in the context of high quality. They produced, along with pre-World War II Webley & Scott, Greener, and Watson, some of the finest boxlock smoothbores in the United Kingdom.

Given the rarity of existing 410s by any of these three makers, and given the unsurpassable quality of material and workmanship, an owner of one must consider himself very fortunate indeed. Producing such a gun today, especially considering the amount and quality of handcrafting, would cost a minimum of $20,000.

As an aside to the Churchill story, the Atkin, Grant & Lang, Ltd. firm that Churchill joined in 1964 before moving to 7 Bury Street in 1967 was, in itself, a union of some interest. Grant & Lang had incorporated at 7 Bury Street, London, in 1925. Joining them over time were such firms as Harrison & Hussey in 1930, Charles Lancaster in 1932, Watson Bros. in 1935, Frederick Beesley in 1939, and Henry Atkin in 1960 [1].

A brown catalog, circa 1946, specifically describes the Watson Bros. "High Grade" boxlock 410 double or single barrel for the "boy of eight or ten." The 410 "Teaching the Young Idea" weighed 4-1/2 pounds in the double and 3-1/2 pounds in the single barrel. A white 1953 catalog describes additional models of the various firms.

The final union in which Churchill joins the combined firm in 1964 made for a company with a remarkable and revered history in shotgun making. Examples of 410s from Beesley, Watson, Lancaster, et al appear in other chapters.

Postscript

Recently, a 36-caliber smoothbore with Damascus barrels appeared at auction, a unique "gauge" in the Churchill records (#4964) (see Photos 1 and 3 in 410 Cartridge chapter).

Today

The resurrected E.J. Churchill from the 1990s to the present is, by anyone's definition, a remarkable success story. They are producing many smoothbores a year, at least one in the 410 bore. In a 2002 Holt Auction in England, the Churchill seal and records, owned by the Harris & Sheldon Group, sold for over 70,000 pounds to the present reconstituted Churchill firm. Their current prosperity bodes well for fine gunmaking.

E.J. Churchill, Ltd. References

1. Original Churchill records at the Harris & Sheldon Group, 1995, then owners of the records.
2. *Experts on Gun and Shooting*, G.T. Teasdale—Buckell, Publisher, Sampson Low, Marston & Company, 1900.
3. Masters, D.A., March 17, 1992, correspondence.
4. Masters, D.A., March 8, 1994, personal communication.

CHAPTER FOURTEEN

COGSWELL & HARRISON

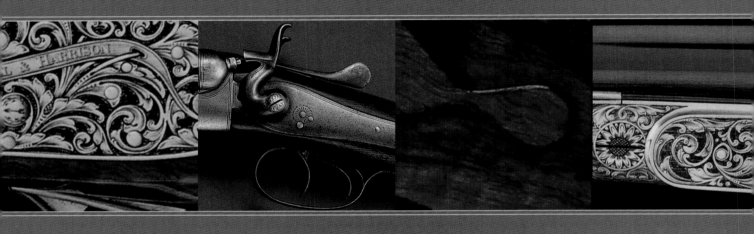

F ounded by Benjamin Cogswell in 1770, this firm, the most ancient name still surviving in British gunmaking, began at 4 Bengal Place, London. As they prospered, the company moved to 224 The Strand in 1842. They took their final title in 1863 when Edward Harrison joined as a partner [1].

In 1879, the 141 New Bond Street London branch opened, and in 1882, the firm moved its first showroom from 224 to 226 The Strand, London. They purchased William Moore & Grey, a gun firm with an illustrious ancestry in 1908.

They closed the 226 The Strand branch in 1917 and moved to 168 Piccadilly. The New Bond branch closed in the 1920s. From 1957 to 1963, the firm fell under the control of an international arms dealer; to what purpose we may use our imaginations.

In 1982, the firm was liquidated, and in 1983, Farlow's of Pall Mall, London, a high-quality fishing and accessory firm, bought the name, goodwill, and record books [2]. This firm's long history of gunmaking ceased to exist.

Miraculously, but not surprisingly, this once revered name was resurrected in 1993 by Professor M.J.E. Cooley and his partner, master gunmaker Alan Crewe. Using the "new" Beesley bar-action self-opener locks, they now will build only a "Best" gun in side-by-side or over/under barrel configuration in bores 12

through 410. This represents a departure from the historical gun pedigree, in which the firm had been a prolific maker of guns in a bewildering array of quality and types, especially from 1875 to 1960.

Hammerless action, ejector, safety device, single trigger, target trap, cartridge and powder patents from 1864 to 1929 marked the firm as innovative and successful, especially in the last quarter of the 19th century and the first quarter of the 20th. Edward and Edgar Harrison had 17 patents related to gun mechanism and function, including those for a single trigger and cocking and ejector mechanisms.

At the turn of the century (19th to 20th), Cogswell & Harrison advertisements described themselves as the "largest manufacturers in London of sporting guns and rifles." It also heralded, "small bore game guns a specialty." An examination of the contemporary records supports that proclamation. In fact, examining the pre-20th century records, courtesy of A.A. Baxter of Farlow's, one became vertiginous at the wide variety of guns manufactured and/or sold [2].

The kind Mr. Baxter sat me in his warm office one cold winter day in London and surrounded me with many volumes of records. According to the large and dusty record books, each page fragile to the touch, they made their first 410 smoothbore in 1880 (SN 10308) in the "walking stick" configuration. From then until January 11, 1889 (SN 15080) they made over 200 410 "walking stick" smoothbores. The 1880 gun is one of the earliest 410s in shotgun history.

The first and only double 410 shotgun made before 1900 is SN 12166, started November 10, 1883, and shipped October 2, 1887. It was a top-lever back-action hammer gun with rebounding locks and 28-inch barrels. It weighed 4-1/2 pounds and had a 14 3/8-inch stock, indicating it was intended for an adult.

During the decade of the 1880s, they made three Damascus double-barrel small-bore guns, two "for a lady" with a "rounded heel" (the stock that is). One, a 30-bore top lever with rebounding hammers, the "Victor," SN 11142; the other two include a 28 bore, SN 14135, A&D boxlock. It had the Doll's head third fastener, barrels of 24-1/2 inches, and weighed 4 pounds 2 ounces. It used 2/8-ounce loads, suitable for the small bird collector. A second 28 bore recorded in this decade, SN 14730, was a rebounding-hammer back action with 28-inch barrels.

The remarkable variety in type and quality of C. & H. smoothbore 410s was evident by the first decade of the 20th century [3]. For example, in 1903, they record a beautifully appointed but now very faded black-powder-proofed top-lever hammer 410 double with rebounding back-action sidelocks, SN 17459 (Photo 1). In the records and on the rib of the barrel it is designated "Made for Cogswell & Harrison, Ltd." by Carr & Son and sold for 3 pounds, 17 shillings, 6 pence. The previously mentioned SN 12166 is identical in description; yet in 1877 sold for 7 pounds, 1 shilling, 6 pence and was "Made By"

Cogswell & Harrison. This is an important fabrication distinction but unimportant as to quality since Carr & Son made very high quality guns.

Examples of their 410 variety are illustrated by a November 1901 top-lever rebounding hammer back-action double, a February 1902 single-barrel walking stick with a detachable stock and safety bolt, and a March 1902 single-barrel side-lever 410. The firm delivered two double 410s with 28-inch barrels December 1903, numbers 17378 and 17430, configuration not detailed. The former may be Cogswell & Harrison's first double 410 of the 20th century sent to Sir James Padgett [3].

These 410s went to lords, knights, captains, and "esquires" and even to other gunmakers. Churchill received a 410 June 1903, SN 17382. It is noteworthy that most of the 410s had stocks over 14 inches and, therefore, were used by adult men and not children or women. This suggests non-recreational purposes, undoubtedly including predator control (rats, rooks, and cats); small wing and ground game for the pot; taxidermy ("collector"); and personal protection ("walking stick for Lord Rossmore") [3].

The 410 folding gun became sufficiently popular by the second decade of the 20th century to have "complete blocks of number allocated" (i.e. numbers 17809 to 17817). A subsequent block from SN 17818 forward was set aside for double-barrel 410s. Throughout World War I, 410s were made, with one elaborately engraved gun, SN 18062, delivered in 1915.

When the firm consolidated at 168 Piccadilly, London, in the 1920s, they made hammerless double 410s in the SN

Photo 1: A double 410 hammer, SN 17459, in poor repair. It was originally built by a quality maker to the trade, "Carr & Son."

G. Allan Brown photo

Photo 3: An example of Cogswell & Harrison's current product in 12 bore.

Cogswell & Harrison photo

17890 block series. They sold some of these guns under the name "Armus" [3].

In addition, during this decade, while the 12, 16, and 20 bore guns were in the 44000 number series, they allocated the firm's 410s sold under their own name the 18000 number series. They built both rebounding hammer back-action 410 doubles (SN 18256) as well as hammerless boxlock doubles using the Anson & Deeley action (SN 18258) during this era.

An example of the firm's A&D 410 double is SN 18242. This is a fully engraved top-lever boxlock gun with an automatic top safety, double triggers, and 26-inch nitro-proofed barrels which sold in 1921 for over 19 pounds (Photo 2). This was a handsome sum for a boxlock smoothbore at that time and the quality of the gun's artistry reflects in the price.

The firm continued to make 410s before and after World War II. In 1946, they exported a single-barrel folding shotgun with 23 1/2- or 24-inch barrels to the United States and provided a spare parts list for the 410, reflecting a significant production quantity. Some of these post-World War II single-barrel 410s featured the "Certus" folding action with 3-inch chambers and 26- or 28-inch barrels with block numbers in the 60467 range. The "Certus" action, the firm's great rifle design introduced in 1900, was a bolt-action positive-lock gun chambered for the 410 shot shell. This 410 became very popular after World War II. It had a semi-hammer mechanism and side lever. The early guns were "made entirely from British material" at a higher standard than later guns, which were imported. In the 1950s, it cost 14 pounds, 10 shillings, 6 pence. Supposedly, a "Deluxe" was also available [1].

Photo 2: A post-World War I ∧ A&D 410 double, SN 18242.

G. Allan Brown photo

Reportedly, they made a hammerless sidelock 410. However, none was specified by serial number nor has one appeared in the marketplace.

Like many great British gunmakers, they made the rook rifle. Because these were of high quality, a 410 conversion was inevitable in some. The barrels were octagonal in form, like a "three penny piece."

The Avant Tout action, developed by Edgar Harrison in the 1880s, is the most common action seen today on the firm's guns brought in for repair. It is a hammerless boxlock with ejectors and assisted opening. If they built some of their 410s on this action, it was never so recorded.

Cogswell & Harrison has resumed production. If a further review of the records reveals that they have never produced a single "Best" bar-action sidelock 410 throughout their history, this represents an opportunity for someone to order a "first" from a modernized yet venerable British gunmaking firm (Photo 3).

Cogswell & Harrison References

1. Cooley, Graham & John Newton, *Cogswell & Harrison*, The Sportsman's Press, London, 2000.
2. Cogswell & Harrison record books examined at Farlow's, 1992.
3. Cogswell & Harrison records and personal communication to writer 1994 and 1995.

CHAPTER FIFTEEN

JOHN DICKSON & SON, LTD.

The Round Actions of John Dickson & Son, Ltd., built on the "trigger plate action" (see Chapter 4), were never married to the 410-bore barrel according to factory records. This is an aesthetic shame because the lovely elegant appearance of the Round Action would be especially fetching in a properly proportioned 410. Theoretically, a miniaturized 410 action could be built but at considerable cost. The result would be a near beatific vision for the eyes gazing upon the simple, pure, clean, and spare architecture of such an ensemble.

According to detailed reviews by Boothroyd and others, John Dickson began gunmaking in 1836 "on his own account," and the last of three John Dicksons, John III, died in 1927 [1,2,3]. They had become, in those 90 years, one of the greatest "best quality" gunmakers in the world. Their fame rests primarily on the supreme quality of craftsmanship and upon the now legendary "Round Action" based upon three patents—one in 1882 and two in 1887. The typical sidelock was replaced by locks mounted on an enlarged and extended trigger plate; hence, the "trigger plate action" nomenclature. Archie Nelson, Dickson's once head gunmaker and a man of quiet kindness, theorized that this action was first developed in northern Europe in the mid-1800s where it came to be known as the "Blitz" action, especially in Germany. Because of strong craft and commercial relations

between Scotland and northern Europe in the 19th century, this action found a home in Scotland. Both Dickson and its Scottish sister firm, MacNaughton, modified the action to suit their respective purposes.

Dickson built guns for a variety of monied and titled people of the British Empire. But, sadly, by the late 1960s they had ceased production.

However, in the 1980s, Boothroyd persuaded David McKay Brown, a former Dickson action and lock maker, and now an independent gunmaker, to manufacture the Round Action for Dickson. This he did in small numbers. When Brown decided to do this under his own name, Dickson then sought suitable production facilities in Europe.

The Dutch firm of gunmakers, Verenigde Geweermakers in Strijkviertel, Holland, agreed to build the Round Action, and in 1991 began delivery. The first "European" Round Action for Dickson, 8001, is machined using digital computer technology. Tom Derksen, owner of Verenigde, says he produced his components within tolerances as tight or tighter than the great Fabbri guns of Italy.

The actions are then case hardened in the United Kingdom, and Dickson completes the gun in Edinburgh with chopper lump English barrels and Circassian walnut wood. The guns are built to handle steel shot.

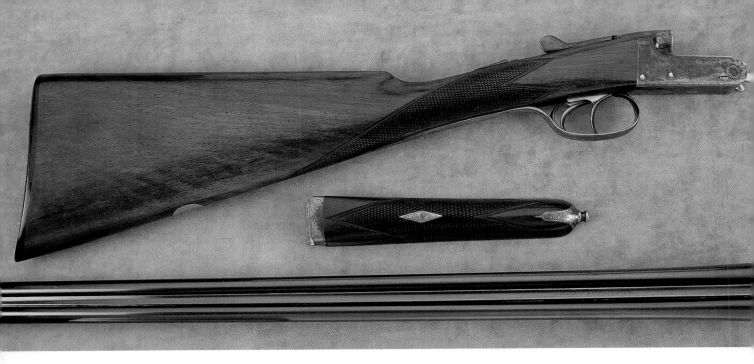

Photos 1A and 1B: (above) A post-World War II A&D ejector 410, SN 7481. (right) Another view of SN 7481, which has the engraving and checkering of a "Best."

Paul Goodwin photo

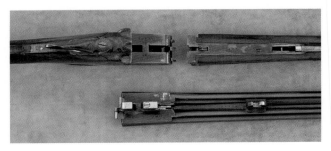

The Dickson Round Action "trigger plate" is significantly different from the James MacNaughton & Son "trigger plate action." The latter, patented in 1879, cocks the mainspring by the top lever that opens the barrels, requiring a very long lever for the necessary mechanical advantage. MacNaughton, the high quality Scottish gunmaker absorbed by Dickson in 1947, never made a 410-bore shotgun using the "trigger plate action."

Dickson, however, and the many Scottish firms it purchased and absorbed, had a long but modest history of 410 production using less expensive configurations.

Dickson has built six double-barrel hammerless 410s on the A&D boxlock, with the first, a non-ejector, completed 4 January 1913 (SN 6485) (Photo 1). Currently, this gun weighs its original 4 pounds 10-1/2 ounces with 27-inch barrels. It goes to the shoulder and shoots as if it were part of the human anatomy. It was shot over pointers in many New Hampshire grouse and woodcock coverts by Dave Tilden, a technical director at Sturm, Ruger & Company. A former British skeet champion and a regular winner of 410 sporting clay championships, Tilden has since "retired" the gun into a collection where it now sits admired but not used—a shame.

Five more were built: SN 6557, 29 October 1913, a non-ejector; SN 7481, an ejector in 1946; SN 7490, a non-ejector in 1947; SN 7537, a 2-inch-chambered non-ejector in 1949;

and SN 7607, an ejector in 1959. The first and last guns are in pristine condition [4].

A recently surfaced Dickson ejector A&D 410, SN 7481, has the engraving and checkering of a "Best" (Photos 1A and 1B).

It is worth noting that guns made "by Dickson" have a four-digit serial number while guns made "for Dickson" have a five-digit serial number.

Other Firms Owned by Dickson Prior to 1996 [5]

Alexander Henry, the great rifle maker, was absorbed by Dickson soon after World War II ended. According to available records, the firm made four 410s, all double barrel, on the A&D action. The first was SN 7471, a "shot and ball" ejector, made in 1906 for an Indian Maharajah. This, together with a non-ejector in 1924 (SN 8107) and the composite paired SN 8531, a non-ejector, and SN 8532, an ejector, both in 1943, are the totality of Henry's 410 production.

Mortimer & Son, whose records end in 1938, and whose dates and serial numbers are often out of sequence, made four 410s. SN 7785 was recorded in 1914 as an A&D "plain" ejector hammerless with 27-inch steel barrels. SN 7906, weighing 4-3/4 pounds, was sent to "Dr. Yieruth" in 1930. SN 7952, made "plain" in 1933, is a rebounding-hammer, double-steel-barrel, back-action ("back work"), top-lever ("top snap") gun, an

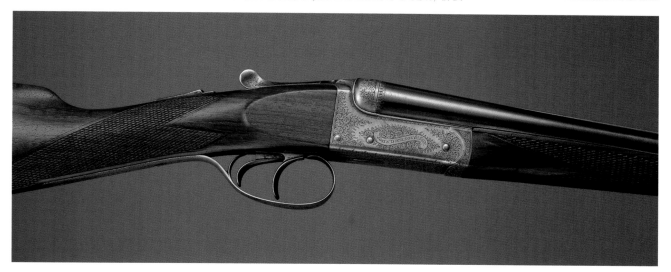

extraordinary configuration for this era. SN 7950, a lower serial number but made in 1934, is an A&D double-barrel Southgate ejector gun, also "plain." Dr. Yieruth's 410, SN 7906, surfaced at a 2001 auction (Photo 2). It is an A&D non-ejector boxlock with 27-inch steel barrels made in 1930. It is representative of a finely made boxlock between the wars.

Alex Martin of Glasgow manufactured eight 410s from 1910 (SN 4977) to 1947 (SN 6859). All were top-lever A&D boxlocks with double barrels and all were non-ejectors, save SN 6253 made in 1926. SN 5996 in 1923; SNs 6026, 6210, 6382 in 1928; and SN 6690 in 1934 round out their total production.

 Photo 1: The first Dickson made according to company records, SN 6485.

G. Allan Brown photo

Photo 2: A Dickson, SN 6485, is shown over a "Plain" but well-made 410 by Mortimer & Son (SN 7906), one of four made by the firm. The forend may be a replacement.

Paul Goodwin photo ∨

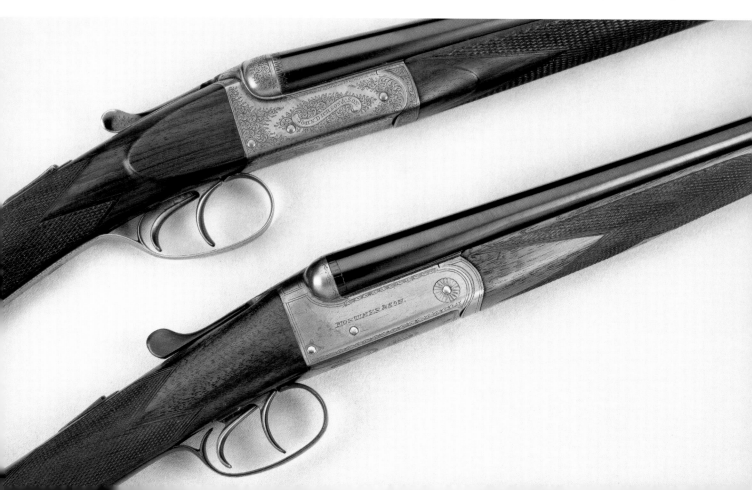

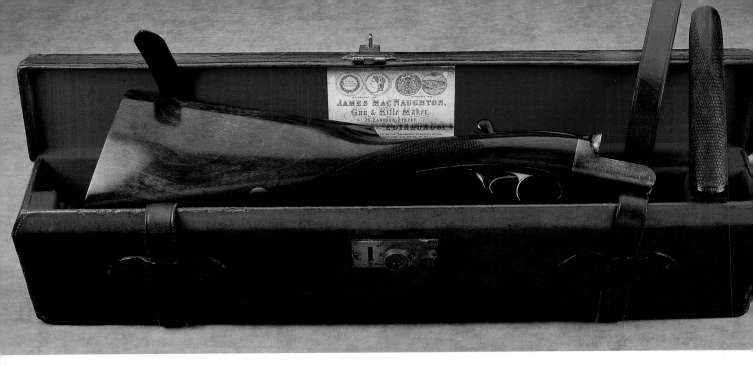

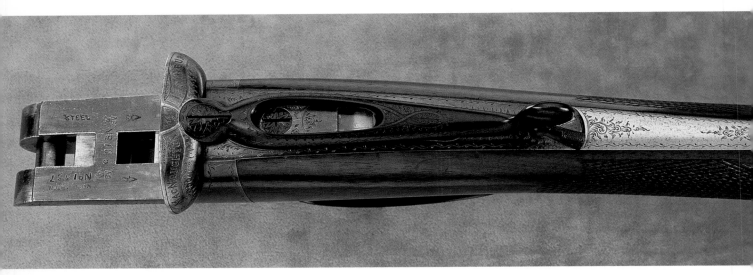

The James MacNaughton firm, founded in 1864, was bought by Dickson in 1947. The records indicate they made 14 410s, all single-barrel guns, beginning with SN 1804 in 1895 and ending with SN 3527 in 1932. Most were designated for the "collector," which meant for those wishing to collect small wing and ground game for taxidermy purposes. I was pleased when I was able to explain its meaning to Archie Nelson, the only occasion when I wasn't his student.

Photo 3: Two views of a remarkable MacNaughton 28-gauge smoothbore originally made with 24-inch barrels.

Paul Goodwin photos

Conclusion

Like Dickson, MacNaughton never made a Round Action "trigger plate" 410. This lock work differs from the sidelock, whose locks are mounted on side plates, and from the A&D boxlock, whose locks are in the body of the action. And therein may be the reason for the absence of a 410 with a trigger-plate action.

The Dickson and MacNaughton Round Action has the lock work mounted on an enlarged trigger plate. The miniaturization necessary for a scaled down 410 poses mechanical and metallurgic problems, which Dickson attempted to solve at great expense with the "Dickson 8011," the first and last Round Action 410 Dickson would have ever built. Alas, the project was abandoned. Pictured is a MacNaughton 28-bore round-action original smoothbore 24-inch gun, SN 1367. The long top lever with a window is unique (Photo 3).

One might think that a small and light action frame such as the Round Action would be fragile. However, the frame is exceptionally strong since there is no removal of steel to harbor the lock works and the ejectors are within the action body. Thus, Dickson has built on the Round Action big-bore shotguns; three-barrel shotguns with all three known Dickson configurations (three barrels in a row, one on top of two and one below two); low silhouette over/under smoothbores; and express double rifles [6].

A 1925 Dickson white and brown catalogue with a roaring lion on the cover is addressed at 63 Princes Street, Edinburgh, where John Dickson III had worked continuously for 65 years. This catalogue, based upon price, places the Round Action higher than the sidelock and boxlock in the pantheon of lock works. Advertised only in 12, 16, and 20 bore, the Round Action was priced at £100 with an extra £10 for a single trigger. The sidelock gun was 85 pounds and the A&D boxlock £55.

The Round Actions were "all handmade" including the forging. There was an intercepting or secondary sear to prevent accidental discharge, and the ejector mechanism was in the action body and not in the forend. Italian walnut was used.

In 1996, the Dickson catalog described its Round Action as having "extra strength." They have accomplished this with high alloy "compax" steel (EN24) that will accommodate steel shot and can be magnum proofed to 1200 bar for duck and geese shooting.

According to Archie Nelson, if steel shot is not to be used, they prefer to use EN32 steel, which is easier to work with in its un-hardened state. It is easier to engrave and is more suitable for gold inlay work and requires a lower hardening temperature.

The Dickson Round Action today, with its French walnut furniture, remains a classic and is among the greatest smoothbores on earth. It is certainly one of the most elegant and suitable for an aesthete's eye with a shooter's soul. Nelson, who has a genuinely kind word for everyone in the gunmaking business, including his closest competitor, McKay Brown, is convinced there will be a place for the Dickson Round Action as long as there are shooters who shoot the classic smoothbore. He also believes McKay Brown will build the first Round Action 410 side-by-side.

Given the resumption of this aesthetically exquisite and mechanically brilliant gun, the Dickson smoothbore is likely to appeal to increasing numbers of game shooters, especially in America. It is ironic that American hunters are becoming more appreciative of the classic British double as the British shooter slides into over/under Japanese- and European-made standardized guns.

John Dickson & Son, Ltd. References

1. Boothroyd, Geoffrey, "John Dickson & Son," *Game & Gun*, Nov./Dec. 1993, Part 1; Jan/Feb 1994, Part 2.
2. Boothroyd, Geoffrey, "Fame and Fortune," *Shooting Times & Country Magazine*, Feb 11-17, 1993.
3. Huggler, Tom, "The Round Action Returns," *Shooting Sportsman*, March-April 1992.
4. Review of Dickson Records.
5. Review of the Firm's records.
6. Boothroyd, Geoffrey, "Three into One Did Go," *STCM*, June 21-27, 1990.

CHAPTER SIXTEEN

W. W. GREENER, LTD.

like Webley & Scott, W.W. Greener must be considered one of the greatest gunmakers of the 19th and 20th centuries. Like Webley & Scott, Greener was a prolific maker of a great variety of sporting guns and rifles of all configurations and grades. These guns ranged from the back-action hammer to the bar-action hammer and hammerless; from the Anson & Deeley (A&D) boxlock to the Facile Princeps of Greener's own design; from the exquisite and expensive to those modestly priced but well crafted.

Like Webley & Scott, they had a large manufacturing plant with many superb artisan employees. Like Webley & Scott, they were great mechanical innovators and promoters of custom gunmaking through exhibitions and shooting matches.

Unfortunately, like Webley & Scott, they did not survive intact the last quarter of the 20th century. This was, in part, because of their very diversity and their over-expanded industrial plant. They had failed to find an economically viable niche among gunmakers as the 20th century came to a close.

In 1910, Greener was the largest gunmaker in the world, employing over 400 artisans. However, just before the turn of the century, legislation by British governments began to exact its toll on the British gunmaking industry. Government regulations at this point prevented the importation of guns manufactured by British firms into British-controlled India, Australia, New

Zealand, and East Africa. Ostensibly, this was to reduce the dangers of an armed "native" population. However, the laws failed to prevent the importation into these colonies of guns made by European and American competitors. Thus, foreign firms prospered, the "natives" armed and eventually freed themselves, and a once flourishing British industry slid into an inexorable decay of attrition and underutilization' [1].

A second and finally fatal bullet that ended one of the great industrial artisan firms in history was the effect of World War II. Greener had capitalized a new factory and machinery just before World War II. The war needs resulted in the firm's conversion to producing military arms. This necessary government requisition continued beyond the war, and eventually in 1965, a labor government confiscated their St. Mary's Row factory property in order to build the Inner Ring Road of Birmingham [3].

Those classic British gunmakers that did survive did so as relatively small specialty houses such as Purdey, Holland & Holland, Boss, John Wilkes, John Dickson, Westley Richards, etc. These houses focused on a best-quality gun in small numbers

---

1 *The Greener Story* by Graham Greener confirms that William Oliver Greener [2], the son of W.W. Greener, ghost wrote for his father, *The Gun and Its Development.* This massive work ran to nine editions from 1881 to 1910.

with a limited number of efficient employees and a small manufacturing plant structure either in-house or on sub-contract.

To detail the highlights of the Greener firm would require a book and one is now published [2]. Indeed, W.W. Greener's *The Gun*, 9th Edition, leaves out much that is available in Greener catalogs of that and obviously later eras [4]. It also neglects much of what Greener's competitors contributed to gun development in the second half of the 19th century. Concise recapitulations of the firm's important patents including the Greener crossbolt and side safety are now available [2,5,6].

The 410

Looking at the 1893 Greener catalog, one is awestruck by the great diversity and quality of sporting guns offered and this appears to be their introduction of the 410 bore.

Greener made their "Miniature" gun for "naturalists and collectors" in the 410 and 28 bore. It was a bar-action hammer gun with Best English 27-inch Damascus barrels and an engine-turned rib. The gun had a top-lever opener, the metal was scroll engraved, and it was a 3 pound, 11 ounce ensemble of delicate beauty. The 410 pictured in this catalog, SN 40552, sold for 25 guineas ($375) in 1893 (Photo 1).

Although this is not the first 410 ever built or even the first 410 Greener ever built, it is the first cataloged 410, along with those available in the Lancaster and Evans catalogs, of a British or American gunmaker in this writer's files.

The Records[2]

Volume I of the existing records begins with SN 20498 (October 25, 1880). During the next 12 years, Greener made 40 28-bore, two 32-bore, and 25 24-bore shotguns. Their first recorded 28 bore was a "Best," SN 26077, made in 1883. In 1881, they made a batch of six top-lever 380-caliber rifles. One, SN 24506, was later converted at an unspecified date to a 26-inch barrel, 2 1/2-inch chamber, 410 smooth-bore shotgun. In 1888, the records begin to detail who made what component of each gun. The 5th Edition (1892) of *The Gun and Its Development* makes no mention of the 410 bore, although some British firms were making the rare 410 for the "collector."

The first original 410 smoothbore appears in 1892, SN 40396. It had 27-inch barrels, weighed 4 pounds 1 ounce, and was a bar-action, top-lever gun. Nothing else was recorded, but almost certainly, it was a double-exposed-hammer gun. During this era, the records specified if a gun was "single barrel" or "hammerless."

From then until 1906, at SN 54097, they made eight 410s. One was a "single" barrel, SN 41696, and one was a "side-lever ejector," SN 49671. The remaining were bar-action, exposed-hammer, top-lever guns. Some were designated as having steel barrels ranging from 26 to 28 inches.

GREENER'S MINIATURE GUNS

FOR NATURALISTS AND COLLECTORS.

Represents Gun No. 40,552, ⅔ actual size. Made on the Hammer System.

AS Hammer Guns of the higher qualities are so rapidly being superseded by those on the Hammerless and Ejector principles, we have deemed it unnecessary to exhibit any above the 25 guinea quality.

The illustration above represents the miniature gun No. 40,552 but it will serve to show the style of our 25 guinea Hammer Gun.

No. 40,552.—**Greener's Collector's Gun** 410 bore, Bar-Top Lever 27-inch Best English Damascus Barrels, Engine Turned Rib, Half Pistol Hand, No Heel Plate, Drop at Bump, 2⅜; At Comb, 1⅜. Length, 14⅜. Weight 3 lbs. 11 oz. Most carefully finished, and well engraved.

Price 25 GUINEAS.

No. 40,651.—**Miniature Gun** 28 bore, Treble-Wedge Fast Action, 27-inch Stub Damascus Barrels, Engine Turned Rib, Half Pistol Hand, Drop at Bump 2¾, at Comb 1¾, Length 14¼. Weight 4 lbs. 10 oz. Shooting Rt. 140, Lt. 150.

Price 20 GUINEAS.

∧ **Photo 1:** Greener's "Miniature" 410 was cataloged as early as 1893.

Paul Goodwin photo.

The next or ninth 410 manufactured, SN 55376 made in 1907, was their first hammerless 410 gun. It had 23 5/8-inch "Siemens" steel barrels. It was designated F20 with "F" meaning Facile Princeps, Greener's patent version of a hammerless boxlock. This gun was clearly distinguishable from an A&D boxlock.

The next two 410s were paired, numbers 55379 and 55380. Greener designated them as A10 "T.W.F." guns with "Cellar" steel 27-inch barrels. The "A" means a rebounding hammer lock system and the "T.W.F." refers to their patented treble wedge fastener; a gun bolted with two barrel lumps and a crossbolt.

The next 10 410s from 1907 (SN 55408) to 1910 (SN 57442) included a trio of A10 T.W.F. hammer guns (numbers 56873, 74 and 75) and a pair of F20 hammerless 410s (numbers 57441 and 42).

The next 410, SN 57553, entered in the records in 1909 and designated D10, was their first A&D classic hammerless boxlock 410. It had 28-inch steel barrels. From then until 1914, they

made 17 more 410s in various configurations from hammer (A) to hammerless (D) or (F), all with a T.W.F. bolting system. Beginning with SN 54097 in 1906, all were made with steel barrels, either Siemens or Cellar.

The next series of 410s, beginning with SN 64351, recorded in 1914 as an FH25, was their first Baker (coil spring) or Southgate (leaf spring) ejector 410 (although not the first "ejector" 410, which was SN 49671 in 1901). The "H" designates the presence of either a straight barred Baker ejector or the more robust and stronger kicking curved talon Southgate system (Photo 2).

Thereafter they made, through 1941 (SN 69641), 25 more 410s, nine with ejectors with either FH or DH lock systems.

Of these 25 guns, 14 used the Greener hammerless lock "F," eight the A&D box-lock "D," and three the hammer bar-action lock system "A." The grades were FH25, FH35, D20, D25, DH35, and A16. Of these 25 410 guns, the record describes only four as having a crossbolt and, therefore, the T.W.F. bolting system. They usually made these 25 guns in pairs or trios destined for the same buyer, with Australia and India receiving the majority of them.

The last 410 was completed in 1957, an FH25 model (SN 69778) with 26-inch barrels, resting and probably rusting away in

Photo 2: A Greener FH35 with T.W.F.

Cameo photo ∧

Photo 5: The "plainest" "miniature" 410 cataloged after 1900. With engraving the cost increased by 25 percent.

Greener catalog photo ∨

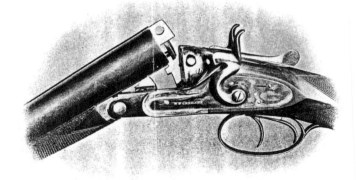

^

Photo 4: A full elegant view of the Greener A-9 410, SN 58747.

Paul Goodwin photo

Photo 3: A Greener A-9 410 with a "miniature" but plain frame, SN 58747.

Cameo photo

v

some overseas attic. The second-to-last 410 built, SN 69641, is a DH35. Sent to Abercrombie & Fitch in 1940, it is presumably still in America.

Existing Guns

A pristine 410 bar-action hammer double 410 with Jonas steel barrels, SN 58747, has recently surfaced (Photos 3 and 4). It was begun in 1911 and finished in 1914 and the record lists 10 separate workers as manufacturing different components of the gun. These included a jointer, an actioner, a stocker, a finisher, a polisher, an engraver, a "freer," a "smoother," and two additional people, one who manufactured the top lever and somebody described as "shooting." The cost attributed to each worker is listed. This gun is a grade A9 or Dominion model.

G.N. Greener, the current director of W.W. Greener, Ltd. said this model was introduced in the first decade of the 20th century. It differed from the Miniature by less engraving, rebounding locks, and a price tag of 9 guineas. The top bolt is a modified rectangular doll's head. The Dominion model was listed in the 1893 catalog as available in the 12 bore, selling for 9 guineas. The 410 soon thereafter became available in this model (Photo 5).

Serial number 58747 has an interesting history. A "knocker" (someone in England who knocks on doors looking for rubbish to buy) bought the gun from a widow "cleaning out her closet" for £50. He, in turn, sold it to a local gun dealer for £100, who sold it to a collector for £800 and a single-barrel Purdey. This English collector sold it to an overseas friend at a handsome profit. Today, only a founder of a now-bankrupt Internet company can afford the gun. (Many founders of such companies sold early!)

A second 410 hammer has surfaced, SN 59327, a virtual mate to SN 58747 with engraving and in excellent condition (Photos 5A and 5B).

Another 410 that is known to this writer is SN 64823. It is one of a trio completed in 1921 and is designated as an FH25 with 26-inch barrels (Photo 6). Although not so described in the records, it has a cross-bolt, thus the complete T.W.F. bolting system. It has double triggers, a straight-grip stock, and a splinter forend. It now weighs 3 pounds, 14 ounces. It surfaced in America in 1984 and now reposes in the state of Texas, where so

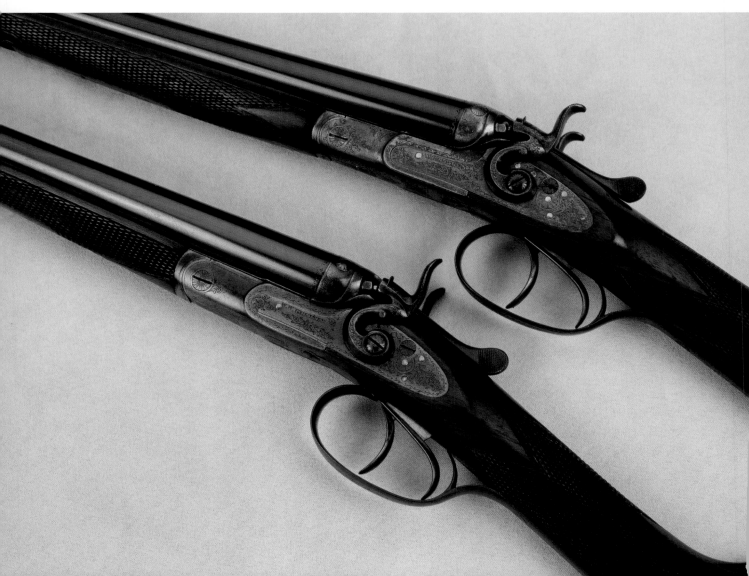

Photo 5A: A full view of a Greener A-9, SN 59327.

Paul Goodwin photo

Photo 5B: A view of SN 58747 alongside SN 59327, nearly mates!

Paul Goodwin photo

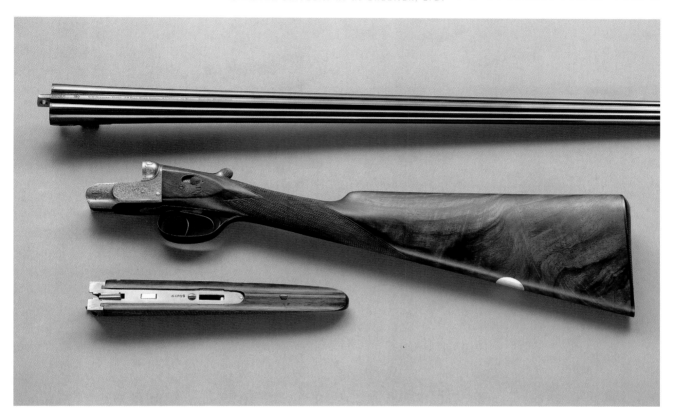

∧ **Photo 6:** A Greener FH25, SN 64823.

G. Allan Brown photo

many brilliant guns are now sleeping surely and beautifully preserved in the vault of a shotgun aficionado or are used to shoot Texas scaled quail.

Two more FH25 410 smoothbores (SNs 68509 and 72589) with a T.W.F. bolting system, double triggers and steel barrels, surfaced in remarkable condition (Photos 7 and 8).

To this writer's knowledge, very few 410s have publicly surfaced over the past 20 years. A series of 1954 and 1955 catalogs, brochures, and price lists do not list the 410 as available. Certainly, there are more 410s still in existence, but undoubtedly, the large majority was eventually destroyed by use, time, and environment in the colonies. The owner of a 410 Greener today has a rare gun indeed.

The Catalogs

The green 1893 Greener catalog was the first to list the 410 smoothbore and did so in the Dominion model. A Greener catalog of 1899 advertised a 410 walking-stick gun. The 6th Edition of *The Gun and Its Development* discusses the 410 for the first time, and then only as a "walking-stick" gun. A number of old 310-caliber rook rifles were made during this era, and undoubtedly more than one was bored out to a 410 smoothbore after the early 1920s when the new Proof House rules took effect together with new gun regulations (see Chapter 26).

A green 1920 Greener catalog, #41, lists various grades of sidelock, the Facile Princeps, and the A&D boxlock guns. Their highest-grade gun cataloged was a "G" ejector Presentation grade. This gun looks similar to the A&D boxlock but has, in fact, the Facile Princeps lock mechanism. Patented in 1880, this lock was deemed sufficiently different from the A&D boxlock for the House of Lords to rule against Westley Richards in a patent infringement lawsuit they brought in 1880 [6].

Boothroyd describes the Greener boxlock action as having cocking rods that curved inward, giving the bar of the action body a "rounded" and more aesthetically pleasing appearance. Baker explains that the forward ends of both tumblers are cocked by engaging a single central lifter, and hence curved inward, and are clearly distinguishable from the A&D boxlock [7]. This allowed for a smaller action body. By comparison, the A&D housed a bigger cocking and ejector system, requiring a "squared" box configuration.

Most of these various models were listed in 1920 as available only in 12 to 28 bore; however, from the records we know that a number of 410s were made in various model configurations and grades. In addition, in the same 1920 catalog, Greener has a chart of "Weights and Loads of Guns" with an entry for the 410. He lists the 410 at 3-3/4 to 4 pounds, and the gun "will use" a 2 1/2-inch shell with 3/4 dram of powder and 5/16 ounce of shot (Photo 9).

∧

Photo 8: A full view of a Greener 410, SN 68509.

Paul Goodwin photo

Photo 7: Two FH25 410 smooth-bores, SN 72589 (top) and SN 68509 (bottom), with a T.W.F. bolting system, double triggers and steel barrels.

Paul Goodwin photo   ∨

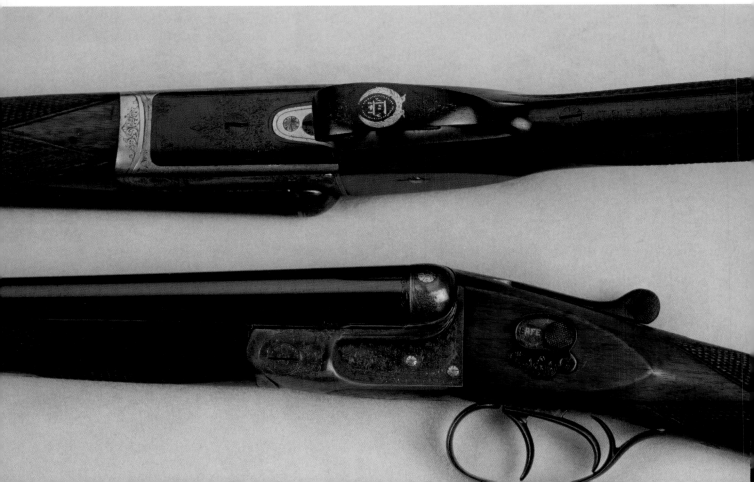

Conclusion

After Webley & Scott purchased the firm, it formally ceased independent life in 1965. Webley continued to produce the famous G.P. single-barrel, single-shot riot police shotgun based on the Martini action. They invented this gun in 1910 for the Egyptian police.

Subsequently the firm passed through several hands, producing a few Greener smoothbores each year, but none in the 410 bore, according to available records.

In 1985, a Greener heir, G.N. Greener re-purchased the company. He and his partner, Ken Richardson, resurrected the firm, a startling and gratifying occurrence. The "new" Greener exemplifies a renaissance of "Best" gunmaking in Britain by many ancient firms that have been re-appearing on the scene to build a select few of the magnificent double guns. In addition to Greener, these resuscitated firms include Watson, Cogswell & Harrison, Churchill, Hellis, and Lancaster.

In fact, Greener in 1992 completed SN 70000, their highest-grade "St. George" gun, a "Presentation" grade, and sold it to an American gun connoisseur. This gun is also designated "L500." There have been two prior "St. George" guns with "G" ejectors. This gun is remarkable for its deeply chiseled relief engraving.

In 1985, when Greener and Richardson re-purchased the firm, they continued to produce the G.P. gun, now called the Mark II. This gun is identical to the previous G.P. gun without the keeper screws. Furthermore, in order to make production easier, investment casting is used in place of forging.

Today they list the single-barrel G.P. Mark II shotgun at £350. Evidently, it is now offered only in 12 bore, but at one time, it was offered in the 410. Attempting to order one in the 410 bore, one is quickly told that this would be a "one off" and would cost £5,000, or $7500. It is a very interesting Martini lever-action, single-barrel gun with a walnut stock, polished, and checkered. Some admirers have called this particular gun the most dependable, the most trouble-free, and the soundest single-barrel shotgun ever made.

Photo 9: Weights and loading data for the 410.

Glenn Campbell photo

Today they offer a full line of side and boxlock shotguns of varying grades from a Presentation sidelock L500 to the Needham boxlock ejector No. 5.

It is with wonder and delight that we witness the renaissance of this revered firm and it is to be hoped they meet with commercial success.

W. W. Greener, Ltd. References

1. Greener, Charles and William Oliver, *The Causes of Decay in a British Industry* ("Artifex" and "Opifex"), 1907, Longmans, Green & Company, London, et al.
2. Greener, Graham, *The Greener Story*, 2000, Quiller Press, London.
3. Greener, Graham N., personal interview January 3, 1995.
4. Greener, W.W., *The Gun and Its Development*, Cassell & Company, Ltd., 1910.
5. Greener, Graham N., personal correspondence 1991.
6. Boothroyd, Geoffrey, "W.W. Greener", *Game & Gun*, July/August 1993, Part 1, September/October 1993, Part 2.
7. Baker, David, "Goodlooking Greener," *Sporting Gun*, July 1995.

CHAPTER SEVENTEEN

CHARLES HELLIS & SONS

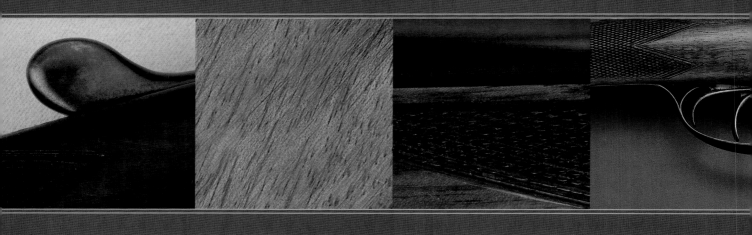

harles Hellis founded his firm in 1884 in London. He moved to 119 Edgware Road in 1897, and in 1902, together with his two sons, formed "Charles Hellis & Sons." They moved again in 1935 to 121-123 Edgware Road. The last Hellis to manage the company was Stuart Charles Hellis, a former captain and commando in the Royal Marines [1].

In 1953, they joined with C.S. Rosson & Company to manufacture cartridges, and in 1956, the firm closed. The name and records became part of the Harris & Sheldon Group and eventually part of Chubbs of Edgware.

In 1994, a hopeful group bought the name and records under the direction of David Ingles and Michael Whittingdale, shooting enthusiasts. They are now building a London "Best" using the peerless Atkin action. This action is essentially a Beesley sidelock with a "spring-loaded" mechanism to open and close the action more "smoothly and uniformly" by incorporating the Southgate ejector system with the locking bolts [2].

The "Stock Book"

Birmingham makers to the trade made and proofed almost all of the Hellis guns in Birmingham. These included the Wright Brothers, G. and S. Holloway, and Joseph Harkom of Edinburgh. However, they may have made their "Best" side-

lock gun in-house by E. C. Hodges, the great actioner from Islington, England. Clearly, however, the Hellis firm occupied a niche in the London trade as a boutique firm, in which marketing and sales were their forte. As a prestigious London gun firm, they provided boxlock "Best," "Plain," and "Second" grades as well as the rare "Best" sidelock gun to a select circle of clientele.

Serial numbers range from 0 to 5882. However, all data from 0 to 1000 is missing. The first gun entry is 1101. The first 410 entry is a trio of double hammer, back-action guns in 1904, serial numbers 1803, 04 and 05.

Their first 28-gauge guns were also a trio, numbers 1680, 81 and 82. They were A&D boxlock guns, the first two without ejectors, the third with ejectors. The listed date is 1906, 2 years after the first 410s despite the earlier serial numbers.

The first A&D double 410 was SN 2172, dated in 1909, along with a second A&D double, SN 2174. In 1910 and 1911, they made the last of their 410 hammer double guns, all with top levers, SNs 2239 and 40 as well as SNs 2285 and 86. Serial number 2286 also had "extra engraving."

Beginning in 1909, they record 41 single-barrel 410s, the first 38 not noted as to configuration. The company described the last three—SNs 4539, 4701 and 4702—as "single A&D" "Standard" quality guns without ejectors. They sent the first two to "Rosson,"

∧ **Photo 1:** A "Best" 410 by Hellis with a large customized forend, full coverage scroll engraving and modest wood, SN 3950.

Paul Goodwin photo

a quality provincial gunmaker, now owned by Gallyon & Son.

The remaining recorded 410s, a total of 65, were all A&D boxlock doubles. Eleven had ejectors, with the first recorded in 1925, a pair, SN 3240 and 41. Prior to 1925, they had already listed 18 A&D double non-ejector 410s. The majority of A&D 410s were consecutively numbered: non-ejectors in 1921 (SN 301 thru 15); SN 3236 thru 41, the last two ejectors, in 1925-26; and SN 3945 thru 50 in 1934. All of the latter guns were non-ejectors; however, for the first time, the word "Best" is attached to four guns, SNs 3947 through 3950 (Photos 1 and 2).

They subsequently described most of their 410 doubles as either "Best or Plain." Six were "Best," eight "Plain," and the rest unspecified. One gun, SN 3977, a non-ejector, had a single trigger. The last two 410s to leave the firm did so in 1954, SN 5807 and 08. Both were 28-inch-barreled non-ejectors. The former at £63 went to the Duchess of Devonshire and the latter at £88

Photo 2: A close-up view of SN 3950.

G. Allan Brown photo ∨

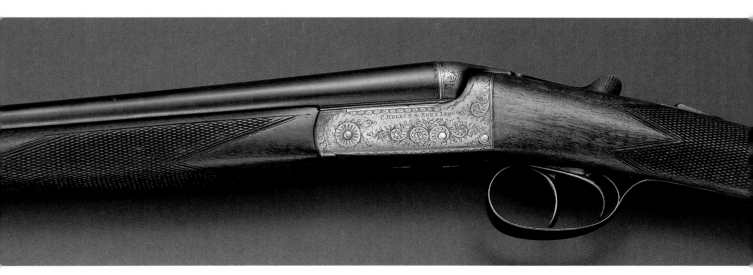

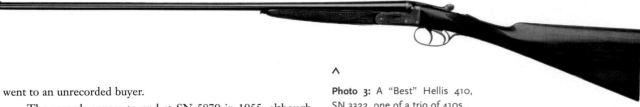

went to an unrecorded buyer.

The records appear to end at SN 5879 in 1955, although there is a cryptic entry in 1985, SN 5882.

A representative example of their A&D 410 is SN 3322, a non-ejector with full coverage scroll engraving, delivered September 27, 1926, at £22. This was one gun of a trio, numbers 3321, 22 and 23 (Photos 3 and 4).

A 1953 price list for a "Standard" A&D boxlock 410 without ejectors was 57 pounds, 9 shillings and 1 pence; the with-ejectors price was over £67. A "Universal" grade was over £74 and with ejectors over £83. A single trigger was available in the "Universal" grade for an additional £25!

British taxes, at that time, were 17 percent on these guns. In fact, the high rate of taxes on British goods, levied to pay for their socialistic welfare state, depressed their post-World War II economy. This almost killed the double gunmakers until the Thatcher revolution in the 1980s, which slashed taxes and privatized industry—a cautionary tale for those who think government regulation and taxes are an unmixed blessing.

∧

Photo 3: A "Best" Hellis 410, SN 3322, one of a trio of 410s.

Paul Goodwin photo

Photo 4: A close-up view of SN 3322.

Paul Goodwin photo   ∨

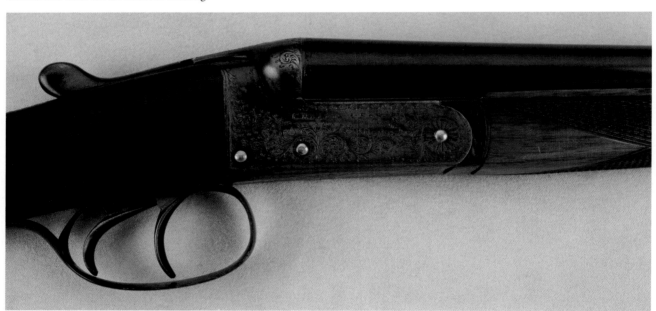

Charles Hellis & Sons References

1. Records were reviewed in 1999 through the courtesy of David Ingles.   2. G.T. Garwood's letter to Atkin, Grant & Lang.

HOLLAND & HOLLAND

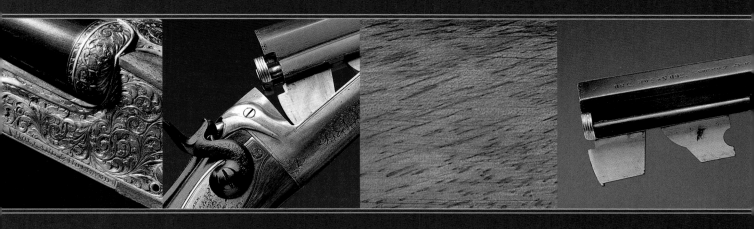

istory

H This company, founded in 1835 by Harris Holland, located to 98 New Bond Street, London, by 1866, and they remained there for almost 100 years. A nephew, Henry Holland, joined the company in 1860, and in 1876 the firm became "Holland & Holland" [1,2]. In 1898, they built their first factory on Harrow Road, London, and recruited their fabricators from the great Birmingham corps of workers. Before this, Webley C. Scott and others in the Birmingham trade made most of their guns. The Birmingham makers built the guns to the highest standards and they proofed them in London.

H&H first made their international name with rifles from the rook to the 4-bore elephant gun, winning all calibers and bores at Mr. Walsh's "London Field Rifle Trials" in October 1883. In 1886, they purchased Colonel George Fosbery's gun invention, naming it the Paradox. This was a smoothbore with the last 4 to 9 inches of the muzzle end machined with deep or shallow fast twist rifling. The rifling would spin the solid conical bullet with stability and accuracy up to 150 yards. The barrels were bored cylinder for a conventional shot shell. The company made them in bores 8 through 28. By 1893, according to their catalog, they manufactured shotguns in all bores from 28 to the then new 2-bore breech-loading goose gun. Like Purdey of that

era, they made a variety of grades ranging from the "Best Royal" to "Good" and finally to "B" and "C" quality.

During the 1890s, the firm made major contributions to shotgun development. In 1893, they patented an automatic ejector with two working parts—a "V"-spring ejector, and a tumbler [3]. In 1897, they offered a unique "three-pull" single trigger, clearly differing from those of Purdey and Boss. By 1908, with Woodward, they patented the easy hand-detachable sidelocks [1]. The breech self-opener was a Holland & Holland innovation in 1922. When opening the gun, the opening spring both forces the barrels down and cocks the hammers.

Most importantly for safety, they may have been the first to use two sears in their bar-action sidelock, one the intercepting or secondary sear used to prevent accidental discharge of the tumbler by something other than a trigger pull. The American back-action sidelocks such as L.C. Smith and Baker had no secondary sear to block the fall of the tumbler should the primary sear be accidentally jarred loose. This became a standard safety feature in all British bar-action sidelocks. Another innovation involved the Holland & Holland "Under and Over." Like Boss, Woodward, Beretta, and the Remington Model 32, Holland never used a knuckle-pin underbolt, thus avoiding the need for a thick frame from top to bottom. This resulted in a low-profile streamlined ensemble that has been the signature of most

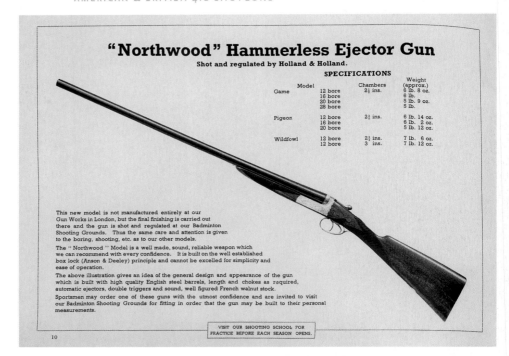

"Northwood" Hammerless Ejector Gun

Shot and regulated by Holland & Holland.

SPECIFICATIONS

	Model	Chambers	Weight (approx.)
Game	12 bore	2¼ ins.	6 lb. 8 oz.
	16 bore		6 lb.
	20 bore		5 lb. 9 oz.
	28 bore		5 lb.
Pigeon	12 bore	2¾ ins.	6 lb. 14 oz.
	16 bore		6 lb. 2 oz.
	20 bore		5 lb. 12 oz.
Wildfowl	12 bore	2¾ ins.	7 lb. 6 oz.
	12 bore	3 ins.	7 lb. 12 oz.

This new model is not manufactured entirely at our Gun Works in London, but the final finishing is carried out there and the gun is shot and regulated at our Badminton Shooting Grounds. Thus the same care and attention is given to the boring, shooting, etc. as to our other models.

The "Northwood" Model is a well made, sound, reliable weapon which we can recommend with every confidence. It is built on the well established box lock (Anson & Deeley) principle and cannot be excelled for simplicity and ease of operation.

The above illustration gives an idea of the general design and appearance of the gun which is built with high quality English steel barrels, length and chokes as required, automatic ejectors, double triggers and sound, well figured French walnut stock.

Sportsmen may order one of these guns with the utmost confidence and are invited to visit our Badminton Shooting Grounds for fitting in order that the gun may be built to their personal measurements.

VISIT OUR SHOOTING SCHOOL FOR PRACTICE BEFORE EACH SEASON OPENS.

10

Photo 1: The third post-war catalog introducing the Northwood model.

Glenn Campbell photo

English over/under guns and subsequently copied by the superb Spanish and Italian gunmakers of the modern era.

In the 1960s, under the direction of Malcolm Lyell, they built a set of five guns from 410 to 12 bore under the title of "Products of Excellence," emphasizing the artistic side of gun decoration.

In 1989, a Chanel Group subsidiary purchased Holland & Holland for over 10 million pounds. They invested in computer numerically controlled (CNC) machinery to produce gun components designed by computer-aided design (CAD) systems. This technology, now in use by virtually all gunmakers, remarkably reduced labor costs and increased precision tolerances. The "Best" guns though are still hand-finished. Holland & Holland has represented innovation and quality in gunmaking for over 125 years.

This brief historical survey emphasizes the point that by the end of the first quarter of the 20th century, the ultimate Holland & Holland shotgun had evolved and they were manufacturing them in various bores. Yet, they did not build or deliver a single bar-action

"Best" quality 410 until 1963. When they did build it though, it incorporated all of the firm's modern shotgun innovations.

410 Bore

The Holland & Holland shotgun records that I reviewed began at SN 16000, July 29, 1883. According to management, the earlier records were lost to the ravages of the past' [4]. David Winks, then director of Holland & Holland and one of the most knowledgeable gunmen in the world, permitted my research. A review of each

1 A recent publication appears to have had more access than this writer had [2].

Photo 2: A matched pair of Northwood 410s, SNs 37140 and 37141.

Gary Herman photo

∧ **Photo 3:** This 410 from the 1990s, SN 41224, is a "Royal Deluxe."

Gallyon & Sons Ltd. photo

smoothbore from SN 16000 thru SN 16999, dates ranging from 1883 to 1903, revealed mainly 12 bore, a few 16 and 20 bore, and a single 28-bore gun. The latter, SN 16502, was a single 28-inch steel-barrel drop-lock Paradox, built by January 10, 1900. They made these smoothbore shotguns in all configurations, bar and back action and boxlocks, with and without exposed hammers. Nevertheless, they apparently did not build a single 410. There is no known original 410 gun prior to 1900, and Holland & Holland did not "do" walking-stick guns, so common in the 410 bore in that era.

A priceless 72-page Holland & Holland catalog, printed between 1910 and 1913 with a grey cover featuring eight gold medals and black and green lettering, did not offer the 410, even in their "Boys' Gun" offering. The smallest bore was the 28. Likewise, a cream-colored 36-page catalog featuring a dog and a 17th-century shooter with a 19th-century hammer gun, circa 1933, did not offer the 410 bore.

From 1900 to 1939, Holland & Holland had highly skilled and experienced craftsmen to hand file, fit, and precision the

∧

Photo 3A: A very rare original 410 smoothbore single-barrel Holland & Holland, SN 13667.

Paul Goodwin photo

∧

Photo 4: A classic rook rifle 410 conversion, SN 10925.

Paul Goodwin photo

metal and wood components of their "Best"-quality bar-action gun including checkering and engraving. In this era, they built "Best"-quality guns in virtually all bores save the 410.

Those 410s that came out during this time under the Holland & Holland name were either single- or double-barrel, back-action or boxlock hammer guns. The double-barrel boxlock 410s were "shot and regulated" by Holland & Holland. Birmingham artisans, craftsmen, small firms, or large-market firms made these original boxlock 410s. Among the firms were Webley & Scott, the largest manufacturer of double guns in Great Britain for nearly 100 years, and Midland Arms. The Birmingham-built guns were however proofed in London.

Holland & Holland would then re-work and precision the barrels, action, ejectors, and safety, and sell the guns under the Holland & Holland name. Holland usually sent these guns to the overseas empire and sold them through the Army & Navy Cooperative Stores, which were found at the frontiers of the British Empire in locations such as Bombay, Calcutta, Port Said, and British East Africa. An example is SN 75654, made by Webley & Scott and "shot and regulated" by Holland & Holland,

Photo 5: A rook rifle with 2-barrel set, SN 10333. The rifle barrel is a 360 caliber while the smoothbore barrel is an original 410 gauge for "shot."

Cameo photo ∨

which was sold by Army & Navy Cooperative Stores under their own numbering system. This is a boxlock ejector with double triggers and 27-inch barrels made between 1939 and 1940.

After World War II, when they returned to non-military gunmaking, they found most of their experienced artisans either too old or off to other post-World War II opportunities. There was no pool of young apprentices to replace them. This was true of all British quality gunmakers of the time.

By 1948, Holland & Holland had produced their first post-World War II catalog listing a number of grades, though none in the 410 bore. They were all sidelock actions. The two top grades were the Modele DeLuxe and Royal, both with hand-detachable sidelocks. The next grade was the Badminton, which did not contain the breech self-opener feature. The next and lowest grade was the Dominion, available only with double triggers, although they did make some with back-action sidelocks. A Centenary, a 2-inch 12-bore lightweight gun, was available in all four grades. The Riviera had two pairs of barrels, one for game birds and one for waterfowl. It was of the Badminton grade but available with hand-detachable sidelocks. A "Best"-quality Under and Over and the Paradox in 12 to 20 bore completed the catalog of shotguns. None of these models were available in the 410 bore.

Their second post-war catalog, published sometime after 1951 but before 1958, added a newly revised Under and Over gun. A 1956 price list refers to all the listed models in the 1948 and post-1951 catalogs.

They published their third post-war catalog after 1958 but before 1960. The address on the catalog is 98 New Bond Street, London. However, in 1960, the company moved to 13 Bruton Street, London, and some of these catalogs with the old address have a new address sticker affixed over the old.

This catalog is most interesting in that they dropped the Dominion grade and the Centenary model actions and added the Northwood Anson & Deeley boxlock with automatic ejectors. This Northwood gun was made "to Holland & Holland specifications" off premises but "shot and regulated" by Holland & Holland to a very high level of workmanship. A Birmingham consortium led by Vic Simmons built these guns. They were available, according to the third post-war catalog, in 12 to 28 bore with double triggers (Photo 1).

However, according to the records[2], they did make at least four such Northwoods in 410 bore.

A pair, SN 37140 and SN 37141, ordered in September 1958 and shipped in September 1960, weighed but 4-1/2 pounds each. Built on a miniature boxlock frame with a checkered butt on a 14 3/8-inch stock of exquisitely beautiful wood, the pair was magnificent. Made for an Englishman and once owned by the articulate aficionado of the English smoothbore and rifle, the

Connecticut gun dealer Gary Herman, they now rest with an American collector (Photo 2).

A third Northwood side-by-side 410, SN 37443, choked one quarter and modified, sold at auction in 1969. It has 26-inch barrels with 3-inch chambers. As an A&D boxlock, it has automatic ejectors, a straight stock, and a beavertail forend. It weighs 5 pounds, 4 ounces with a long 15 3/4-inch stock and recoil pad. A fourth 410, SN 37021, sold in May 1961. It has double triggers, ejectors, and 27-inch barrels.

Holland & Holland made two other "shot and regulated" boxlock 410s and one Badminton sidelock 410 in the same timeframe. The latter grade was available until the early 1980s.

The Northwood boxlock remained available in 12 through 28 bore into the 1980s, but by then, they were made entirely in the Holland & Holland factory.

In the 1980s, they introduced a high-quality Cavalier model in 12 through 28 bore. This was the first boxlock designed and completely made by Holland & Holland with a detachable cross pin in their action. They made approximately 500 guns in the 50000 serial number range, but none in the 410 bore (through 1992, the H&H numbering system for all other guns had reached just above 41000).

For a short time in the 1990s, they reintroduced the Dominion sidelock in 12, 16, and 20 bore. As of 1993, Holland & Holland will make only the "Best" quality Royal or DeLuxe bar-action sidelock in any bore from 12 through 410.

410 Sidelock

The affable and courteous William McKelvey, the senior and now-retired director of Holland & Holland's gunroom, reported to me in 1985 that between 1963 and 1984, they had produced 22 bar-action sidelock 410s, almost exclusively for the American market. For example, they produced one in 1967, one in 1968, four in 1969, six in 1982, and four in 1983. All were side-by-side doubles.

Holland delivered a typical 410 in 1973, SN 40052. This is a double-trigger Royal DeLuxe, splinter forend, hand-detachable side-by-side with a game-scene-coin-finished action body, made for an American hunter. Sadly, he died soon after receiving the gun and it has remained to this day unfired.

Of the 22 "Best"-quality bar-action 410s made between 1963 and 1984, six of them have successive serial numbers, 40584 through 40589, although all with different owners. Eight had been publicly identified as to serial number and specifications. An example is SN 40498 with two sets of barrels and a single trigger, smothered in gold overlay by Ken Hunt, a preeminent engraver of our era.

H&H built 12 additional 410s in the Royal or DeLuxe grade from 1984 to 1993, all for the American market. An example is SN 40708, a double-triggered, coin-finished, game-scene-engraved gun. Roger Mitchell, then managing director, described an especially brilliant "Royal DeLuxe" 410 (SN 41224) with an

---

2 David Winks has confirmed that less than six were made.

exhibition Circassian walnut stock as one of the "finest Royals we ever produced." It has 26 1/2-inch barrels and weighs 4 pounds, 13-1/2 ounces (Photo 3). Two additional post-1993 410s are SN 41227, engraved by Ken Preater, with 27-inch barrels and a single trigger, and SN 41228 with hand-detachable locks.

The first Holland & Holland Under and Over is provisionally numbered 5100 with a single trigger. This is the prototype, and as of the year 2000, they are in full production of the Royal or DeLuxe over and under 410 bores.

The Rook Rifle Conversion

Today there are various other existing Holland & Holland 410 smoothbores. All or nearly all are converted rook rifles (Photo 3A). Built before or shortly after the turn of the century, these guns were converted to the 410 bore after the change of proof laws and gun regulations went into effect after World War I. Hence, they are all nitro proofed and the cartridge chambers lengthened to at least 2-1/2 inches (see Rook Rifle chapter).

According to Holland & Holland's 1893 catalog, the rook rifle was primarily manufactured as a single-barrel, hammerless top-lever A&D boxlock ejector, offered at that time in the 295 and 360 caliber. This catalog also offered a less expensive side-lever, ejector, single-barrel rook rifle in the same calibers. Interestingly, a double-barrel rook rifle of an early vintage (pre-1900) has surfaced for public identification. Serial number 19369, with 26-inch barrels, semi-pistol grip, and border engraving sold at auction at Bonham's, London, in 1998.

All of these rook rifles appear to have had a pistol grip stock with a cheek piece. Their barrels are octagonal with some becoming rounded at the muzzle end. All of those converted to the 410 bore are nitro proofed from 2 1/2- to 3-inch cartridge chambers. Usually, the actions are scroll engraved with casehardened colors.

The earliest rook rifle 410 conversion that I known about, SN 8945, was originally built in 1880. It is uniquely double-barreled and was originally a 295/300-caliber rifle. It once belonged to a Holland & Holland employee. A somewhat later single-barreled rook rifle conversion, SN 9846, has a side-lever breech opener with an octagonal barrel and 2 1/2-inch chambers with scroll engraving. This appears identical to the lower-priced side-lever single-barrel ejector rook rifle advertised in the 1893 catalog. This gun sold at auction in 1990 in London.

Serial number 10370, a top-lever hammerless single barrel, sold in 1993 in France. Another conversion, SN 10925, sold in 1990. It is a single octagonal barrel boxlock top-lever, hammerless, nitro-proofed, with a foliate scroll-engraved action. It has a pistol grip and a steel buttplate stock (Photo 4).

Additional 410 rook rifle conversions include SN 18126, built in 1911 as a 295 rook rifle, and SN 21253, both of which sold at auction in London in 1992. SN 18928, a side-lever hammer 2 1/2-inch 410, sold in France in 1993 along with SN 10370. Another conversion, SN 18312, sold in 1966, and numbers 21246 and 24264 sold at auction in 1967.

An important example of Holland & Holland versatility is a rook rifle with a second barrel in 410 smoothbore for "shot." This back-action hammer gun (SN 10333) is beautifully made, in pristine condition, and once resided in the home of a man who shoots on one of the Queen of England's dairy farms (Photo 5).

Most Holland & Holland rook rifles that have appeared in the public market in the past 30 years have been converted to the 410 bore.

Conclusion

Holland & Holland was late on the scene with their "Best"-quality 410 in comparison to Purdey, Boss, Westley Richards, or the premier American double gunmakers of the 20th century. However, when it did appear, it was in all of its resplendent beauty and technological genius. It is a work of art, wondrous to behold. It is also a tool that becomes an inseparable extension of the human body.

In the past 20 years, Holland & Holland, together with Purdey, have developed a strong in-house apprentice program that has spawned a young generation of skilled gunmakers. The charming presumption of William McKelvey's assertion that the "past, present, and future of fine shotgun making" lies with his firm and a few British and European brother firms, is difficult to debate.

Holland & Holland References

1. Boothroyd, Geoffrey. 1992, *S.T.C.M.*, April, 2-8.
2. Brown, Nigel, *London Gunmakers*, Christie's Books, London, 1998.
3. Greener, W.W., *The Gun and Its Development*, Cassell & Company, Ltd., 1910.
4. The Holland & Holland Records, reviewed in 1990 and 1994, courtesy of David Winks.

CHAPTER NINETEEN

PURDEY

ased upon known guns and with factory record confirmation, Purdey manufactured the 410 bore as early as 1883. A formal review of the factory production records may indicate earlier manufacture, but the company, so far, will not allow such a review. A brief recapitulation of the development of the Purdey shotgun from the time of Joseph Manton will set the stage for the evolution of the Purdey 410 bore [1-6].

History

James Purdey, the founder, apprenticed with Joseph Manton, the father of modern shotgun makers, from 1804 to 1808. This apprenticeship was especially illuminating and valuable to Purdey because Manton represented the pinnacle of British gunmaking of that era. Purdey then worked with Alexander Forsyth from 1808 to 1814, helping to perfect Forsyth's detonating lock—the percussion system that revolutionized all gun making in the early 19th century. By 1814, he was on his own at 4 Princes Street, Leicester Square, London, and began, in 1818, an unbroken period of gun manufacturing and recording that continues to the present. In 1826, he moved to 314-1/2 Oxford Street, Joseph Manton's old address, and, in 1882, moved to South Audley Street, where they are still located today.

Although LeFaucheux's breechloader appeared in London in 1851 at the Great Exhibition, it was not until 1858 that Purdey built a breechloader—a 12-bore pinfire, SN 5642. From the 1818 muzzleloader to the end of the 1890s, Purdey preferentially used the back-action, hammer sidelock, although in diminishing numbers after 1880 when he purchased the Beesley bar-action hammerless sidelock patent. The hammer muzzleloader with a bar action goes back to 1816 in the flintlock and to 1821 in the detonating lock. When the pinfire emerged mid-century, both back and bar actions were used. (It is interesting to note that the records revealed the manufacture of a 12-bore back-action muzzleloader as late as 1880.)

In 1863, the company patented the "Purdey bolt," a double under bite to hold the barrel to the water table. This consists of two barrel lumps, each with a locking groove. In 1878, Purdey developed the third fastener, a top cross-bolt hidden from view. A barrel extension from between the cartridge chambers mates with a recess in the standing breech that contains the hidden horizontal cross bolt that locks the barrel extension. This completed the famous and much emulated "Purdey triple bolting" system seen in subsequent generations of gun making worldwide. It remains unclear if this third fastener development was part of a collaborative effort with W. & C. Scott. The latter, in 1867, patented a top lever and spindle method of opening and closing a gun, later used in Purdey guns.

By the 1860s to 1870s, using the W. & C. Scott patent, Purdey began converting from an underlever to a top-lever breech-opening system with the centerfire system. Very quickly, the pinfire was extinguished as a viable product. In 1880, Purdey began making guns using the Frederick Beesley-invented hammerless bar-in-the-wood sidelock, centerfire action, with barrel cocking ejectors. This action was a true self-opener. It was in the 1860s that Purdey developed their distinctive and exquisite rose and scroll engraving attributable to John Lucas, an engraver for Purdey for almost 60 years. We know little of him but he may deserve to be called a giant in his field. Eventually replacing him was Henry Albert Kell, a peerless engraver of the early half of the 20th century. Kell trained a current master, Ken Hunt.

By the 1880s, the Purdey hammerless gun used fluid steel barrels from Joseph Wentworth's firm. In this era, Joseph Brazier or Edwin Chilton, lock makers for London's "Best" guns made the locks. Also in this era, they converted from the bar-in-wood configuration, a most beautiful ensemble, to the standard bar action seen almost exclusively in the 20th-century "Best" sidelock.

Purdey continued to make elegant first-quality hammer bar-action guns well into the 1890s, in addition to the lesser quality (although beautifully fashioned) back-action hammer guns. By the turn of the century, Purdey had turned almost exclusively to first-quality bar-action hammerless guns, with the occasional exquisite and graceful hammer gun made for the odd shooter, such as the King of England and Lord Ripon, the greatest game shot in British history.

Gone, however, by 1900, were the long, stylish back-action guns. The bar action offered a better angle between sear and

Photo 1: A workshop in action showing some of the great Purdey craftsmen of the inter-war period.

Purdey photo

1933
THE ACTION SHOP. IRONGATE WHARF ROAD PADDINGTON.
① BEN. DELAY ② FRED. WILLIAMS ③ ARTHUR DEAN. ④ FRED. SCALES ⑤ BOB HORSCROFT.
⑥ MR E.C. LAWRENCE (FACTORY MANAGER) ⑦ BERT. WOOLMER ⑧ BILL HOLLAND.
⑨ WALTER FIELD. ⑩ PHIL. SUMPTER ⑪ LEN HOWARD. ⑫ C. HARRY LAWRENCE.
⑬ HARRY WHITEHOUSE ⑭ PERCY WILKES ⑮ ALF. SMITH ⑯ MAURICE TIMBERS.
⑰ ERNEST LAWRENCE.

tumbler, which provided a crisper trigger pull. The Purdey bar action, unlike those of Holland & Holland and others, has two cams on each lock. There is one at the end of the cocking rod and one contacting the upper limb of the "V"-shaped mainspring for a more efficient use of energy. The mainspring had two arms. The upper—heavier and stronger—cocked the lock while the lower and weaker arm, fired it.

The final phase of development began in the 1930s in response to the American market, which wanted a "Best"-quality Purdey over/under. Purdey chose the Edwinson Green action that Harry Lawrence redesigned to four locking bolts. This gun, though very strong, was too heavy for the typical game shooter. By 1938, the company had made 18 such ensembles, but none in the 410 bore. In 1948, Purdey bought the James Woodward & Sons firm and its exquisite low profile over/under first introduced in 1908.

The Purdey 410 Pedigree

The immediate background for the manufacture of the first 410 includes the fact that the back-action hammer breechloader gun was manufactured from 1858 to the end of the 1890s. Several grades were available from "Best" quality to "B," "C," and "E" grades. The bar-action sidelock became more generally available in the 1880s, first with external hammers, then with the hammer-less Beesley action. After 1900, the bar action became the exclusive gun built and only in the "Best" grade quality. This evolution explains what we do know about the Purdey 410 story, gleaned from known existing guns and historical comments by Purdey personnel over the years. The full story will not be available until Purdey permits a historian to go through the records, gun by gun, which up to now they have not allowed for privacy reasons.

The first very small smoothbore Purdey built, for which we have evidence, was a hammer side-by-side, top-lever, double-triggered, bar-in-the-wood action gun. Purdey built it for Lady Marion Scott, a well-recognized ornithologist and bird collector. According to the records, it left the factory in 1883, originally as a 360 "caliber" (smaller than a 410) smoothbore shotgun, SN 11358, weighing 3 pounds, 15 ounces and with no engraving. Currently, this unique gun has a skeletal steel butt, weighs 3 pounds, 11 ounces and has been engraved and inlaid by George

Photo 2: On top is the third original 410 made by Purdey, SN 13074, with partial coverage rose and scroll engraving. Shown on bottom is a Westley Richards single-barrel original 410 with a side-lever opener.

Purdey photo

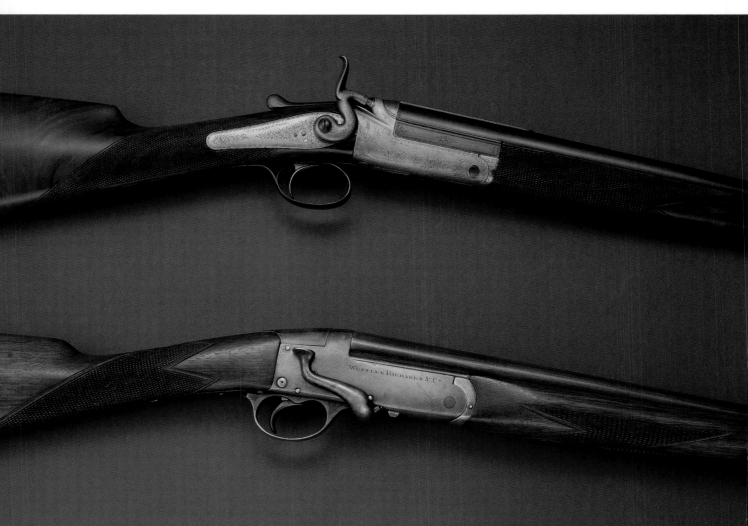

Photo 3: A full view of SN 13074 illustrating the remarkable wood is shown above a double-barrel Purdey rook rifle 410 smoothbore conversion of considerable elegance, SN 8625.

Paul Goodwin photo

Spring. The original double barrels were 26 1/8-inch Damascus, black powder proofed. According to Gary Herman, a Connecticut fine gun expert, John Foster of London re-barreled the gun in the late 1970s with 26-inch barrels in the 410 bore with 3-inch chambers.

Recalling the Purdey gun development, they made the Scott gun soon after they began to make the top-lever bar action. This was also in a timeframe when women and boys became more involved in recreational shooting, for this was a gun built for a small person.

The Beesley hammerless bar action had been available for 3 years and the third fastener for 5 years at this point. The transition to these technological advances was rapid, especially in the "Best"-quality guns, as almost certainly the Scott gun was. This gun appears just when we begin to see 410 cartridges advertised by cartridge companies.

Details and photos of a Churchill and Reilly 360-"caliber" smoothbore for shot shell are located in Chapter 2.

The Vintage 410

Purdey shipped the first recorded 410 on September 27, 1883. The gun (SN 11739) weighed 3 pounds, 15-1/2 ounces, was a grade "E" back-action hammer gun with a single steel barrel, and was chambered for the "gastight" 2 3/4-inch cartridge, an unusual length for that time.

The same person ordered the next two documented Purdey 410 bores as well. The first, SN 12239, shipped January 1888, and was described in the Purdey records as a 28-inch steel double-barrel hammer back-action shotgun with rebounding locks. It was an "E"-quality gun chambered for 2-inch "gastight" Eley cartridges and weighed 4 pounds, 6 ounces. The second 410, SN 13074, shipped May 23, 1988, is likewise an external hammer back-action gun of "E" quality bored with a modified choke. This gun is a 26-inch single-Siemens-steel-barrel ensemble with 2-inch chambers. Although it was of "E" quality, an "extra handsome stock" is recorded at 12 5/8-inch with a "bend" of 2 3/16-inch to 1 3/8-inch, obviously made for a small woman or a boy.

This third 410 reveals fine scroll engraving on the locks, action, hammer, and breech end of the barrel. The under bolts are doubled with no top bolt. It is a top-lever straight stock gun. The wood is spectacular despite the gun's designation as "E" quality. It may not have been a "Best," but the gun is magnificent (Photos 2 and 3).

It is interesting that the same person received these two guns, 4 months apart, yet the serial number of the first gun would date it prior to 1885. This suggests not a strict concordance between some of the serial numbers and the various dates ascribed to them in various references outside of the Purdey records themselves. These guns, SN 12239 and SN 13074, are well documented in the Purdey archives.

Starting in 1876 with SN 9841, until 1888 with SN 13074, Purdey made only the above-mentioned three 410s. I base this information upon an inspection of factory records by an employee of the firm. Further inspection revealed the company built no 410 guns before 1876.

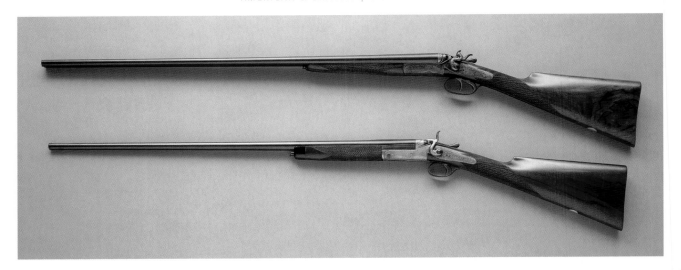

Yet they made a number of 28 bores from 1876 to 1888, undoubtedly due to its popularization by W. Greener for small game shooting. Between 1895 and 1900, they built two 32 gauge, numbers 16421 and 22, at least one 28 gauge, and one 24-gauge shotgun. The first three were back-action hammer guns with ejectors and 27-inch barrels. The 24-gauge gun, also with 27-inch barrels, was a hammerless "Best," SN 16177. Also at this time, Purdey made several "410" blackpowder rifles for big game hunting. These were rifled bore and the actual caliber of the guns was 450/400.

Photos 4, 5: Original 410s by Purdey show SN 13667, a single barrel, and SN 13668, a double barrel. SN 13668 reveals exceptional wood and generous case colors set off by rose and scroll engraving from the workbench of J. Lucas and assistants at Purdey.

G. Allan Brown photos

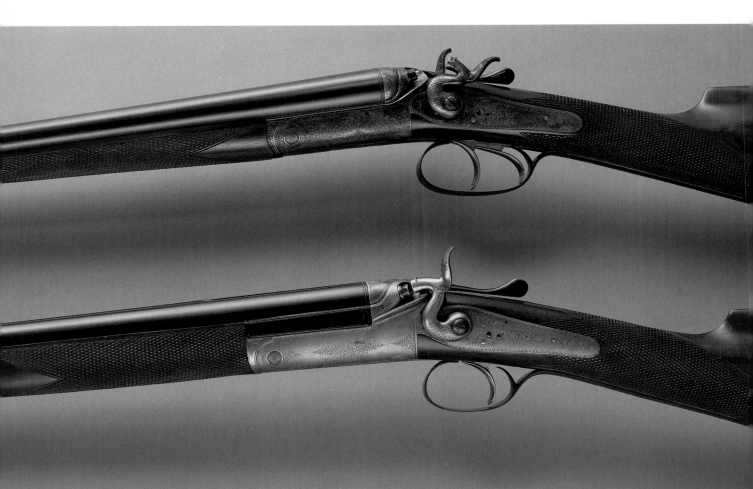

Photo 6: (Above) A single-barrel rook/410 conversion by Purdey, SN A558. (Below) A very early single-barrel rook rifle 410 smoothbore conversion by Purdey, SN 87.

Paul Goodwin photos

The next known 410 guns are a pair, SN 13667 and 13668, built in 1892. The former is a single-barrel gun, the latter, a double side-by-side. Both are steel barreled with 2-inch chambers with a top lever and with rebounding external hammer back actions of "E" quality. They were "patterned with 3/8-ounce of #7 shot." The SN 13668 gun has superb wood and a fine fancy dense scroll engraving with rich case colors. The SN 13667 gun has good wood with fine scroll engraving (Photos 4 and 5).

Both guns feature engraving on the locks, action body, hammers, and breech end of the barrel. Both have double bite under bolts, rebounding hammers, and no top fastener. All of the above five back-action guns have push-button forends. These are the only Purdey 410 bore shotguns built prior to 1900 to publicly surface, and according to an employee's perusal of the records, Purdey built no other 410s between 1876 and 1900.

Two double rifles converted to the 410 smoothbore have surfaced. The first, SN 8625, is interesting in that Purdey built it in 1871, 10 years before they moved to South Audley Street. The records describe it as a double breech-opening, centerfire, hammer "P"-grade rifle (caliber unspecified). The Purdey researcher states that it was probably a 360 caliber. Today the barrels and back-action locks say "J. Purdey, 314 1/2 Oxford Street, London." The barrels, now nitro proofed, were originally blackpowder proofed and are probably Damascus under blackening. Currently it has a straight stock, splinter forend, checkered butt, with toe and heel plates. The breech opener is an underlever and the action is coin finished. It now belongs to an obscure gunshop in England, and the owner was told years ago that it was originally a "300 caliber Express long case rifle," not a "rook" rifle (Photo 3).

A second 410 conversion was a 300-caliber double rifle, SN 12863, built in 1896. It is an "E"-quality, back-action hammer gun, fully engraved and with rebounding locks. The stock has a pistol grip with a cheek piece converted to a steel plate and a push-button forend. The gun weighed 6 pounds, 14 ounces when Purdey shipped it with a 14 3/16-inch stock and 26-inch steel barrels. It has now been re-barreled by Rigby's to a 410 with 3-inch chambers, fitted with a new rib and splinter forend, and weighs 5 pounds 2 ounces.

A third 410 conversion, SN 87, a number far too early for the address,[1] was a single-barrel "rook" rifle (Photo 6). It is a beautifully engraved and maintained hammer, side-lever breech-opener gun with a 24-inch smoothbore barrel chambered for the 2 1/2-inch 410 shot shell. Purdey made it when the firm was at 314-1/2 Oxford Street, London. There may be other original Purdey 300+ caliber rifles re-bored to the 410 shotgun such as these.

There is a heretofore-unknown story in the Purdey records that is revealed by two 410 smoothbore rifle conversions. SN A1091 is listed in the Purdey records as a 360-caliber single-barrel

#5 rifle made by Webley & Scott, SN 84897. The Purdey firm received it new on 18 October 1908, added a Purdey number, and sold it to an Earl. The "A" designation means that Purdey named and retailed the gun. It is a boxlock top-lever gun with a 25-inch barrel, a 3-inch chamber, and is in marvelous condition. The octagonal barrel was rounded at the breech and muzzle ends by Peter Stevenson, a long-time Purdey jobber who also owned the gun for many years.

The second 410 conversion is a single-barrel hammerless gun, originally a 300-caliber rook rifle made "By Allport Dec. 1892" "4-5." The serial number is A558 on the trigger guard (Photo 6). This and all "A" numbered guns are in an "A Book" which states, "retailed not manufactured." Thomas Allport was a rifle maker to the trade at the end of the 19th century.

These guns exemplify the fact that all gunmakers, no matter how exalted, at one time had guns and components of guns made by the "trade." The firm would then finish, regulate, name, and retail the gun. It is also a tribute to the greatness of Webley & Scott and others as "gunmaker to other gunmakers" in London and Birmingham. In America, there is a gun, SN 15387, which the Purdey records lists as a hammerless 12 bore, but which today is a back-action, hammer 410 bore. It illustrates the need for the buyer to check, if possible, the original records.

The Modern 410

The next publicly documented 410 shotguns are those built under the supervision of Harry Lawrence [7]. He personally built the first bar-action hammerless "Best"-quality 410 from 1927 to 1928. Purdey built a total of six before World War II and another 18 after World War II up until 1982. All except two were side-by-side doubles (Photos 6A and 6B).

Purdey shipped a pair of 410s that Ken Hunt masterfully engraved in 1981 (SNs 28345 and 28346). They have 28-inch barrels and double triggers with a straight stock. Harry Lawrence planned, measured, and supervised their construction. The rose and scroll engraving is the trademark of Purdey, established by James Lucas, Harry Kell (who trained Hunt), and Geoffrey Casbard (Photos 7, 8, 9).

James Lucas has been credited, most recently by Donald Dallas, as the "man behind rose and scroll" engraving, the hallmark of the Purdey Best gun. He was Purdey's chief engraver from 1855 to 1915 [8].

The two exceptions to side-by-side configurations were over/under guns made in the early 1980s. These are the first of the 410 over/under guns ever built and they were crafted for two Texans no less. The firm built these guns to the Woodward over/under specifications with a Purdey modification—the Edwinson Green over/under was already discontinued when Purdey purchased Woodward in 1948. William Jaqua ordered a third 410 over/under in the early 1980s as part of a set of four in 12, 20, 28, and 410, all elegantly gold engraved by Ken Hunt. By 1993, Purdey had built six over/under 410s with two more in the mid-1990s. By comparison, a

---

[1] Purdey is unable to explain this.

Photo 6A: Bottom view of Purdey side-by-side 410, SN 28090.

Levasheff photo

Photo 6B (bottom): Side view of Purdey side-by-side 410 (SN 28090) with a single trigger originally sent to Abercrombie & Fitch in the 1970s.

Levasheff photo

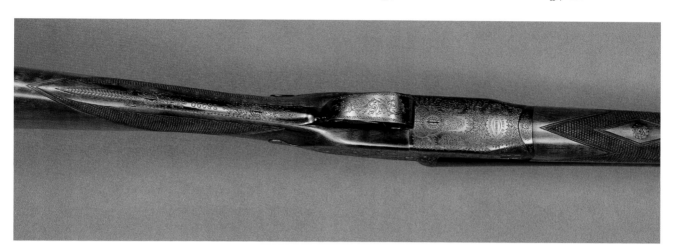

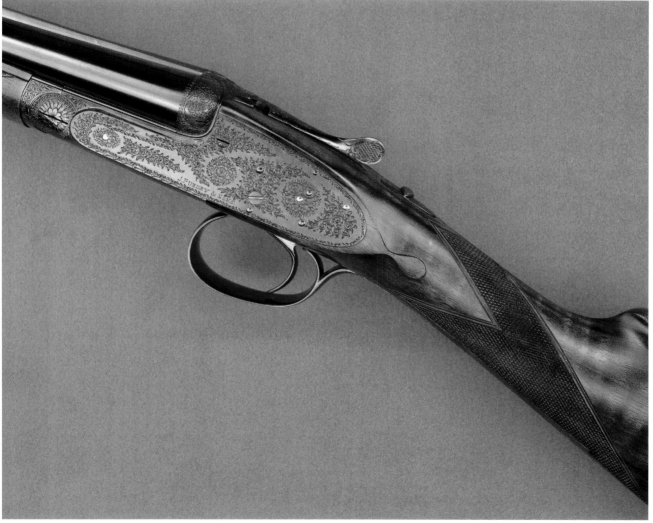

total of 21 28-bore over/under guns have been built since 1948 when Woodward and its over/under ensemble was purchased. Two more 28 bores were in production in the 1990s.

Public records detail nearly 30 Purdey 410-bore shotguns going back to the 19th century. However, an old Purdey barrel maker, Alf Harvey, said that over 50 410 double barrels have been made [9]. Furthermore, he maintained that they provided no new barrels for old guns or extra barrels for new guns. This means that a good number of 410 bore guns exist or Purdey has a good supply of 410 barrels waiting for customers.

There may be other back-action hammer or hammerless 410s built prior to 1927, and it will be interesting to see if a

Photo 8 (bottom): A Purdey 410, SN 28346, shown above a Boss 410, SN 8745A.

G. Allan Brown photo

Photo 7: A Purdey 410 engraved by Ken Hunt, SN 28346.

G. Allan Brown photo ∨

Photo 9 (right): Full views of a Purdey 410, SN 28346, above a Boss 410, SN 8745A.

G. Allan Brown photo >

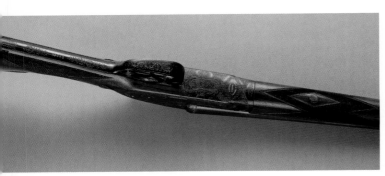

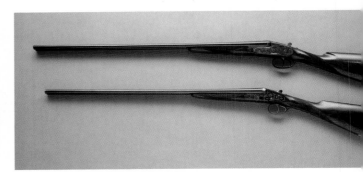

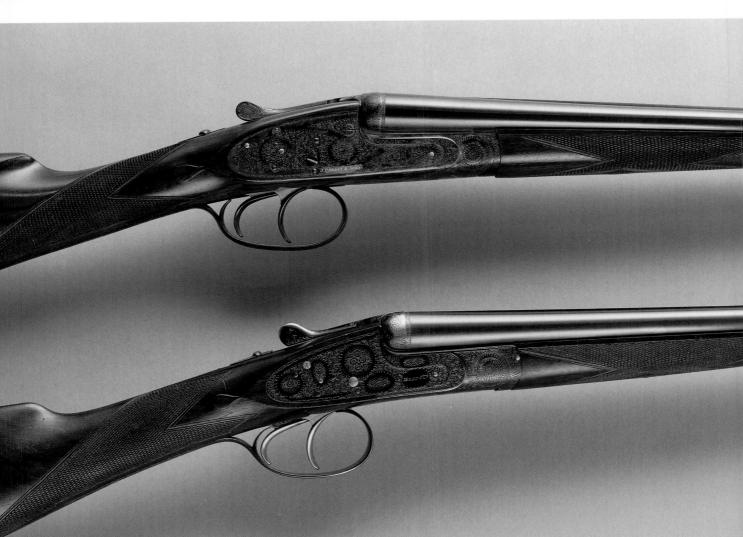

bar-action hammerless double built before the Harry Lawrence gun in 1927-1928 should someday appear.

A Personal Observation

Harry Lawrence, a physically small man, was modest, unassuming, and greeted visiting Americans warmly. He was a constant source of gunmaking information, given out with the quiet assurance of a man who was a preeminent gun artisan in the middle 50 years of the 20th century. He was one among the few who maintained Great Britain's productive excellence before the world as she otherwise slipped into decline from World War II until the Thatcher revolution in the 1980s.

Lawrence, who apprenticed in 1914 and rose to managing director after World War II, said his two greatest gun making pleasures were building the first bar-action hammerless 410 and building

Photo 10: A painting of the trio of (left to right) Harry Lawrence, Honorable Richard Beaumont, and Larry Salter, who kept the firm together from the 1960s through the 1980s.

Purdey photo

<

the set of three miniature guns for the Silver Jubilee of George V in 1935, numbers 25000, 25001, 24707. In 1938, the firm presented the consecutive pair to the king and SN 24707 to Tom Purdey. The latter resides today in Purdey's revered Long Room. All three Lawrence-built guns have cartridges and are capable of firing them, unlike the non-working pair Purdey built for Queen Mary, the Mother of Elizabeth, in 1923 (see Photo 2 in Chapter 1).

He further stated that his greatest challenge was his effort before World War II to convert the Green over/under with six bites to a more usable proportioned over/under with four locking bolts. This evidently remained a source of permanent frustration [7].

Today

The Honorable Richard Beaumont, Purdey's former Chairman, had nursed the firm from the brink of closure to a prominent place once again among producers of greatly artistic and functional firearms that enrich the human spirit. He strikes one, on first impression, as soft. Yet this is a calculated pose. It is best not to underestimate him for he is, in fact, a steel barrel inside a velvet sheath.

He needed all of his business toughness to see Purdey

Photo 11: A classically configured straight stock double-trigger "Best" 410 by Woodward, SN 7196.

Paul Goodwin photo

Photo 12: A closer view of the Woodward 410, SN 7196.

Paul Goodwin photo >

Photo 13: A Woodward 410 over/under in fabrication.

v *Purdey photo*

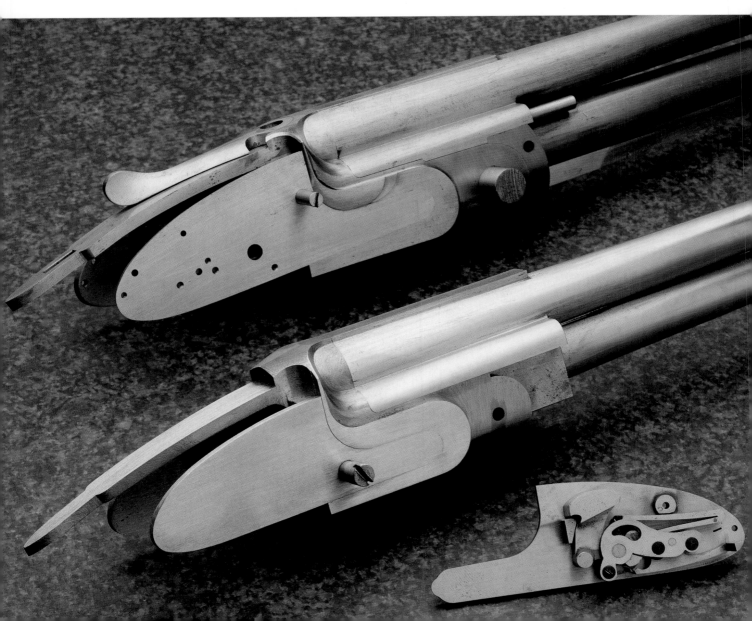

through the recession of the late 1970s and early 1990s. He succeeded, and then concluded that for Purdey to remain successful and thrive into the 21st century, a major corporate sponsor was required. Thus, Vendome, a European holding company, purchased the firm for a reported 13 million pounds in the early winter of 1994 with the promise that Purdey will remain a singularly preeminent gunmaker. The holding company, now Richemont Group, has honored that pledge (Photo 10).

Today, starting with CAD/CAM systems and CNC technology equipment, they hand-build only "Best" guns—approximately 60 to 70 guns per year. A 410 side-by-side requires over 700 man-hours to complete with a dedicated 410 action. The barrels are English chrome nickel steel using the chopper lump technique, with a wall thickness of 40 thousandths of an inch (.040). The guns are pressure proofed at 1200 bar.[2] The gun, with its Beesley locks, cocks on closing, thus releasing the tension on the springs when the gun is disassembled.

Finally, hopefully someday Purdey will permit someone to catalog the production records going back to 1818. This is the greatest consecutive record of gun making in British history. Perhaps the new owner will reevaluate the balance between privacy and public history.

Postscript—The Woodward Story

The Woodward 410 story is pure melodrama—a mixture of murder, thievery, mystery, speculation, frenzied bidding, and renaissance. At one time, there was one known 410, an over/under ensemble (SN 6930) circa 1930 that, according to open FBI records, was stolen in Cincinnati, Ohio, in conjunction with a murder. This gun has not been recovered, although another gun, a Woodward 20-gauge over/under (SN 6940), also stolen in that same murder-theft crime, was recovered.

According to the Woodward records, owned by Purdey, SN 6930 is a 2 1/2-inch gun with ejectors, double triggers, 26-inch barrels, and a 14-inch stock with an ebony butt. Unless destroyed, it is likely to reappear sooner rather than later.

The reason very likely for its reappearance is the emergence

of a wholly unsuspected second Woodward 410 over/under, SN 7158, delivered in 1939 with double triggers, ejectors, 26-inch barrels, 3-inch chambers, and Prince of Wales 14 1/2-inch stock. The name "W.C. Teagle," a former Chairman of the Standard Oil Company, is inlaid in gold. It was sent to the customer with a medallion in the stock that said, "To a straight shooter from a friend." The retail price was $1100, enough to purchase a luxury sedan such as a Packard in 1940. It sold at an American auction in 1999 for $200,500!

A third 410, SN 7196 built in 1997, is the first bar-action sidelock side-by-side known. It has 28-inch barrels, double triggers with ejectors, and a straight 15 1/2-inch stock. It has the classic Woodward fine scroll engraving by Martin Bublick. The gun has side clips, the unique arcaded Woodward detonators and the "T"-shaped safety, an original Woodward feature. It features a rounded frame with the Woodward name in gold (Photos 11 and 12).

Woodward traditionally creates their side-by-side guns using the Rogers action, which cocks the mainspring on opening the breech (vs. the Beesley action). However, there is no existing prototype Rogers action for a 410 frame; therefore, SN 7196 uses a Beesley action.

A fourth Woodward "Best" 410, this one an over/under, is under fabrication by Purdey under the supervision of Nigel Beaumont, now Managing Director. A cousin of Richard Beaumont, he has married modern manufacturing and steel technology to the incomparable hand finishing so distinctive in the Purdey Best gun (Photo 13).

The records between 1908 and 1918 reveal one A&D boxlock 410 (SN 6460) recorded in 1916 made by "Claborough & Johnson," gunmakers to the trade, and sold under the Woodward name. In 1908, "Osburne" made a 36-gauge smoothbore non-ejector A&D boxlock for Woodward and it is so named. The gun, SN 6030, has 27-inch barrels and a straight stock, and now reposes in the United States (see Chapter 20).

More 410s may surface when the records receive a formal review. Fortunately, Purdey reintroduced the Woodward in the early 1990s and hopefully it will be a great success. Woodward is an important and brilliant part of gunmaking history.

---

2 The pre-1989 nomenclature was in tons.

Purdey References

1. Dallas, Donald, *Purdey Gun & Rifle Makers,* Quiller Press, London, 2000.
2. Beaumont, Richard, Purdeys, *The Guns and the Family,* David & Charles 1984.
3. Yardley, Michael, "Making of a Masterpiece," *Shooting Times & Country Magazine,* 15 Feb. 1996, 29 Feb. 1996.
4. Venters, Vic, "The 'New' James Purdey & Sons, Ltd.," *Shooting Sportsman,* Jan/Feb 1999.

5. McIntosh, Michael, *Shooting Sportsman,* 47-49, Nov/Dec 1996.
6. Brown, Nigel, *London Gunmakers,* Christie's Books, London, 1998.
7. Lawrence, Harry, Personal communications from 1977 to 1982.
8. Dallas, Donald, "Purdey's Unknown Engraver," *Shooting Sportsman,* July/August 2002.
9. Harvey, Alf, personal communication 1980.
10. Woodward factory records reported in 2001 by Purdey, personal communication.

CHAPTER TWENTY

WEBLEY & SCOTT, LTD.

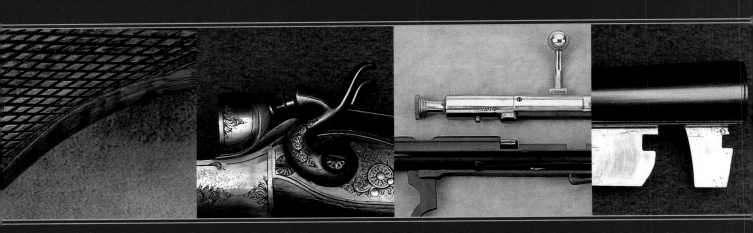

P hilip Webley & Son was established in 1838. W. & C. Scott & Son, founded between 1834 and 1843, merged with Philip Webley & Son in 1897, and by 1906, under the name of Webley & Scott, Ltd., the firm was making 2500 guns per year. They were the "largest producer of quality double guns in Britain" [1]. They made these guns in all configurations: back- or bar-action sidelocks, boxlocks, with and without exposed hammers. Over 75 percent of the guns they made were for the "trade."

In the years after World War I, double gun manufacturing gradually declined to an annual low of 100 guns by 1932. Joe Brown, one of England's greatest gun engravers in the early part of the 20th century, was Webley & Scott's chief engraver for 20 years. His work is seen on the Scott Premier and Imperial Premier bar- and back-action sidelock doubles with hammers or hammerless. In fact, many double gun cognoscenti, in part because of Brown's work, consider the early 20th-century Imperial Premier the best smoothbore ever made.

Following World War II, the firm concentrated on various quality boxlocks and production reached 1000 double guns per year by the 1950s. This continued into the 1960s and early 1970s with 60 percent exported to the United States and Europe. The decline to a few hundred per year by 1979 prompted an end to the double gun manufacturing, thus ending, after 80 years, the

reign of probably the most prolific and profitable manufacturer of quality double guns in Britain's history.

During the first three quarters of the 20th century, Webley & Scott was the chief supplier of quality barrels and actions to the gun trade in Britain and America and became known as the "gunmaker to the gunmakers." From the 1960s to 1980s, they were the only barrel maker of significance in England.

They made many double guns, actions, and barrels for such firms as Holland & Holland, Grant & Lang, William Evans, Churchill, and Cogswell & Harrison. During this period the prefix "Specially made for" or "Shot and regulated by" followed by the seller's name had been added to many guns actually fabricated in large measure by Webley & Scott. The seller would often do no more than engrave and number the gun.

The "W. & C. Scott & Son" name after the Webley & Scott merger continued to grace the Rogers action hammerless sidelocks built from 1897 to 1939. This included the Imperial Premier grade. It was priced higher than the "Best" of Boss, Purdey, Holland & Holland, or Woodward! Additional high grades on the Rogers action included the Premier and the popular "Monte Carlo B," a game and competition gun much in demand. Subsequently, additional sidelock models were built through the 1920s including the Unique, the Model 180, and the Model 158. They built 6000 of these Rogers sidelocks under the

W. & C. Scott name over 43 years, but none in the 410 bore that can be verified by factory records.

The best W. & C. Scott & Son boxlock was the Reliance with 4000 made from 1890 to 1935, apparently none in the 410 bore.

The best sidelock under the Webley & Scott name was the W & R. Produced from 1906 to 1940, this sidelock was a lower grade than those made under the W. & C. Scott & Son name. The top Webley & Scott boxlock was the A & W. In 1900, they introduced the "Proprietary" hammerless boxlock with a Webley rib extension, later called the top screw grip, patented in 1882. *The Field*, the gun and shooting journal of the day, described this new top bolt as "absolute" in its effect, confirming the firm's claim as the "simplest and soundest" in existence.

Based upon a W. & C. Scott & Son 1891 catalog and the 1914 green Webley & Scott catalog, the 410 bore was not available prior to World War I. After World War I, the 410 bore finally became available in the "Proprietary" boxlock, then called the Model 400, with the top screw grip bolt. There were three different grades—I, II, III—defined by quality of engraving and wood. The Model 300, made with a Greener cross bolt, and the Model 500, a 12-bore game gun, were not produced in 410 bore. The Model 600, introduced in 1927, was a lower grade boxlock without ejectors or a rib extension and was in production until 1946. This model was available also in the 410 bore.

Between 1920 and 1940, 128 410-bore double guns were made in either the "Proprietary" Model 400 with ejectors or the Model 600 without [1]. Interestingly, a 1939 off-white Webley & Scott catalog and price list did not list a 410 bore as available in any of these shotgun models. However, the Stoeger 1932 (No. 18) catalog shows the 410 bore available in the "Proprietary" Model 400 in three grades. The 410 was not available in the sidelock guns, most of which appeared under the name "W. & C. Scott & Son." After World War II, Webley & Scott introduced, in 1947, the Model 700 series, and one 410 is recorded as having been built in this model in 1967.

The Model 800, identical to the Model 700 with decorative sideplates, and the Model 900, a Beretta-like over/under, were never available in the 410 bore [2]. After 1967, it appears they never again made a double 410.

After 1910 and through the 1970s, Webley & Scott made single-barrel guns in 410 bore. Finally, in the 1950s and 1960s, they made a number of "diminutive bolt-action" 410s that were researched in the archives and noted below.

When Webley & Scott discontinued shotguns in 1979, a reformed W. & C. Scott Ltd., under new corporate control, resumed the manufacture of quality sidelock and boxlock double guns in 1980, but none are recorded in the 410. Furthermore, they again began to produce actions and barrels "in the white" for the "trade."

The Original Records

Researching the factory ledgers confirmed the essential accuracy of Crawford and Whatley's "History" regarding the 410-bore data [2]. However, these dusty and dry ledgers have a number of historical morsels worth exploring. Although not cataloged in the 1914 green Webley & Scott booklet, their first 410s, all doubles, were made on the eve of and during World War I.

Serial numbers 90395 and 90396 were paired 26-inch 410 boxlocks made in 1913. SN 91536, also a boxlock, shipped in 1914. Numbers 91851, 93513, and 93514 were shipped between 1915 and 1928. The three latter guns were the A & W model boxlocks with an automatic safety, their highest-grade boxlock of that era. The first of the three was shipped in 1915 while the pair came out sometime between 1919 and 1928 and shipped to Holland & Holland, who regulated and finished the guns and sold them under their own name.

There were five grades of the A & W model. The "1st" was the basic A & W, which was the 29 1/2-inch barrel double 410, SN 91851, shipped during World War I. The pair that went to Holland & Holland is listed in the ledgers as "A & W 2nd." The "2nd" was a higher grade and included "patent tumbler safety catches." The "1st" was catalog priced at £21, the "2nd" at £26. The top grade A & W model was called the "51" and sold for £50. This compared to the highest-grade gun in their inventory, the W. & C. Scott Imperial Premier at £120. The Imperial Premier, then the most expensive gun in the world, was a bar-action Rogers sidelock with ejectors and Whitworth steel barrels. The popular Monte Carlo "B," by comparison, was £41.

The above six were the only 410s recorded in the ledgers encompassing the years 1912 to 1923 (SNs 89047 to 95570). These are the earliest existing detailed records from this firm on the smoothbore.

From 1923 to 1939, they built 114 410s with the first (SN 97568) in 1924 and the last (SN 115034) in 1939. They were all double-barrel Anson & Deeley (A&D) boxlock guns with the single exception of SN 114237, shipped in 1934 to William Evans Company as a double sidelock ejector "2nd quality" with 26-inch barrels and 3-inch chambers.

Of the boxlocks, all were ejector guns with two exceptions, and virtually all were designated as their Proprietary model grade "2." This model, introduced in 1900, had a characteristic "top screw grip" and came in three grades. The "3rd" grade was plain without engraving, the "2nd" had full coverage engraving, and the "1st" was even more elaborate.

The grade "2" price was £22, similar to the lowest grade A & W boxlock in 1914.

The two non-ejector 410 guns were the Model 600, and, therefore, did not have a rib extension or the patented "top screw grip." Twenty-five were 26-inch barrel doubles and 89 were 28-inch guns. All of the 113 boxlock guns were chambered for 2 1/2-inch cartridges.

The majority of guns were shipped to well-known gunmakers such as Churchill, Holland & Holland, William Evans, Westley Richards, Army-Navy, and Watson. Interestingly, one was shipped to Woodward in 1924 and another to Rigby in 1931. These firms regulated and decorated the guns, put their name and number on them and sold them as their own. This was

Photo 1: Two views of a "Deluxe" bolt 410, a very rare gun.

Paul Goodwin photo ∨

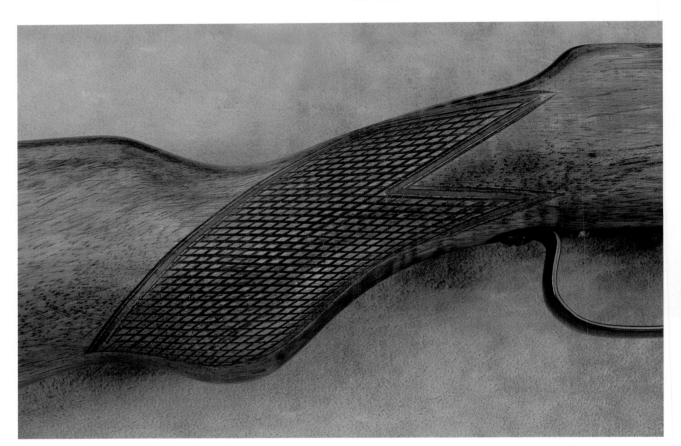

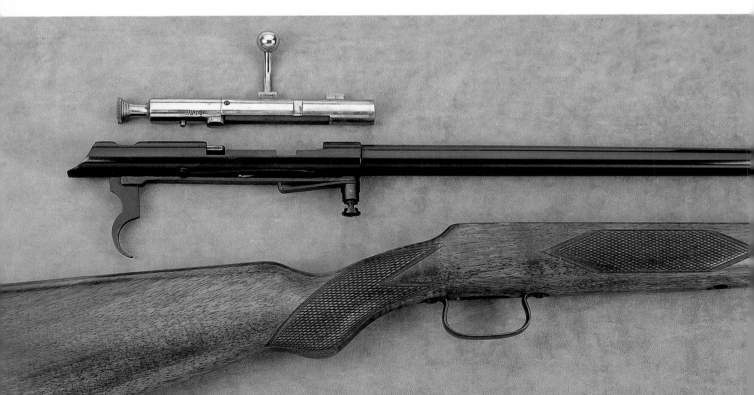

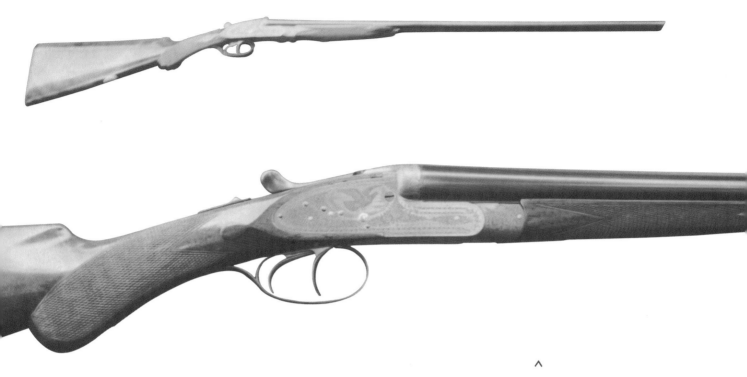

Photos 2 & 3: Two poor quality photos of an important 410, SN 78614.

Paul Goodwin photo

common practice in Great Britain during the first three-quarters of the 20th century, with Webley & Scott supplying actions, barrels, and complete guns to the "trade"—truly a gunmaker's gunmaker.

A relatively small minority of these 119 410 boxlock guns carried the Webley & Scott, Ltd. name and number. A few did though and were shipped to wholesale and retail dealers such as C.B. Vaughan and Hoffman Arms who sold them to the public. The fact that only a minority of all of the 410s built had the Webley name, and of these, many went abroad to colonies, explains why so few are surfacing today on the resale market. The barrels corroded with mercury salts and the actions rusted with humidity in the various colonies of the tropics and subtropics. However, when one does appear for sale, it is usually in pristine condition, lovingly cared for by a single long-term owner.

Another 410 (SN 114155) was shipped as an A&D boxlock, a 26-inch double-barrel gun, with one barrel 410 smoothbore and the other barrel a 250-caliber rook rifle. This was sent to William Evans and sold as an Evans gun.

From 1939 to 1967, no additional 410s are recorded. In 1967, SN 137990 was exported to "Service Armament." It was

the only Model 700 built as a 410, an A&D boxlock with 28-inch barrels, 3-inch chambers, and a beavertail forend.

Neither the Deluxe Model 701, built from 1978 to 1980, nor the even higher-grade Model 702, built from 1971 to 1979, was built in the 410 bore.

Two additional 410s appeared from the firm under the W.C. Scott name. Serial number 103057 is an A&D boxlock ejector with 26-inch barrels. Serial number 103058 is a bar-action side-lock Rogers action, a "2nd quality" ejector, also with 26-inch barrels. These two consecutive numbers are in the sequence of a 1925 timeframe. However, these guns were "dispatched" in 1946, destination unknown. It is likely they were sent to another gunmaker and, thus, never appeared publicly as a W.C. Scott gun. Time may prove otherwise.

Including the 410 smoothbore/250-caliber rook rifle ensemble, 123 double 410s are found in the records. This differs from Crawford and Whatley's *History* in which they recorded 128 Model 400 (Proprietary) with ejectors or Model 600 without ejectors from 1920 to 1940. I was unable to reconcile the difference. Two additional small-bore stories emerge from the records.

The Bolt Action 410

There appears to have been two "bolt-action" 410s. The first was a single-barrel semi-hammerless ejector "bolt action," first built just after World War I. From 1921 (SN 4700) to 1928 (SN 14799), 159 semi-hammerless bolt-action Webley & Scott 410s were built. From 1928 (SN 14800) to 1949 (SN 24799) an additional 335 bolt-action 410s were built. None are recorded thereafter. These 494 single-barrel bolt-action guns were generally used for pest control or as a youngster's first gun. Information on the precise action type remains to be identified.

The second "bolt-action" 410 was a true bolt action and was introduced, according to Chris Dunn, in the early 1950s [3]. No records had been retained on these guns until 1967, at which time Britain required an individual to have a government-issued Shotgun Certificate to own the bolt action or any shotgun.

From 1967 to 1976, at which time the gun was discontinued, approximately 13,227 were recorded (SNs 50000 to 63227) although not all serial numbers were used. This suggests that, including years from the early 1950s to 1967, between 20,000 and 30,000 were made. Their ubiquity on today's resale market would support that.

Photo 4: A rare Webley & Scott 410 under the rarely applied "Webley & Scott, Ltd." name. A large majority of Webley & Scott 410s were sent to other makers who applied their own names. This is a "proprietary" Model 400, SN 98543.

G. Allan Brown photo ∨

The gun has a tapered 25 1/2-inch fully choked barrel chambered for a 2 1/2-inch shell and a breech stock with an uncheckered grip. This was primarily an agricultural gun. From 1966 through 1972, a "Sportsman" model was produced, according to Dunn [4]. This gun, numbered from 1 to 1755, had a two-cartridge magazine in the wood under the bolt, resulting in a three-shot ensemble. With No. 6 shot, the gun patterns with 77 pellets in a 30-inch circle at 40 yards. *The History of W. & C. Scott Gunmakers* describes this gun as "rugged and sound" at an "extremely low price and using the most economical gauge of ammunition." This three-shot magazine gun was produced for both 2 1/2–inch and 3-inch cartridges, nitro proofed to five tons per square inch pressure.

A "deluxe" version was made according to Richard Gallyon, who was a gunmaker apprentice at Webley & Scott in that timeframe. According to a 1956 Webley brochure, this is characterized by a "copy turned" walnut stock and a hand-checkered and polished grip and fitted with a heel plate (Photo 1). Gallyon explained that for every 50 to 100 standard guns, the company would run one "deluxe" version, resulting in a very small number of existing "deluxe" guns.

The Garden Gun

A second story is the "No 3 Bore Garden Guns" built from 1954 to October 17, 1974. This was a 9-mm-caliber smoothbore with a rimfire cartridge filled with "dust shot." According to the 1968 green Webley & Scott catalog, these cartridges were "useful for destroying rats … with a minimum of damage to the structure." It was a single-barrel bolt action, identical to the 410. It had a "robust" 24 1/2-inch cylinder-choked barrel and a one-piece birch stock. The No. 3 rimfire cartridge has a "special" paper tube, which separates from the metal head on firing. This paper tube

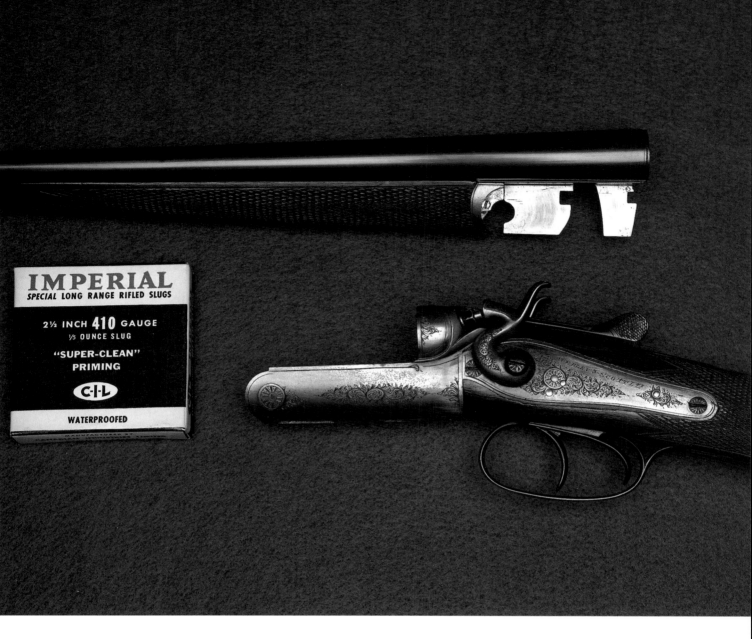

travels intact through the bore and then upon emergence from the muzzle, disintegrates, with the metal head remaining to be ejected by the bolt. "Unconventional functioning," boasts the Webley *History* [4]. They were proofed to 3-1/2 tons.

Prior to World War II, a number of inexpensive continental 9-mm guns with bolt actions and folding barrels were imported into England for self-defense and pest control. The serial numbers before 1967 have not been retained, but records from 1967 (SN 13600) to 1974 (SN 18855) indicate that over 18,000 guns were built.

A parallel but earlier story of the 9-mm or 36-caliber smoothbore was seen in the Model 36 Winchester. This was a single-shot bolt-action gun made from 1919 to 1927 with an 18-inch single barrel. It shot a blackpowder rimfire cartridge, both "ball and shot." Approximately 25,000 were made and were especially popular in Europe and South America but are almost never seen today.

Photo 5: A back-action hammer double smoothbore 410, SN 83491.

Glenn Campbell photo

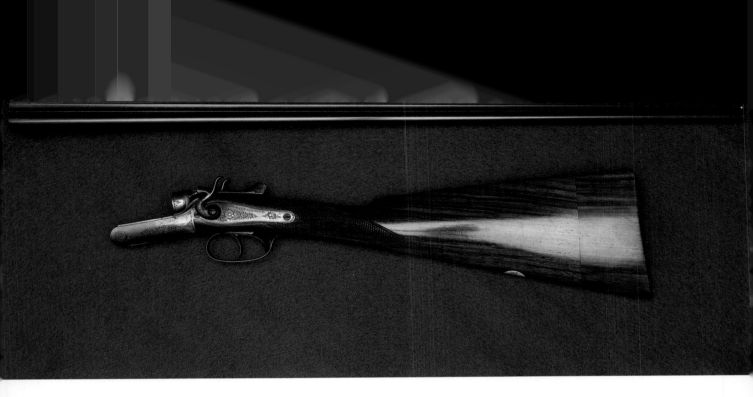

This gun is equivalent in bore diameter to the centerfire 36-gauge double smoothbores made rarely by Churchill, Bland, E.M. Reilly, and Greener prior to World War II for the "collector" (see Photos 1 and 2 in Chapter 2).

Postscript

Based upon the W. & C. Scott & Son 1891 catalog and the Webley & Scott 1914 gun catalog, together with the *History of W. & C. Scott Gunmakers* and the original records, a double 410 was not made until shortly before World War I, and then only in a boxlock action with the above-noted two exceptions.

An additional exception may be a W. & C. Scott 410 "Monte Carlo B" sidelock (SN 78614) with 28-inch barrels, double triggers, and 3-inch chambers. The barrels have a double under bolt and a square-configured cross bolt as the top fastener. It has been proofed according to the 1904 rules of blackpowder proof with no subsequent nitro proofing. The steel barrels have been re-blued and the chambers lengthened to 3 inches. The serial number places it in a 1909 to 1911 manufacturing range with the Rogers action. It is not a rook or high-velocity rifle conversion because the firm never made one on the Rogers sidelock (Photos 2 and 3).

This would be a unique gun except for the fact that the serial number cannot be confirmed because the 78000 serial number register "has vanished." This is indeed unfortunate for the gun appears to be an authentically original 410 with one caveat. That is, although nitro proofing of barrels was not mandatory until 1925, the firm "regularly" submitted for nitro proof all their sidelocks after 1900.

A typical example of a Model 400 Webley & Scott 410 boxlock, SN 98543, was manufactured in 1924 (Photo 4). It is characterized by automatic ejectors, splinter forend, straight grip

Photo 6: Full view of SN 83491 ∧ with a stock extension—a one-of-a-kind 410.

Glen Campbell photo

checkered butt stock, and 3-inch chambers. The gun now has 90 percent case colors. This gun is grade 2 and was originally shipped with 2 1/2-inch chambers and 28-inch barrels. It is fascinating to note that it was shipped to Mr. C.B. Vaughan, a gun retailer, who purchased seven guns (SNs 98542 to 98548) all in 410 bore. Guns SN 98539 to 98541, also Model 400 410s with ejectors and 28-inch barrels, were shipped in 1924 to Hoffman Arms Co., another retail firm.

An existing second example is number 98914, a 410 boxlock with ejectors and 26-inch barrels reproofed to 3-inch chambers. It is a 1924 Model 400 gun.

A third example of a "Webley & Scott, Ltd." boxlock with ejectors is a Model 400, grade 2, SN 110416, completed in 1925 and shipped in 1931. It has double triggers, splintered forend, and a checkered butt. The 3-inch chambers were probably a later change. Two additional Model 400 410s have surfaced in the resale market, SNs 110362 and 110390, with ejectors and double triggers.

A unique 410 hammer double Webley & Scott, SN 83491, with nearly full coverage scroll engraving appeared in the first decade of the 20th century (Photos 5 and 6). No other hammer 410 has been reported in the records available.

A Premier back-action hammer miniature 410 W. & C. Scott gun with 2-inch chambers was said to have been completed in 1921. This gun cannot be verified because the serial number cannot be obtained.

Summary

This firm made a large number of quality boxlock 410s. However, very few are accounted for. The twofold reasons were stated earlier but warrant repeating. Many were sent to the colonies in India and Africa between the wars from whence to never return or even survive by virtue of human use and environmental abuse. Secondly, over 80 percent of their 410 production consisted of complete guns "in-the-white" or blued with or without engraving, sent to such firms as Churchill, Holland & Holland, William Evans, Rigby, Army-Navy, Watson, etc. These firms then numbered, named, and sold the 410s as their own after they "shot and regulated" them.

Just how good are the Webley & Scott 410s made from 1920 to 1940?

In 1932, Webley's lowest grade boxlock was $225. This was economically nearly equivalent to the Parker CHE grade at $236.50 and the L.C. Smith Crown Grade at $248.95. The highest grade Winchester Model 21 with all the options including single trigger, ventilated rib, and selective ejectors was $120.50.

The year 1932 was deep into the Great Depression and the money paid for a product reflected both free market forces and product usefulness and quality. Therefore, there are good reasons to believe that the least expensive Webley 410 boxlock was a very high quality gun.

In fact, when an American examines such a gun today, side-by-side with comparably priced American guns of 1932 as noted above, one is shocked and dismayed to see that the Webley is indeed better built. One would easily be persuaded that the quality of wood and checkering, the metal-to-wood fit, the engraving, the finish of the internal metal surfaces and locks are superior or at least equal in the Webley. In fact, John Wilkes, the London gunmaker, opines that the Webley & Scott gun was the "best built smoothbore."

This, of course, does not necessarily translate into today's financial values because rarity, condition, and American history, in significant measure, determine present "collector" value.

It would be interesting for those readers who have a Deluxe Smith or an A-1 Special Parker to compare them to Webley's top gun, the W.C. Scott & Son Imperial Premier grade. In 1932, the Imperial Premier was $1200. The A-1 Special was $875.60, and the Deluxe was $1,203.30. How does the quality of these great guns compare? By the way, none of these grades was originally built in the 410 bore.

Webley & Scott, Ltd. References

1. Crawford, J.A. and P.G., Whatley, *The History of W. & C. Scott Gunmakers*, 2nd Ed., 1985, Rowland Ward of Bruton Street Limited.
2. Factory ledgers at Harris & Sheldon corporate headquarters 1990.
3. Dunn, Chris, Webley & Scott historian, personal correspondence 2001.
4. *History of Webley* 1790-1968, a company produced monograph.

CHAPTER TWENTY ONE

WESTLEY RICHARDS & COMPANY

Although Theophilus Richards' family originated a gunmaking business in the late 1700s, his son, William Westley Richards, who began a gunsmith business in Birmingham in 1812, must be credited as the founder of one of the greatest firms in gunmaking history, a firm very much alive today and thriving. In 1813, William helped petition the British Parliament to establish the Birmingham Proof House. He established, in 1815, a London outlet on Bond Street. William Bishop, the "Bishop of Bond Street," superintended this branch's great success until he died in 1871 [1]. This firm's patent achievements were to British gunmaking what John Browning's were to American and European gunmaking: a continual cascade of gunmaking genius. Their first patent in 1821 was an improved percussion lock of the original Forsyth detonating system. For the next 99 years, until their last patent in 1919, they recorded 100 patents, many of seminal importance to gunmaking of the 19th and 20th centuries [2,3].

History

Westley Richards, the son of William, took command in 1855. While William was a man of charity and exhibited the spirit of noblesse oblige, the son was a legendary Dicksonian scrooge who was a hard and successful taskmaster. He oversaw the conversion to the breechloaders and the development of the world-

renowned "falling block" breech-loading rifle, the forerunner of the British Martini-actioned rifles. Before retiring in 1872, he nursed the doll's head top bolt to perfection. This was the first and remains one of the three types of top bolts in current use. Many side-by-side shotguns and rifles use some form of this system today in order to maintain a tight fit between the barrels and the standing breech of the action.

They began the doll's head development in 1858 and completed its final version in 1871. This top bolt is, in essence, an expanded end of the barrel extension that interlocks with a machined groove at the top of the action body. This fit counteracts the detonating forces that would tend to separate the barrels from the action along the standing breech. Parker and Lefever modified the doll's head bolt configuration to control forces that would otherwise cause a loosening of action and barrel at the breech edge. They did this by redesigning the doll's head to prevent the groove in the action body to be forcibly and permanently expanded. Lefever retained the Westley Richards horizontal cross bolt; Parker did not. Both American guns enormously benefited from this example of English gunmaking evolution.

John Deeley became managing director in 1872 and supervised the most revolutionary change in gunmaking since Forsyth's 1807 percussion ignition invention. It was in 1875 that

William Anson and Deeley patented the boxlock action breech-loading hammerless gun. This action reduced the heart of the gun's operating parts from 22 in the sidelock to three main limbs: a tumbler with sear and sear springs, a mainspring, and a cocking rod. The fall of the barrels cocked the tumbler. The cocking principle depends upon leverage created by the barrels as they pivot on the hinge. Upgrades in the safety tumbler, cocking, and cartridge ejection followed. In 1884, they developed the first forend cartridge ejector [4].

Finally, Deeley and Leslie Taylor patented the fabled "drop-lock" in 1897. This allowed the conventional boxlock action, now mounted on a steel plate, to be hand inserted into or removed from the base of the action body. The lock, consisting of the cocking lever, sear, tumbler, and mainspring, attaches to a removable steel plate rather than to the action frame. Being held in place by a sliding or hinged plate rather than by permanent pins provides a great advantage. When secured by pins, the pins pass through the entire action body to secure the frame from one side to the other. The absence of traverse pinholes through the tumbler and sear axles gives greater strength to the drop boxlock frame than that found in the fixed boxlock or sidelock. The Westley Richards "drop-lock" inspired the detachable sidelock developed by Holland & Holland and modified by Westley Richards in the second decade of the 20th century (Photo 1).

Both the fixed boxlock and the drop-boxlock actions have remained essentially unchanged for nearly 100 years. For example, the American boxlock side-by-side, such as the Parker, the Ithaca, and the Winchester Model 21, and almost all European side-by-side boxlocks such as the Francotte, have tumbler-sear arrangements identical to the Anson & Deeley action. They differ only in the use of a coiled rather than a V-shaped mainspring. The Prussian-built Charles Daly featured a lengthened water table and an added intercepting or secondary sear. The former improved the gun balance by allowing for a scaled-down frame and the latter enhanced safety.

The purpose of this preamble is to illustrate that all the known and recorded Westley Richards "Best Quality" 410s, built in either drop-lock or sidelock configurations, included all the advanced features of these locks. This firm reached its ultimate zenith in gunmaking evolution prior to World War II. Like the 410s of other great British gunmakers, the Westley Richards "Best" incorporates most or all of the innovations of the prior century.

The Catalogs [5]

By 1902, Westley Richards had a special catalog, "Reliable One Trigger," promoting the single selective trigger and all of the refinements of the late 1800s. They offered gauges 10 through 28 in boxlock, with or without the drop-lock option (detachable boxlock). Another catalog in the first decade of the 1900s details many shotgun types including hammer or hammerless, sidelock or boxlock actions in all grades 10 through 28. No 410s were available.

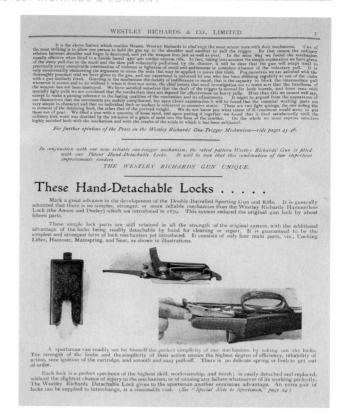

Photo 1: A page from a turn-of-the-19th-century catalog illustrating the "drop lock" and single trigger mechanism.

Glenn Campbell photo

Photo 2: A "boy's" 410 illustration from a post-1924 Westley Richards catalog.

Glenn Campbell photo

While still at 178 New Bond Street during the reign of George V (1910 to 1936), a purple-covered catalog, issued sometime between 1910 to 1913 (by 1914 they had moved to 23 Conduit Street, London), offered the 410 bore in drop-lock or sidelock with ejectors and with double or single selective triggers. WR priced a medium-grade gun up to 65 guineas and charged up to 210 guineas for a "Best"-quality gun. However, there is no public record of a drop-lock 410 being built prior to World War I or of a sidelock 410 prior to World War II.

The Westley Richards '410 Shot Gun and its Cartridge
(continued from previous page).

For occasional use about the place, and for Ladies.
Carefully bored—even grouping and deadly effect.

Light, Handy and well balanced. Chambered for the long cartridge (2½ inches).
A High Grade Gun in miniature, every part proportional in size to its bore.

Extract from "Shooting Times," December 5th, 1925.
"We say that the '410 is an excellent little weapon for the beginner, and has the advantage of being light and registering a minimum of recoil. Yet even the "old hand" need not despise this little gun. . . . . The '410 in its own realms of possibility, is not a gun to be treated with contempt. Its main use is undoubtedly for the training of the young sportsman who will presently exchange it for a heavier weapon. All the same, it is a most useful addition to the gun room if only for the express purpose of keeping down the vermin in the close season."

Henry Sharp in "The Daily Telegraph," December 16th, 1927, says:—
"I have now a '410 Double Hammerless Ejector (Westley Richards), and while by reason of its diminutive size and tiny dose of ⅜oz. shot, no such bags of game can be expected as from larger guns, it is undeniable that the keenest possible satisfaction is to be derived from its shooting. For picking off rabbits stealing about in thick cover such as brambles, briars and brackens, when disturbed by the ferrets, the '410 bore is an admirable little weapon and in such situation on its first trial my gun accounted for Nineteen Rabbits from the first box of Twenty-five cartridges shot away."

. . . . . . ' One of the keepers there was using a four-ten, there were plenty of pigeons about, and he brought down bird after bird which, till I actually witnessed his skill, I had imagined could only have been done with a larger bore. Every other description of game fell to this little gun just the same and he by no means selected his shots. Forthwith I ordered a double four-ten. .
"Hoverer," "Shooting Times," Nov. 19th, 1927.

20 yds.   30 yds.   40 yds.

The Patterns reproduced here illustrate the results of independent tests at 20—30—40 yards in 15-inch Circle with a Westley Richards '410 Bore Gun.

PAGE FIFTEEN

< Photo 3: Ballistics of the 410 cartridge from post-1930 Westley Richards catalog.

Glenn Campbell photo

A green-covered catalog published sometime after 1924 advertised a "boy's" single-barrel top-lever boxlock hammerless 410 with automatic ejectors for £21 (Photo 2). They also advertised a stag-horn-handled, Malacca-covered 410 walking-stick gun for 2-inch cartridges, priced at £3.

A large catalog with green-gray covers and published after 1930 lists a hammerless sidelock ejector shotgun available in the 410. It was triple bolted and priced at £75. Also listed in this catalog were single- and double-barrel Anson & Deeley boxlock hammerless ejectors 410s for 2 1/2-inch cartridges using 3/4-ounce shot. This catalog provided testimonials from the shooters who had shot the 410. These included "nineteen rabbits" with 25 cartridges and "bird after bird." It illustrated 410 cartridge test patterns of a pigeon silhouette showing at least 27 pellet hits at 20 yards, 13 hits at 30 yards, and five hits at 40 yards (Photo 3).

A brown-covered catalog published after 1938, but pre-World War II, lists a boxlock double- or single-barrel 410 with 2 1/2-inch cartridges. The double was available with automatic ejectors for an additional five pounds (Photo 4).

The Ledgers

The Best [6]
The well-kept records are voluminous and the serial numbers/dating system is complex. We spent many hours reviewing the data. A 1995 printout helps provide some order to this complexity:

Westley Richards SINGLE BARREL Hammerless Ejector, '410 Shot Guns
MINIATURES OF OUR BEST GUNS.   ::   ::   Excellent for Rabbits.

SPECIFICATION—Westley Richards Patent Top Lever and Automatic Safety Bolt, Scroll Back Action, Finely Engraved, well figured Walnut Stock, Pistol Grip, Horn Cap to Fore-end, Silver Crest Plate, Superior finish, constructed for the '410 2½in. Cartridges. Weight: about 4⅛lbs. As A Plate IV... £21 . 0 . 0

This weapon is recommended for beginners, also for use round the fields and in the orchards, and, furthermore, it is undoubtedly a weapon which teaches anyone how to shoot. Every shooter will find pleasure in its possession and use.

Westley Richards Special Models of Double Hammerless Shot Guns, '410 bore

Westley Richards Best quality, fixed locks, two triggers, scroll back action, engraved and finished as B Plate IV   Price £45 . 0 . 0

Do.   do.   Plainer finish, line border engraved, plain checker   ...   .   Price £35 . 0 . 0

Do.   do.   as C Plate IV   ...   ...   Price £15 . 15 . 0

If Ejector to either model, £5 Extra.

Weights from 4⅛lbs.

PAGE FOURTEEN

Photo 4: A Westley Richards catalog showing the firm's pre-World War II 410 models. ∧

Glenn Campbell photo

GUN NO.	DATE
624 – 1695	1839-1850
1615 – 3030	Book Binders
1695 – 3591	Book Binders
2060 – 3915	1830 – 1839}
70 - 623	1830 – 1839} Same Book
3592 – 5886	1866 - 1882
3914 – 6920	1839 - 1848
5001 – 6000	1875 - 1882
6921 – 9999	Book Binders
8001 – 9000	1899 - 1906
9001 – 10000	1906 - 1913
10000 – 11000	Book Binders
11001 – 12000	1865 – 1871
13745 – 16000	1883 – 1901
16001 – 18000	1900 – 1924
18001 – 19000	1924 – 1957
19000 -	1957 – Current
39000 – 40000	Magazine Rifles
40001 – 41000	1917 – 1921 – Magazine Rifles
41001 – 43020	1921 – 1955 – Magazine Rifles
T1001 – T2000	1902 - 1905}
G5008 – G5106	1903} Same Book
T2001 – T3000	1905 – 1909
T3001 – T4000	1907 – 1910
T4001 – T5000	1910 – 1912
T5001 – T7000	1912 – 1923
T7001 – T9000	1915 – 1926
T9001 – T11000	1926 – 1938
T11001 – T11787	1935 – 1926
G5200 – G6617	1903 – 1960
O 1001 – O 2000	1914 – 1936
O 2001 – O 2189	1936 – 1950
K36 – K1000	1885 – 1899
K101 – K1214	1899 – 1919
1-323	1853 – 1857

WR recorded no 410s prior to the turn of the 20th century. From 1883 (SN 13745) to 1924 (SN 18019) is a sequence of numbers that designate the "Deluxe" or "Best" or "Highest Quality" shotguns. The firm recorded no 410s in the records during this time. However, during this era they made at least 20 "Best" 28-bore guns, double-barrel and hammerless. Configurations included the bar-action sidelock, the drop-lock boxlock, and the A&D boxlock. Examples include the first "Best" 28 bore (SN 15007), an 1891 hammerless ejector gun, and a "Highest Quality" pair of "one trigger" drop-lock ejector doubles (numbers 15935-36) shipped just before World War I. SN 16000 marks the year 1901; however, the guns were often "allocated" a number long before they were built or shipped.

The next ledger, spanning numbers 16001 to 17000, years 1900 to 1908, lists no 410 guns. The next span, numbers 17001 to 18000, again lists no 410s manufactured.

Suddenly and uniquely, in the next ledger book cataloging "Highest Quality" guns, numbers 18001 to 19000, years 1924 to 1957, there appears a series of six 410 shotguns, SN 18020 through SN 18025. WR made these for "H.H. the Maharaja of Patiala" and shipped them in 1924 and 25. All were identical 28-inch steel double guns with "cylinder"-choked barrels. They had double triggers and the hand-detachable drop-lock actions. The actioner was "Ward," a great name in British craftsmanship.

There was then a span of 30 years before, in 1955, they made the next "Best Quality" 410, a drop-lock, SN 18933. It has a beavertail forend with a single trigger, a pistol grip stock, and a game scene engraved action. It has 28-inch barrels with a ventilated rib. It is one of a pair; the other, a 28-gauge gun, wore SN 18934.

WR built the next "Highest Quality" 410 soon thereafter, SN 18949. It has 24-inch barrels with 3-inch chambers and is built with a beavertail forend and a single trigger. The action is unspecified but it is probably a bar-action sidelock or a drop-lock.

The current ledger, ranging from SN 19001 to SN 19821 and from 1957 to 1995, lists an additional 13 410s. Two are paired with a 28-gauge gun: SN 19342 and SN 19343 (28 gauge), both sidelock guns shipped in 1968, and SN 19520 and SN 19519 (28 gauge) also sidelock guns shipped in 1976. A third 410 is a 410/28-gauge two-barrel ensemble (SN 19784) with a single stock, housing a drop-lock action, which shipped in 1992.

Individual 410s include the first in the 19000 series, SN 19276, a 26-inch gun weighing 4 pounds, 8 ounces and shipped to Abercrombie & Fitch in 1965, action unspecified. The next two 410s are paired (numbers 19293 and 94) sidelock guns with non-selective "one triggers," and also shipped in 1965. SN 19292 is a 28-bore gun and has, in recent years, been matched with SN 19293.

The fourth is the remarkable Homer McCoy sidelock, SN 19321, shipped in 1967. Detailed below, it may well be the finest Westley Richards gun in existence for quality, beauty, rarity, and uniqueness (Photos 5-9).

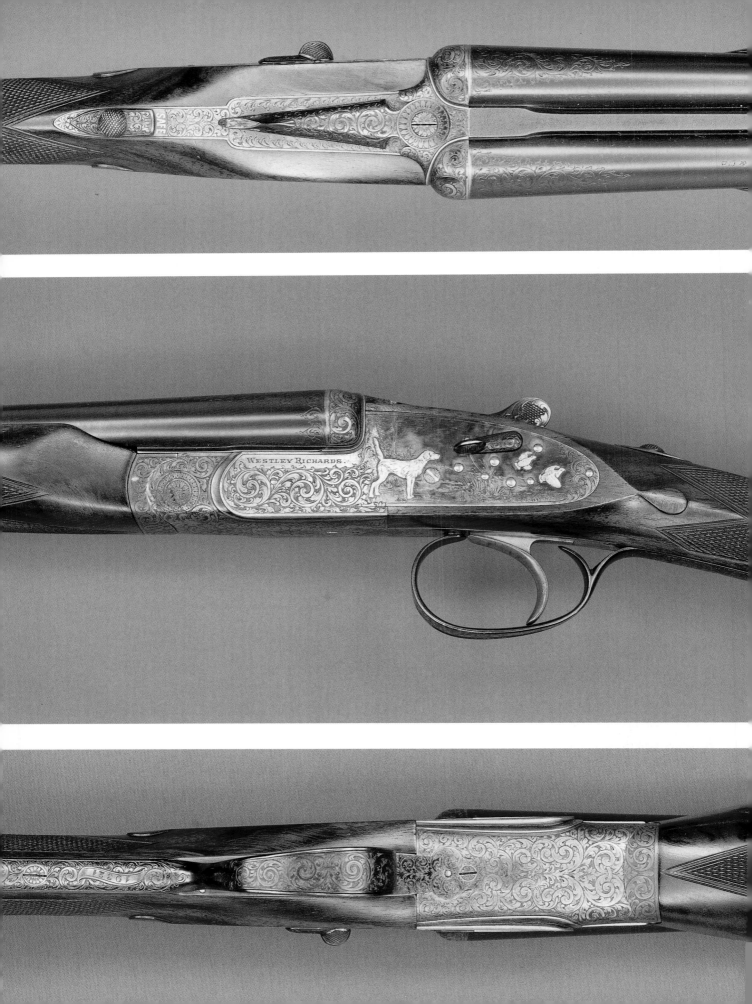

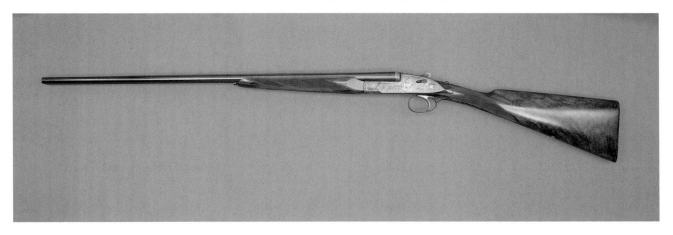

Photos 5-8: Four views of SN 19321, truly a work of art.

Levasheff photos

Photo 9: SN 19321 with Homer McCoy's favorite hunting companion in gold.

G. Allan Brown photo

The next group of 410s, beginning with SN 19725, shipped from 1987 through 1993. The first action is unknown, but all others are "Best" drop-locks with two pairs of 410s, SNs 19790 and 91 and SNs 19802 and 03.

In 1994-95, Westley Richards invested 1.5 million pounds in new computer-controlled machinery, and underwent a marketing and production renaissance to match those of Holland & Holland and Purdey. Westley Richards is making best-quality smoothbores and double rifles and finding a ready market throughout the world, especially in Europe and the United States. They are using precision technology, the most modern metal forgings, and hand finishing. And, like Holland & Holland and Purdey today, are uniquely British. They have no superiors for quality or beauty — Italian, German, Spanish, or American makers notwithstanding.

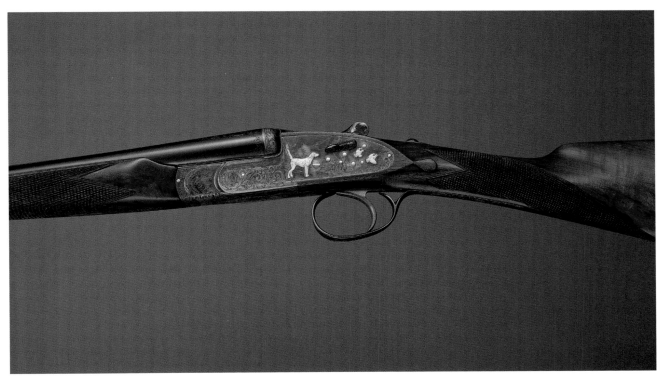

Other 410s

There is a series of guns, beginning in 1902 with SN 7801 and ending in 1945 with SN 10040, that denote a lower-quality gun, and here we see the emergence of Westley Richards' first 410, SN 7867. It is a double-barreled top-lever back-action hammer gun with 28-inch barrels and shipped in 1903. Two more were made in 1907 and 1909, numbers 7987 and 7988, their actions not specified.

WR designated the next series of record books with the letter "T" prefixing the serial number. It begins in 1902 with SN T1001 and ends in 1942 with SN T11787. At least 58 410s were manufactured in this series, almost all A&D boxlock double-barrel guns. The exceptions were a 410/rook rifle combo (SN T11049) in 1935 and a pair of 12-inch-barreled 410 over/under smoothbore pistols (SNs T10750 and 51) made in 1935 for the Charles Lancaster firm.

The ledger books include what appears to be the first "T"-series 410s built in 1909-11, numbers T3031-32-33-34, and the last in 1942, SN T11356. The A&D 410s are almost evenly divided between ejector and non-ejector guns.

Existing A&D 410s includes SN T11036 with 26-inch barrels and 2 1/2-inch chambers, manufactured in 1935. Also included is SN 11129 with double triggers and a horn butt plate, listed in 1936. The cost of these two guns is listed in a post-1930, pre-World War II catalog at 26 pounds with ejectors.

Two ejector guns, numbers T11136 and T11146 from 1938-39, were described as "Southgate ejectors," to be distinguished from the usual ejector system of the period, the "Baker." Virtually all of the "T"-series 410s are A&D boxlocks and many

were exported. For example, SN T3033 was shipped to "Buenos Ayres" in 1911.

Three additional serial number nomenclatures of guns occur in the ledgers. These include a "G" series from number 5008 to number 6617, manufactured from 1903 to 1960; an "O" series beginning with number 1001 to 2189, from 1914 to 1950; and a "K" series beginning at SN 36 and ending at SN 1214, made from 1885 to 1919. These three series of guns, in which the serial number begins with a designated letter, contain no 410s.

The five-digit number series, SN 13745 to SN 19803, from 1883 to 1993, represent Westley Richards' "Highest Quality" guns.

The last serial number nomenclature to be analyzed began in 1830 and extended to 1945. It starts at number 1 and ends at number 11000. This series includes all guns Westley Richards made from 1830 to 1885 and a large percentage of guns made from 1885 to 1945. It includes all conceivable variations of smoothbores and rifles built in those eras.

Several ledgers are exclusive after 1875 for A&D boxlocks. For example, noted are SN 3592 through SN 5886, from 1866 to the 1880s, and the "B" guns in which the letter nomenclature precedes the numbers, from SN 5887 through SN 7000, manufactured in 1882 to 1902. In these various series of guns, there are no 410s recorded until 1903 (SN 7867). This gun was followed by numbers 7987 and 7988 in the first decade of the 20th century as mentioned above.

Thereafter, these various series of ledgers record no further 410s until 1938. In 1938, WR made a pair of guns, SN 9996 and 97, single-barrel side-lever-opener 410s. These were followed in 1939 by another pair, SNs 9959 and 60, also single-barrel 410s. (Note the out-of-sequence serial number regarding years.)

The next and final group of 410s in this series was made from 1942 through 1945. These were a total of nine A&D double 410s, all non-ejector, double-triggered smoothbores, numbers 10026 through 10034. The first one was made for a "Lady Belker." All were 27- or 28-inch guns with the exception of one, SN 10027, which had 30-inch barrels.

Thus, it is clear that although Westley Richards built many thousands of guns over the years, very few were built in the smoothbore 410.

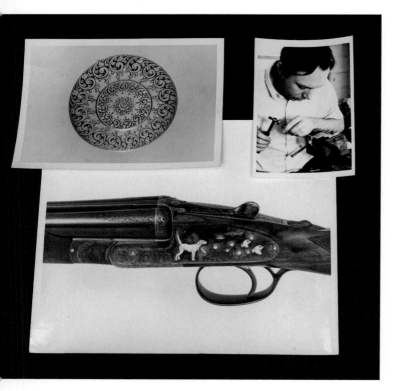

<

Photo 10: Lynton McKenzie engraving the Homer McCoy gun, SN 19321.

Glenn Campbell photo

The photograph shows a magazine feature titled "THE MAKING OF A MASTER ENGRAVER" with inset text:

> The uphill struggle of Lynton McKenzie to reach his goal of absolute mastery of the gun engraver's art.
> By Homer McCoy

Known 410s

Drop-Locks

Based upon known 410s and the available factory records, all "Best" sidelock and drop-lock 410 guns were built after World War I. Walter A. and Simon Clode, the late 20th-century father-son managing tandem, reported that factory records show that the only 410 drop-locks built before World War II were actioned by Ward and barreled in 1924 with consecutive serial numbers from 18020 through 18025. All six guns had scalloped frames, 28-inch barrels, double triggers, matted ribs, 2 1/2-inch chambers, straight stocks, splinter forends, and were made at the highest or "Deluxe" grade. These are the drop-lock guns built for and sent to the Indian Maharaja of Patiala in 1924, mentioned earlier. All six have resurfaced and are now in collector hands in the United States and Great Britain. These are the only "Best" original 410s built before World War II in any lock configuration.

Westley Richards refurbished and added 3-inch chambers to a seventh drop-lock 410, SN 18933, in conjunction with a drop-lock 28 bore, SN 18934, for William Jaqua and returned them to him in the late 1970s. This "Best Quality" gun pair was originally made for an American in 1955. They had pistol-grip stocks, beavertail forends, ventilated ribs, game-scene engraving, and single triggers. They were sent to Philadelphia, Pennsylvania, with extra sets of locks. The eighth and final "Best" in the SN 18000 range is number 18949, and the particulars will remain unknown until the gun comes to public light.

Additional "Best" drop-locks are in the 19000 serial number range and include the two recent pairs mentioned earlier, SNs 19790 and 91, and SNs 19802 and 03, shipped from 1987 to 1993. The Clode's were building at least six more drop-lock 410s and were offering them with an extra set of locks for £15,500 as of 1994. They promised to be of the highest quality.

A ninth drop-lock 410, SN 17127, was originally shipped in 1910 as a 300-caliber rifle. It was subsequently re-bored and re-proofed to a 410-gauge, 26-inch-barrel smoothbore for

∧ **Photo 11:** A *Guns and Ammo* feature on SN 19321.

G. Allan Brown photo

WALT DISNEY PRODUCTIONS

500 SO. BUENA VISTA ST. • BURBANK, CALIFORNIA 91503 • CABLE ADDRESS: DISNEY

3856 Dixie Canyon Ave.
Sherman Oaks, Calif.91403
Oct.14, 1968

Dear Lynton:

You must accept my apology for the lateness of this thank you
note for the gold-plated and engraved oil flask. It is a gem
and I shall treasure it.

The reason for my tardy reply should be understandable to all
shooting people. I returned this past week-end from a month of
bird-shooting (woodcock and ruffed grouse)(partridge) in Northern
Minnesota and Canada. During this absence, mail piled up at home,
including the gift from you.

The .410 proved a deadly little gun on both woodcock and
partridges in the thick coverts, although I didn't use it as
much as a Westley Richards 28-bore that has been a long-time
favorite of mine.

I am having the GUNS & AMMO Magazine people mail you a copy
of their new gun annual in which both the W.R. 410 and the
Purdey are pictured and described. I have an article in the
book beginning on page 136. I apologize for certain editing
errors in the text, such as confusing .410 with 28-bore.

You will find your W.R. specimen and Ken Hunt's Purdey in black-
and white on pages 138 and 140; both guns in color on page 192,
with descriptions on page 190, and again in black-and-white on
page 313.

The captions on page 190 give rather loose values on the two
guns. I refused to evaluate the worth of the guns for the editors,
considering the matter of price a personal and private matter,
but the editors apparently went to another source for their
figures.

Sincerely,

Homer McCoy

Homer McCoy

Photo 12: Interesting correspondence to McKenzie, one of the 20th century's greatest engravers, about SN 19321.

Glenn Campbell photo

<

3-inch cartridges. It is game-scene engraved with gold inlays, a single selective trigger, partial beavertail forend, straight stock with steel toe and heel plates, and a miniature frame. At one time the butt plate was horn. The action now has a hinged floor plate with fixed locks. Although not an original 410, it is nonetheless a very interesting and attractive gun.

Sidelocks

All "Best" 410 sidelocks are post World War II and are in the 19000 serial number range. Several have surfaced for public scrutiny. Number 19252 is the last of five consecutively numbered sidelock guns from 10 through 410 bore. It has double triggers and hand-detachable sidelocks. The scroll-engraved action is by the Brown Brothers, a firm noted for gun engraving. The chopper lump barrels are 26 inches long and the gun weighs 5 pounds, 2 ounces. The stock is straight English and the forend is a splinter form.

Another known 410 is SN 19293 and is matched with a 28 bore, consecutively numbered. This 410 sidelock gun is smothered in seven inlays of gold by Geoffrey Casbard. Originally, it had a non-selective single trigger but now it has double triggers. A straight stock with checkered butt completes the gun. The pair once went through the hands of Bruce Hunt, a gun-marketing entrepreneur from Georgia, whose influence in the 1970s and early 1980s on shotgun collecting as an investment was enormous.

A third sidelock, SN 19321, was built for a Hollywood personality, Homer McCoy. Shipped November 7, 1967, it is truly a work of art (Photos 5-9). It has hand-detachable locks, single trigger, modified beavertail forend, and a straight stock of remarkable walnut. Lynton McKenzie, one of the greatest gun engravers of the 20th century, did the engraving. He was originally from Australia, lived and worked in Great Britain for a time, and spent the last years of his life in Arizona (Photo 10). Delicate, extremely fine scroll engraving surrounds six gold inlays—two dogs and four birds—of the most exquisite detail and authenticity based upon the gun owner's own dog. The inner surfaces of the lock plates are extraordinarily damascened, and portions of the locks themselves are scroll engraved. This gun was featured in the 1969 and 1973 *Guns & Ammo* Annuals. McKenzie turned the oil bottle into "an object of art" by gold plating and scroll engraving it (Photos 11-12).

The fourth known sidelock, SN 19343, was built in 1962 and has 26-inch barrels with 3-inch chambers. It has double triggers, a straight stock, beavertail forend and concave rib. The locks are hand detachable.

The other 410 sidelock guns, all in the 19000 serial number range, remain hidden in gun cabinets around the world. Through 1993, Westley Richards had made 21 "Best" 410s in drop- or sidelock configuration. More have been produced since then, principally drop-lock models according to Simon Clode, and are priced very reasonably for a British Best. Given this firm's recent technical and marketing resurrection, it will almost certainly thrive well into the 21st century.

Like the 410s of great British gunmakers, virtually all the side-lock 410s incorporate most or all of the innovations of the prior century. Furthermore, they were built after World War II and mostly for the American market.

A Falling Block Rifle-410 Conversion [7]

An interesting historical sidelight is the "Falling Block" rifle manufactured by Westley Richards from 1872 to 1929. This gun was based upon the Martini falling block action bolted to the Henry barrel. This was known as the Martini Henry rifle, first produced for British troops in 1869. The few guns made under the 1872 patent, the first of six patents, were rook rifles of 300 or 360 caliber. Three known to exist are numbers 1686, 20, and 449. Number 449 has been re-bored as a 410 shotgun and it sold at a London auction in 1992. All three guns have miniature actions with an underlever separate from the trigger guard. Identical to the drawings of the first patent, the second patent of 1873 was almost entirely made in the 450 caliber, with approximately 300 recorded. There are no known guns with the third 1876 patent. Over 1000 were made on each of the fifth patent of 1881 and the sixth patent of 1897. These guns were made through to 1929 in the 450 or 300 caliber. It would be of interest if any reader possesses such a rifle now converted to the 410 smoothbore like SN 449.

Westley Richards & Company References

1. Carey, A.M., *English, Irish & Scottish Firearms Makers,* Arms & Armour Press, 1967, London.
2. Boothroyd, Geoffrey, 1990, *STCM,* June 18-July 4.
3. Tate, Douglas, *Birmingham Gunmakers,* Safari Press, Inc., Long Beach, CA, 1997.
4. Akehurst, Richard, *Game Guns & Rifles,* G. Bell & Sons, Ltd., 1969.
5. Author's review of original catalogs.
6. Author's review of factory records.
7. Kirton, Jonathan, *The British Falling Block Breechloading Rifle from 1865,* 1985, Armory Publications, Tacoma, WA.

WATSON BROS.

This firm must be considered one of the greatest, if not the greatest, of small-bore shotgun makers in the history of smoothbores. It was started in 1875 at 4 Pall Mall, London, by the father of the Watson brothers. The latter were given the firm by their father in 1885, renaming it Watson Bros. In 1895, they moved to 29 Old Bond Street. Another move in 1930 found them at 13A Pall Mall, and in 1935 they were absorbed by the London gunmaker Grant & Lang. Eventually, after World War II, Chubbs bought the records and the name from Atkin, Grant & Lang, and in 1987 the firm once again became independent. It was bought from Chubbs by a former Purdey barrel maker, Michael Louca.

Louca has begun to manufacture only best quality bar-action double guns, starting with serial number 19980.

The Records

Like so many old handwritten records of British and American firms, the serial numbers and dates are often out of sequence. The serial number from Watson's first gun in 1884 is SN 1012. However, the earliest date is 1880, with SN 1276.

Similarly, the first 410 by serial number is SN 1493, recorded in 1883. The two earliest by date are SN 1494, recorded December 29, 1882, and SN 1583, a "double," dated December 4, 1882.

SN 1493 is an under-lever hammer gun with a 22-inch single barrel. SN 1494 is a top-lever ("T.S.") breech-opening hammer gun.

The next recorded 410 from 1883, number 1495, was a border engraved gun. It had a 26-inch single barrel with an exposed hammer ("solid striker").

The fifth 410 was a single-barrel side lever, SN 1560, made in 1885. The next 410 was a double gun, SN 1562, made in 1885. It was the first Anson & Deeley (A&D) boxlock top-lever gun and was recorded as "engraved." The next, number 1563, also in 1885, was a "plain" A&D under-lever gun.

Over the next 10 years, they made approximately 42 410s in different configurations: top-, side-, or under-lever; Damascus or steel barrels from 22 to 26 inches long; single or double guns; "engraved" or "plain"; straight or "pistol" grip stocks. These encompass serial numbers from SN 1576 to SN 1871, ending in 1895.

In 1895, the serial numbers jumped to the 4000 range, entirely bypassing the 2000 and 3000 ranges. In this sequence, SN 4580 and SNs 4612 through 4617, all 410s, are dated respectively 1895 and 1896. The latter guns are designated "collector guns," the first use of such a historically important term. These were single-barrel side-lever guns used to collect small birds and animals for the taxidermist. Such a single-barrel gun was priced at 1 to 2.5 pounds compared to 4 to 7 pounds for a double gun.

From 4580 to the end of the 4000 range, they manufactured 29 more 410s, either top-lever doubles or side-lever single "collector" guns.

The 5000 range, beginning approximately 1896 and ending 1899, records 91 410s. These included the third A&D hammerless boxlock (SN 5307) and the first A&D 410 with Baker ejectors (SNs 5475-5476), paired 27-inch double 410s. All prior guns, with two exceptions, appear to have been hammer guns (see SNs 1562 & 1563). Interestingly, the price for the plain hammer top-lever double was 4 to 7 pounds compared to the A&D hammerless non-ejector at 10 to 11 pounds and the A&D ejector at 16 pounds.

The 6000 range, beginning in 1899 and ending in 1906, saw the production of 60 more 410s. Twenty-two were A&D hammerless boxlocks, 24 top-lever hammer doubles, and 13 single-barrel side-lever "collector" guns. SN 6999 was an A&D non-ejector 410 made in 1906, selling for 8 pounds.

The 7000 range from 1906 to 1919 records 66 410s. This includes SN 7000, an A&D boxlock Baker ejector, at 14 pounds. This also includes SN 7713, an A&D boxlock with the first

Photo 1: A classically engraved 1920's 410 with an A&D ejector action, SN 8472.

Glenn Campbell photo ⌄

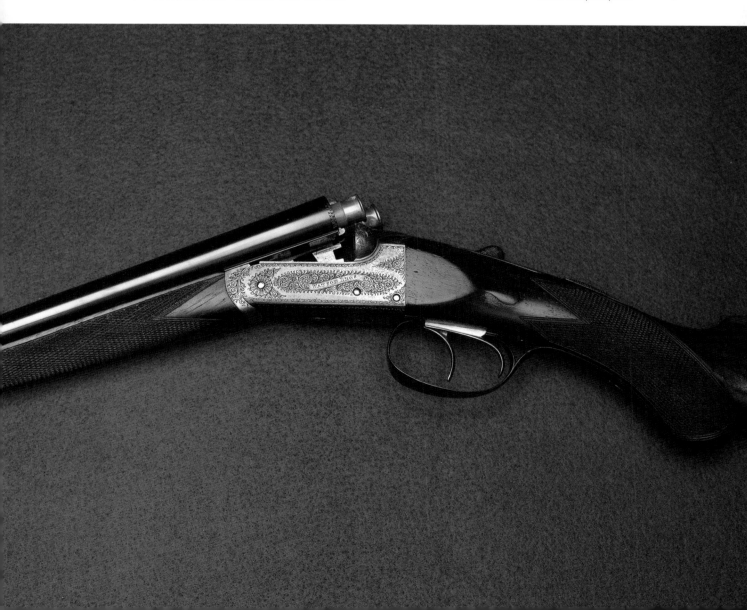

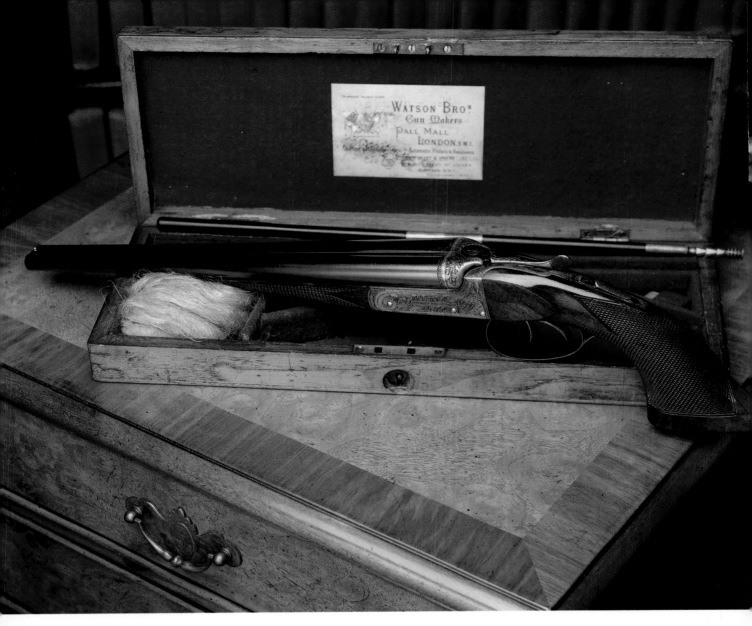

Southgate ejector system, made in 1914. Thirty-eight were A&D doubles, five were top-lever hammer doubles, and 23 were side-lever single-barrel "collector" guns.

The 8000 range, beginning in 1920 and ending in 1928, saw the appearance of the Watson "walking stick" 410. They also introduced in the 410 bore the BSA bolt action, the folding stock gun, and the "Game Getter" gun. The latter was a 410/22-caliber smoothbore/rifle ensemble with the first (SN 8232) being made in 1922. An A & D ejector is pictured here, SN 8472 (Photo 1).

In the 8000 range, they made 109 410s. This included 31 of the newly introduced walking stick 410s.

The firm made a total of six guns in the 9000 range, numbers 9010 to 9015, none in the 410 bore. They then jumped to the 10000 range, beginning in 1928 and ending in 1935. During this time, they made 79 more 410s.

It was in this era they made their handsome 12-inch-barreled smoothbore hammer or A&D hammerless pistol. The first one was introduced in 1929 and wore SN 10186. They ended

∧ **Photo 2:** A "Pistol" 410 smooth-bore with original oak case and cleaning equipment, SN 10193, one of 21 made.

Cameo photo

production of this gun in 1932 with SN 10462. Approximately 21 were made. The ejector 12-inch 410 smoothbore pistol had the Southgate system.

Serial number 10462 was sold at an English auction in 1991. It is a 12-inch double-barrel smoothbore with ejectors, a single trigger, top-lever opener, and 2 1/2-inch chambers. Amazingly, these can no longer be held legally in America and Great Britain except on a special dealer's license.

Pictured is SN 10193, a cased double A&D smoothbore 12-inch-barreled "pistol" shipped in the early 1930s (Photo 2).

The last Watson made in any gauge before absorption by Grant and Lang was a 410, SN 10580, in 1935. It was a single-barrel hammerless ejector gun. The second-to-last 410 gun was SN 10578, a double hammerless 28-inch gun with "side clips." "Side clips" prevent excess movement of the barrels across the standing head of the action, thus re-jointing is less necessary. In view of the "side clips," this may be a bar-action sidelock. If so, this would be the only bar-action 410 recorded.

Of the 79 final 410s in the 10000 serial number range, 21 were the 12-inch smoothbore hammer or hammerless pistols. The others were a mixture of an A&D boxlock double, hammer (single or double), single-barrel hammerless (some with ejectors and some with folding stocks), and the final five walking stick 410s.

Although Watson's last numbered gun in any gauge is the 410 (SN 10580), in the record book there is a gun, SN 10854, that is a 410/28-gauge double-hammer gun with a "straight hand" stock and a "snap on forend." It was not nitro proofed and was unnamed. It was made in 1950. This was the time when Atkin, Grant & Lang owned Watson, and the gun may have been sold under a different name. The word "Birmingham" is recorded in the ledger next to this number — a minor mystery unless or until the gun surfaces for public scrutiny.

Considering the number of 410s produced, Watson must be considered the king of small-bore guns among the quality London firms. Happily, the Watson story has a living sequel.

Today

In 1987, Louca resumed production and is making a London "Best" gun. In-house independent contractors working on current production include Mark Upsher, a former Purdey actioner; Ryan Glyde, another barrel maker; Tom McGuire, the ejector maker; Steven Sinclair, the finisher of a "Best" London gun; and Martin Smith, a magnificent young engraver. The stocker, using Turkish walnut, is "in the trade," a venerable English tradition.

As of 2001, they were making approximately 12 guns per year, all sidelock models. Of the total, 50 percent are over/under models and 50 percent are side-by-sides. They make one 410 every 2 or 3 years, having made a total of three over/under and one side-by-side. Both configurations weigh 5-1/8 pounds with 28-inch barrels, which have a thickness of .04 inch.

The guns are crafted and finished by hand, resulting in a London "Best." The over/under has a Woodward round body action with a Louca patented ejector system. Louca has also patented a "Registered Design" for the over/under and the aesthetic shape of the side-by-side.

Watson has been commissioned to build a three-barrel side-by-side sidelock gun in 20 bore, a 5-year project.

The new Watson guns have few peers in modern gunmaking. Long live the Watson Bros. renaissance!

Watson Bros. References

1. Watson Bros. Records located at 39 Red Cross Way, London Bridge, London, England.

2. Louca, Michael, Personal interviews September 1996, April 2001.

CHAPTER TWENTY THREE

JOHN WILKES & SONS

This firm, a "Best London Gunmaker," started in Birmingham in 1830. Its most recent move to 79 Beak Street, London, occurred in 1927, and therein lays the story. John Wilkes, the great-grandfather of the two present Wilkes (John and Tom), founded the firm in Birmingham, England, and for reasons that time and reticence have obscured, he sold all his assets and fled to America. His son, also John Wilkes, resurrected the firm at 59 St. James Street, London, and prospered as a small but superb gunmaker. The two grandsons now carry on the business, the last "Best" firm operated and controlled by the progeny of the founder. And, the future at one time held another generation of Wilkes gunmakers: John's daughter Fleur and Tom's son Jonathan, who in the 1980s worked in the factory as artisans.

Photo 1: A full view of the Wilkes "Best" A&D ejector 410 with a stock extension, SN 13407. The gun was made for a "Lady."

Paul Goodwin photo

These days, they make only the "Best" sidelock or boxlock in their own factory, approximately 10 to 20 smoothbores per year. However, at one time they offered moderately priced hammer and boxlock guns, many of which were exported to various parts of the British Empire and America.

Very few survived the rigors of the tropics or hard use. Unlike many other firms then as well as now, all of their guns had been and are fabricated in-house, except for the barrels and, in some guns, the locks. Wilkes needed few other outside contracts for any other aspect of gunmaking.

Unfortunately, the company record books prior to 1895 were lost, supposedly due to trash men picking them up as waste. This sounds more fiction than fact, but who knows.

The fourth-generation Wilkes to build guns, John Wilkes, a genial and voluble man dressed in his oil-stained white smock, states that their first recorded 410 bore was built in 1895, SN 4010. It was a top-lever, 2-inch chamber, hammer gun with a back-action sidelock and double barrels. Although John states

Photo 2: A closer view of SN 13407.

∨ *Cameo photo*

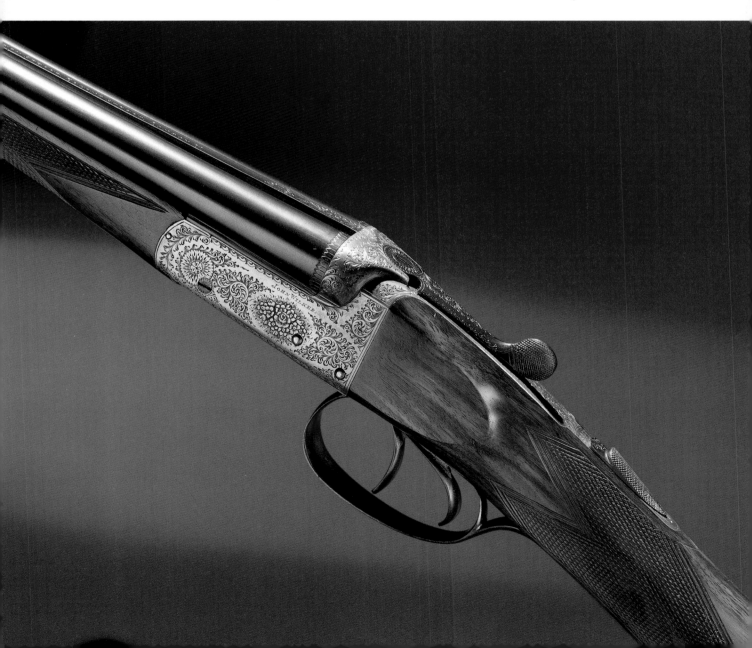

Photo 3: A more detailed view ∧
of the tight scroll engraving on
SN 13407.

Cameo photo

they made a number of 410s in the early part of the 20th century, very few seem to exist today[1].

Craig Whitsey, one of Wilkes' gunmakers, reviewed the records for me from the first 410 in 1895 to the beginning of the Great War in 1914. During this period, they manufactured, in 410 bore: back-action hammer doubles, single-barrel hammer guns, two "boxlock" doubles (SN 4920 in 1904 and SN 8125 in 1913), and one non-ejector double "sidelock" in 1910 (SN 5435). During this time, 24 hammer doubles and 44 hammer singles were made.

Three of the hammer doubles have surfaced on the resale market, numbers 5073, 5599, and 8118. All have 28-inch barrels, rebounding hammers, and foliate scroll engraving.

The earliest 410 boxlock unearthed by this observer was made on 30 August 1930 on an Anson & Deeley (A&D) boxlock action, SN 10446 (see Photo 6 in Chapter 24). It is a non-ejector, double-trigger, double-steel-barreled, "B"-quality gun. The proof marks are from Birmingham and the concave flat rib uses the "79 Beak Street" address. The forend is a splinter style and the straight stock has a checkered butt. There is border scroll engraving. The metal/wood fit and lock mechanisms are of remarkably high and surprising quality for what was a modestly priced gun without ejectors.

A more recent example is SN 13407, an early 1930s A&D ejector with extensive scroll engraving, in superb condition (Photos 1-3). This gun is described as a "Best" with London proof marks.

These 410s were designed for the "boys'" market and for Indian, African, and Australian colonial export. There they were used as camp or farm guns for small wing and ground game shooters, taxidermists, and pest controllers.

They made one documented "Best"-quality bar-action sidelock before World War II in 1936, originally selling it for 46 pounds. This eventually sold in 1982 at auction for 10,000 pounds (nearly 20,000 1982 dollars), a huge price for a resale gun at that time.

Since World War II, they have made several 410s, all "Best"-quality, bar-action sidelocks. Two known guns, SN 15126 and SN 15242, have 26-inch barrels with 3-inch chambers and double triggers. The latter gun is engraved by Ken Hunt and includes a gold inlaid quail and was manufactured in the mid-1980s. It was one of a set of different gauge guns. Another 410, SN 15205 and made in 1986, is also from a set. It is a Rashid-engraved, double-triggered 410, bathed in gold and sold, along with its 20- and 28-bore mates, for a staggering sum at a mid-1990's Christie's auction in London. A final "Best" sidelock 410 that has surfaced publicly is number 13559, also one of a set. The serial number dates to 1932, but the gun was apparently finished in 1984!

This boutique firm is a joy to visit. It is contained in a small decrepit stone building with creaky, yet solid wooden oil-stained stairs and floors, in the heart of London's commercial district. The rooms induce claustrophobia—the workbenches and tables are scarred and ancient, the tools hand-forged, and the artisans from another time, another world. Fleur, when I met her in the mid-1980s, was a working heiress. She was a delicious mixture of openness, guile, charm, and reserve, a young woman seemingly at peace with her destiny. May someone from her generation carry on the tradition. Long live the Wilkes!

---

[1] John's memory includes a 2-inch back-action hammer 410 that came through his shop years earlier for repairs. He judged the gun to be circa 1870s based upon both "proofmarks and other aspects" of the gun.

John Wilkes & Sons References

1. Wilkes, John, March 1994, a series of personal communications, dates 1988 and 1994.

2. Whitsey, Craig, 1997, personal correspondence.

CHAPTER TWENTY FOUR

OTHER BRITISH GUNMAKERS

T he great British gunmakers of the past 100 years define the quality and character of the 410 bore. Some of the most illustrious have been discussed in individual chapters. Yet, other British makers, some of comparably superb craftsmanship, contributed to the 410 bore as a specialty weapon often encased in a work of art.

Rigby

John Rigby & Company, famously London based, was originally a Dublin, Ireland firm specializing in high-quality sporting rifles. It began in 1735 and has been in business ever since. By the turn of the century, they were making smoothbore sporting guns. It was to one of their rifle customers, the Maharajah of Gwaliar, that they supplied the first and only 410 bore built before 1900. A hammer back action with rebounding locks, it was a top-lever breech-opener double-barrel gun with the action supplied by Webley & Scott. The gun was delivered in 1894, SN 16360. This gun is almost certainly a jewel and hopefully may someday emerge.

Paul Roberts, one of Rigby's recent owners and directors and an Englishman of enormous gun knowledge, reports that prior to the 1990s they had never built a "Best"-grade sidelock 410 in their factory [1]. Factory records do show a high-grade "Best" boxlock 410 shipped in 1912, SN 17535, eventually going to the Raja of Manpara to complement his many hunting rifles

(Photo 1). This gun exists today in pristine condition. It is an Anson & Deeley boxlock ejector gun with 27-inch steel barrels and semi-pistol grip French walnut stock. It weighs 4 pounds, 6 ounces. The action was made by "C. Osborne" of the famous gunmaking firm to the trade, and it is perhaps the highest quality boxlock this writer has seen (Photo 2). It was originally sent to Major Sir W.N. McMillan in Nairobi, Kenya, who was President Theodore Roosevelt's host for his Kenyan safari. The inscription "43 Sackville St., London" on the barrel rib confirms the gun's era. And the tight, rich, delicate full-coverage scroll engraving on all metal parts is very similar to a "Best" London sidelock gun of that era. How this gun went from Kenya to the Raja is unknown.

Another 410 was shipped in 1927, SN 18076. It has steel 26-inch barrels, a 15-inch stock, and it is the economy or "D"-grade boxlock made for Rigby by the Birmingham action maker Ilsley Bros.

Correspondence with the firm indicates that before World War II, they had built "three or four" boxlock 410s which were "trade guns" finished by Rigby. After World War II, in the 1950s, they sold a number of Belgium-made 410s, and in the 1980s, made two boxlock 410s on Webley actions.

Rigby built the rook rifle, and like so many of the great makers, it was of such high quality that a 410 conversion was inevitable. Indeed, David Marx, once a Rigby director, reported that a dou-

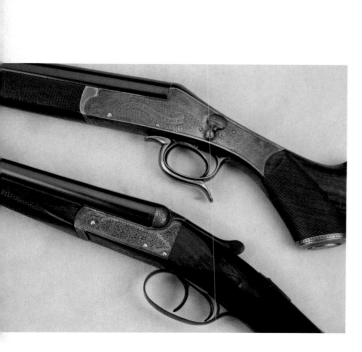

∧

Photo 3: A Rigby single-barrel rook rifle/410 smoothbore conversion, SN 9139 (top) shown with a "Best" Rigby 410, SN 17535. Note the full coverage engraving on SN 17535.

Paul Goodwin photo

<

Photo 1: A "Best" Rigby 410, SN 17535.

Paul Goodwin photo

ble-barrel 24-inch side-by-side 360-caliber back-action hammer rifle, SN 13951, was shipped January 1873 to Captain E. Merrow. This action was subsequently attached to a set of post-1924 nitro-proofed 410 barrels. The barrels are unlikely to be Rigby-made since the top rib is silent. Rigby guns will be identified on the rib by the maker's name: "Dublin & London" if made before 1898 and "London" after 1898 when the Dublin branch was closed.

A pre-1898 rook rifle 410 conversion appeared on the resale market in the mid-1990s (Photo 3).

A circa 1970 red-and-gold-trimmed catalog did not offer the 410 bore, nor does a 1992 brochure. However, a 1994 letter to a customer outlined Rigby's willingness to build a sidelock 410 for 21,000 pounds. Indeed, in 1992, a Southern California gunsmith ordered the first Rigby 410 "Best" double sidelock, paired with a 28 smoothbore. Ken Hunt was to do the engraving on this diminutive 3-pound 10-ounce gun with 26-inch barrels and 2 1/2-inch chambers. The gun was to be beautifully stocked with French walnut. It is unknown whether this gun was completed.

The firm was acquired in 1997 by a California consortium led by Geoffrey Miller, with Craig Boddington, the big bore rifle authority, as director and consultant. They use CNC technology followed by hand finishing. The barrels are made from chopper lump blanks from Austria. High-wear parts are titanium-nitride coated, taking a million cycles to erode away. The wood is English walnut. Today they will build a sidelock 410.

W.J. Jeffery of London

William J. Jeffery established a small but quality London firm in 1885, the date of his first gun patent, at 60 Queen Victoria St. He moved to 13 King St., St. James, in 1897 where the firm remained until 1915, William having died in 1909. By 1927, they had moved to 9 Golden Square, and after World War II, found themselves at No. 5b Pall Mall, where they were bought, first by Westley Richards in 1957 and then by Holland & Holland in 1960 [2,3].

They finished and sold a wide variety of rifles and smooth-bores from their inception to the early 1950s. The record book begins in 1894 at SN 1516 and ends at SN 39822. They were among the most prolific sellers of quality boxlock 410s in Great Britain. Most of their 410s were made by Birmingham makers "For the Trade" such as John Saunders, George Ellis, Harry Leonard, and Webley & Scott.

Their first 410, a "collector" (to collect small ground and wing game often for taxidermy purposes) single barrel with a side-lever breech opener, SN 1633, was shipped July 26, 1894, and sold for 3 pounds, 10 shillings. By 1900, they had built 76 such guns. From 1900 to 1905, they made an additional 113 single-barrel "collector" 410s. And, from 1906 (SN 17501) to 1921 (SN 24480), they made a final 108 guns.

These single-barrel 410s sold for between 1 pound, 10 shillings and 3 pounds, 10 shillings with one spectacular exception.' Made in 1894, SN 1705 is described as a "saloon gun" with a "side lever" breech opener and it sold for 21 pounds, 50 shillings.

---

1 In 1900, 6 pounds was equivalent to almost 2,000 U.S. dollars in 1995 purchasing power. A Jeffery rook rifle in 1900 was 6 pounds and a "best" side-lock shotgun was 70 pounds. The yearly wage for the highest skilled gun craftsman was 150 pounds.

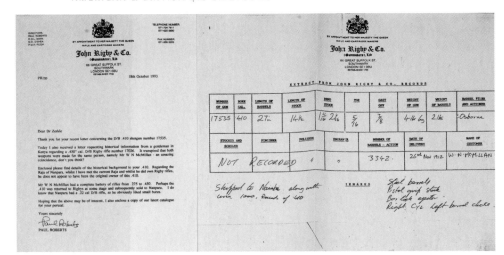

Photo 2: Data from Paul Roberts regarding SN 17535.

Glenn Campbell photo

Given the price, this was probably a double-barrel 410 of high quality. In 1900, they manufactured their first-described double-barrel 410 shotgun, a "best bar lock," SN 10027, which sold for 63 pounds. The gun is not further detailed but the price indicates a gun that could not have been better built by anyone in London.

In 1901, they produced two double 410s, both with side-levers, numbers 10708 and 10709. Also, in 1901, they built SN 10710, their first-described "top-lever" 410. It was a bar-action gun with rebounding hammers and sold for 4 pounds, 15 shillings. In 1904 and 1905, they produced six more top-lever bar-action hammer double 410s. From 1901 to 1926, they produced a large number of double 410s. Sixty-eight double 410s were made with rebounding hammers in either bar- or back-action locks.

The first Anson & Deeley (A&D) boxlock 410 was made in 1909 (SN 18200), described as "Best" quality, at a cost of 2 pounds! The first A&D ejector was produced in 1910, SN 21317.

From 1909 to 1947, they made 55 A&D boxlock 410s, 43 non-ejectors and 12 ejectors. Of these guns, seven were made from 1945 to 1947, two of which were ejectors. Between the wars, the serial numbers and dates are not sequential.

The last two 410s were shipped in 1947: SN 39695, an ejector A&D boxlock, and SN 39696, a non-ejector A&D. Both had 26-inch steel barrels and were foliate scroll engraved. Both sold for 55 pounds, although the ejector gun cost 39 pounds and the non-ejector 24 pounds to manufacture. The former gun's cost included 9 pounds for "tax" while the latter gun was "tax free for export" to "Major H. Barker."

The Barker gun has a straight grip stock and weighed 4-1/2 pounds. This gun, SN 39696, was the last 410 Jeffery made, and is in superb condition, having been refurbished and converted to an ejector gun by Holland & Holland in the 1960s (Photo 4). It retains 80 percent of its case-hardening color and the gun was re-proofed in London in 1994 when the chambers were lengthened to 3 inches. "S. & W." (referring to Webley & Scott) supplied the action for SN 39696 (Photo 5). They supplied high-quality A&D boxlock actions for many London, Birmingham, and provincial gunmakers.

While still at 9 Golden Square, W.J. Jeffery, in 1952, produced a white 8-3/4 by 11-inch catalog and price list. They noted that "small-bore guns" were available only in a single-barrel folding-hammer ensemble called the "Certus" gun. This was priced at 12 pounds and was described as "cheap and reliable." By contrast, their "Best" sidelock was 150 pounds.

It is unlikely that many of the pre-World War II Jeffery 410s still exist. The pre-World War II 410 ammunition was very corrosive to barrels, resulting in deep pitting and eventual destruction of the gun. However, considering the numbers manufactured, more are bound to surface over the years. For example, SN 21416, an A&D non-ejector, and SN 29114, an A&D ejector, have recently appeared on the resale market.

Beesley

The Frederick Beesley firm was established in 1880 in London, the same year Beesley received patent approval on one of gunmaking's greatest innovative designs: the self-cocking hammerless sidelock action that became the long-lived Purdey action of now over 100 years' duration. McIntosh explains that rather than the "tumbler moving the mainspring in cocking, the mainspring moves the tumbler and cocks the locks when the action is closed" [4]. One spring activates the functions of cocking, firing, and breech opening.

The firm prospered until the 1930s, when it was bought by Grant & Lang in 1939. More recently, the firm has re-established its independence as Frederick Beesley, Gunmaker.

They made very few small-bore guns and only 21 410s, the last in 1937. These 21 guns were built from 1892 to 1937. The first was a "sidelock," SN 1287. The second, a hammer back-action double (SN 2463), appeared in 1915. All the rest were A&D doubles, save SN 2728, a sidelock built in 1929.

The only known existing example of the Beesley 410 emerged in 1993, SN 2749, manufactured in 1931 (Photo 6). It is an A&D boxlock auto-ejector gun with 26-inch barrels with full-coverage scroll engraving. The barrel rib identifies it as a "2 St. James Street, London" gun, the address of the gunmaker

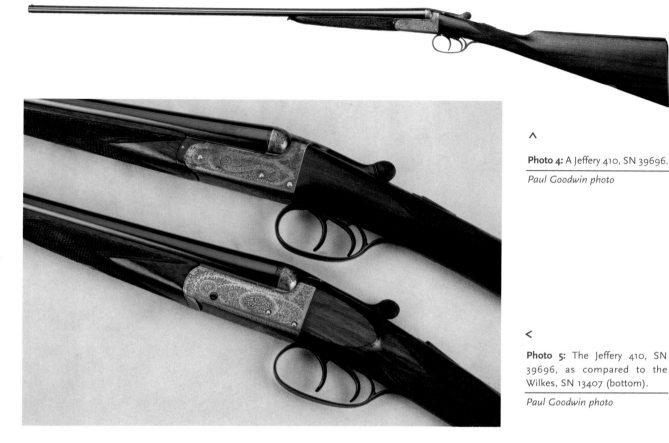

∧

Photo 4: A Jeffery 410, SN 39696.

Paul Goodwin photo

<

Photo 5: The Jeffery 410, SN 39696, as compared to the Wilkes, SN 13407 (bottom).

Paul Goodwin photo

from 1891 to its absorption by Grant & Lang in 1939. It cost 27 pounds, 10 shillings at a time when 7 dollars equaled 1 pound. In 1931, 7 US dollars had tremendous purchasing power.

Evans

Another firm of both historical and current interest, William Evans, is still making guns in St. James, London. Starting in 1883, William Evans "from Purdey's" made and sold an extensive line of guns. Of particular interest is an Evans catalog from their "4 Pall Mall Place" address that dates the catalog between 1888 and 1896 (however, there is one testimonial dated 1897!).

They offered the "collector's" 410 bore in several versions: The classic English-made "walking stick"; the single-barrel hammer side lever; and the double-barrel top lever with back-action rebounding sidelocks.

Their 410 was capable of shooting a cartridge with 21 grains of powder and 150 grains of No. 8 shot and "will put 100 pellets on a 30" circle at 35 yards, evenly distributed," a remarkable boast.[2]

These guns were used for small-bird collecting and for target, rook, and rabbit shooting. They were priced from 2 pounds,

7 shillings to 10 pounds, 10 shillings (in 1890 1 pound had the purchasing power of 300 pounds in today's currency).

Eventually they moved to 63 Pall Mall, where, during World War II, on February 23, 1944, part of the premises and record books were destroyed by a high explosive German bomb [5]. A review of the Evans records before 1900 uncovered several 410 "walking stick" guns manufactured between 1884 and 1895. The first had a "moveable butt" and a "patent safety trigger" and sold for 2 pounds, 5 shillings and had no serial number. In 1887, they recorded their first side-opener 410, again unnumbered. In 1895, they manufactured their first double-barrel 410, SN 3183, along with a single-barrel 410, SN 3184. Both of these actions were made by "C. Osborne," a gunmaker to the trade.

At the turn of the century, they offered a 250-bore side-lever ejector rifle with an interchangeable 410 smoothbore barrel for the "collector."

Rarely is an Evans 410 offered for sale, although one such sale occurred in 1992. It is a 26-inch steel double-barrel top-lever back-action hammer gun, SN 12456, made in 1923, weighing 4 pounds, 11 ounces. The gun frame is border engraved and it now reposes in Texas. Unfortunately, the Evans record book containing this number (numbers 10426 to 13222, spanning the years from 1919 to 1924) has been missing since World War II. An A&D boxlock double non-ejector 410 (SN 17743), circa

---

2 This compares with modern 410 cartridges in which 11 grains of nitro powder and 130 pellets are packed into 2 1/2-inch cases and 19 grains of powder and 220 pellets into a 3-inch case.

Photo 6: A "Best" Beesley 410, SN 2749, is shown above a minimally engraved Wilkes, SN 10446.

G. Allan Brown photo

Photo 6A: An Evans 410 bore from 1937, SN 17743.

Paul Goodwin photo

1937, sold in 1999 (Photo 6A). Additionally, another Evans 410 appeared on the auction market in 1995. It is a rebounding hammer double, number 9808 (Photo 7). It has back-action sidelocks with scroll engraving, illustrating the labor-intensive high quality gun of the early 20th century.

Another 410 Evans surfaced in 1993. It is described as an auto ejector A&D boxlock double. Unfortunately, this gun (SN 97342) is far beyond the Evans numbering system. Evans does record 15 410s sold between 1945 and 1959.

Today they offer a "Best" sidelock or boxlock in any conventional bore including the 410. In 1999 they completed an over/under 410 sidelock, SN 20031, a "Best" gun in all respects mechanically and aesthetically (Photo 8).

Their present premises are cloistered amongst Victorian and Edwardian buildings, rehabilitated relics of a remarkable and now ancient age in gunmaking and gun sports. Inside the shop the senses awaken to the aroma of gun oil and solvent, the cold touch of blued steel, and the svelte vision of Circassian walnut. The guns may be new or from the 19th century. The transition seems seamless.

Lancaster [6]

Charles Lancaster's firm has vanished. Fortunately, however, the record books still exist to reveal a remarkable past. Many of their guns survive and continue to function, a monument to the productive genius of the firm. Started in 1826 as a gunmaker at 151 New Bond St., London, the firm survived independently until 1932 when it was bought by Stephen Grant and Joseph Lang, Ltd. Originally, the founder started in 1811 as a barrel maker of the highest quality, servicing the London trade including John and Joseph Manton. You will find Lancaster's initials on the barrels of the great guns of the first quarter of the 19th century including those made by the Mantons.

Charles Lancaster, who died in 1847, had earlier brought his two sons into the business. However, in 1859, Alfred Lancaster, the younger son, left the founding firm to start his own gunmaking firm at 27 S. Audley St. He moved to 50 Green St. in 1886, and when he died, in 1892, his business returned to the original firm. Fourteen years earlier, in 1878, Henry A.A. Thorn had acquired the original firm from the older son, Charles William Lancaster. Thorn, in a stroke of clever marketing, retained the Lancaster name, even to a point of signing letters "Charles Lancaster."

The 410

An 1893 8-1/2-by-11-inch brown 39-page catalog from 151 New Bond St., lists a 410 "collector gun" (Photo 9). It was available with single or double barrels, a top-lever opener, and back-action locks with rebounding hammers. It was available also in a high-grade hammerless gun with detachable sidelocks. The gun ranged from 4 to 50 pounds depending upon configuration. Their most expensive gun was a 12-bore hammerless sidelock ejector at 60 pounds.

They also cataloged, in 1893, a 410-gauge "walking stick collector's gun" with a "moveable butt," a steel barrel, and a "safety bolt" for 2 pounds, 6 shillings.

An 8-1/2-by-11-inch beige 1924 catalog from 99 Mount St. Berkeley Square, London, catalogs the 410 bore only as a single-barrel breechloader. However, the records, as noted below, confound the promotional material, as it so often does.

The recent owners of the records, Jonathan Boydell and his sister, T. Boydell, kindly allowed me to review them one wet, cold and late January night in a warm sitting room by a coal-stoked fire. Outside, in a stone-quiet Georgian-era village near Birmingham, a dark night gradually turned to dawn and the smell of hot Indian tea aroused me from my preoccupation with often-indecipherable handwritten entries. When finally finished, an English breakfast was my reward.

Volume I of the records, from 1826 to 1884 (SN 100 to SN 5448), documents a wide variety of rifles or rifle barrels from 30 to 90 "gauge." There were scores of 40 gauges built through the 1860s and numerous 50 gauges through the 1870s. There were a smattering of 30-, 70-, 80- and 90-gauge rifles listed until approximately 1880 when the firm began using the term "caliber" in the 300 to 500 plus range.

The firm's first small-gauge smoothbore was a 28-gauge shotgun, SN 4973, built in 1880. It was a "top snap" breech-opener gun that used a 3/4-ounce load.

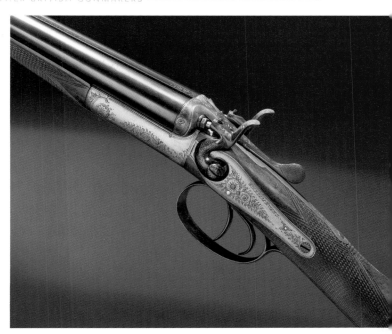

Photo 8: An Evans over/under 410 sidelock with game scene engraving, SN 20031.

William Evans photo

Photo 7: An Evans 410 bore from 1910, SN 9808.

Cameo photo

Photo 9: An ad for 410 "collector's guns" from an 1893 Lancaster catalog.

Paul Goodwin photo

Volume II, SN 5449 to SN 11949, reveals the first 410 smoothbore to be a "collector's gun," number 7318, built in 1883. Subsequently, through 1903, they had built 18 more 410s, all with a single barrel, a side or "top snap" opener, and rebounding hammer back-action sidelocks. In 1902, SN 11569 to 11572, the single-barrel 410 was described as a nitro-proofed ejector gun.

Volume III (SN 11950 to SN 14685 and from 1903 to 1933) describes the first double-barrel 410 (SN 12113) in 1905 as a rebounding-hammer, back-action sidelock. Twenty-two more double- or single-hammer guns were built through 1910. In 1910, they built their first hammerless 410, an A&D top-snap gun, SN 13264. From then until 1933, the records reveal six more 410s. All, with one exception, were A&D guns without ejectors: numbers 14527, 14607, 14634-36. They have double triggers, 2 1/2-inch chambers, and 28- to 30-inch steel barrels. The exception is SN 14685, a single-barrel, side-lever hammer 410 built in 1933.

Built in 1932, SN 14635 weighs 4 pounds, 5 ounces with 28-inch barrels and has been in Texas for many years (Photo 10). Its owner, Perry R. Bass, a gentleman from the school of classical manners, enjoys Texas quail hunting with this and other 410s.

Bass is the nephew of Sid Richardson, a Texas oil man of the mid-20th century, who, in the 1950s, wrested control of the Del Mar Race track in Del Mar, California, from my father, Philip Louis Gabriel. Dad said he, "a Californian, got beat by a Texan in California using California law. It was a square win." The gun's mate, SN 14636, recently appeared in England and has found a home also in America.

Finally, an additional A&D non-ejector 410, SN 17405, was sold recently in England. It is a double-trigger 28-inch gun in excellent condition, made in 1935, and is virtually unused. It was owned and cared for by three Norfolk, England, families for over 60 years. "Saunders," a quality lock maker, made the A&D action, which is fully engraved, retaining 50 percent of its case colors (Photo 11). This gun is recorded in the "Grant & Lang" book (see chapter) and is one of a trio, numbers 17405, 06, and 07.

Records after 1933 (SN 14685) are owned by Atkin Grant & Lang. Many of their recorded 410s left their firm under the name of one of the old firms they bought including Watson, Lancaster, Beesley, etc.

William Powell & Son

There were and are so many other fine gunmakers in the British Isles that built the 410. However, this chapter would be incomplete without a word about Powell, a firm still in the hands of the original family. Founded in 1802 by William Powell and a gunsmith, Joseph Simmons, it is the second oldest gun firm in the British Kingdom to be continuously controlled by the founding family. Presently, two great-great grandsons, Peter and David Powell, run the firm. The records are rich in detail on each gun manufactured and they reveal that a large part of their business was to repair guns from other makers.

The records were reviewed at the firm in 1997 in Birmingham. They reveal that from the late 1800s to the onset of World War I in 1914, they produced only three 410-bore shotguns [7]. In 1895, they made a hammerless A&D action, Siemens-steel, 28-inch, double-barrel, automatic-ejector 410, SN 9984. It weighed 4 pounds, 13 ounces and sold for 30 pounds. A second 410 (SN 10493) is described in 1902 as a "collector gun" with "rebounding locks"[3] (a hammer back action), 27-inch steel barrels, and a "lift lever." A third 410 (SN 11071), also produced in 1902, was a steel double-barrel A&D hammerless gun with Southgate ejectors. It was made for "Lady Lambert," weighed 4 pound, 13 ounces and sold for 30 pounds, equivalent to 1000 pounds in purchasing power today.

During this era, they made one 32-bore shotgun and 11 28-bore shotguns. The large bulk of guns were big smoothbores and this has continued to the present, although they do offer today boxlock and sidelock 410s in various grades.

---

[3] They used their own rebounding locks patented in 1886. A year later, John Stanton patented a rebounding lock which became the industry's standard.

The current lower-grade guns, the "Heritage" series, are fabricated initially by Famars, a high-quality Italian gunmaker, sometimes known as Abbiatico & Salvinelli. The rounded actions, locks, and barrels are delivered to Powell, who then proofs the barrels, stocks, regulates, and engraves the guns. Their high-grade shotguns are made entirely in England. They have been in Carrs Lane, Birmingham, since 1830 and, judging by the success of their mail order dry goods business, will be there indefinitely into the future. The Powell brothers are a fund of knowledge, especially about the Birmingham trade.

Various Other Makers

This section will review a few additional British makers for whom there is some 410 data including two 20th-century gun-making giants: Midland Gun Co. and Birmingham Small Arms Co. or BSA.

Charles Osborne & Sons, whose records were with the Harris & Sheldon Group in Birmingham, kept a ledger book that was, with few exceptions, undated and ran from SN 101 to SN 3175. Seven 410s are listed including numbers 1180 and 1181, two "ejector" guns without further description. The last was a "Hammer Pro DIZZ," SN 2202, made in 1929. This firm appears to differ from "Charles Osbourne" of Birmingham [8].

The Midland Gun Company, founded in 1888, became a pow-erhouse for the retail and wholesale trade [9]. They provided a huge inventory of smoothbores between the world wars and sold a large volume direct to the retail customer. Occasionally a maker of a high-quality side-lock gun, most of their guns were of lower quality, within the price range of the average shooter. In the 1930s, guns ranged from 65 pounds for a "Best" sidelock to 2-1/2

Photo 11: Two views of a Lancaster 410 in pristine condition, SN 17405.

Paul Goodwin photo ∨

Photo 10: A plain, well-used ∧ Lancaster 410, SN 14635.

Perry Bass photo

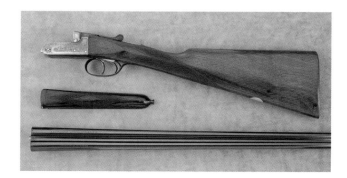

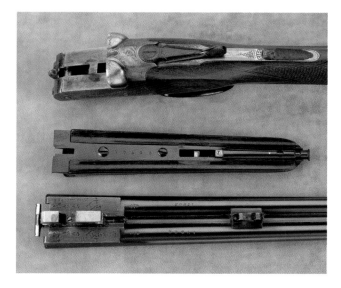

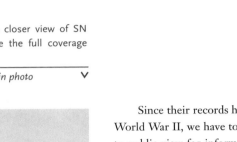

Photo 12: A delicate miniature hammer double 410 from Midland, SN 29610. Note the elegance of the back action.

Paul Goodwin photo

Photo 13: A closer view of SN 29610. Note the full coverage engraving.

Paul Goodwin photo ∨

Since their records have vanished or were destroyed during World War II, we have to rely on the occasional 410 that comes to public view for information. Pre-World War II 410s include SN 76507, a top-lever back-action rebounding-hammer double with 30-inch newly sleeved barrels. In 1999, a 410 ejector A&D gun, SN 97251, circa 1935, was publicly offered. Other 410s include a delicate miniature hammer double, SN 29610, in supreme condition (Photos 12 and 13).

Gallyon & Sons, Ltd., a major provincial firm, has manufactured 410 doubles of high quality and deserves special mention in gunmaking history. A Cambridgeshire firm, it was founded in 1784 in Cambridge. It has remained in the family continuously and is now under the guidance of Richard Gallyon, of the sixth generation of the family and one of the most knowledgeable and respected men in British gunmaking. Guns are still manufactured under this name. The current Gallyon, after a brief odyssey at Cambridge University, apprenticed at Webley & Scott. Now a master gunmaker, he puts raw steel to a stump of Tajikistan walnut and magically produces a British "Best" gun. Twice he has been Master of the British Gunmakers Guild, the "Worshipful Company of Gunmakers."

pounds for a Belgian-made folding 410 [10]. Hence, they helped to make the shooting sports more egalitarian. Their demise in 1966 reflected the general socialistic-engineered poverty of post-World War II England, an economic system that delayed Britain's post-war recovery by two generations.

They supplied 410 boxlock actions to many British gunmakers. Based upon the resale market, they must have made relatively few 410s under their own name, apart from the cheap 2 1/2-pound folding "collector" 410 listed in their late 1930's catalog. They may have been the first British firm, in their 1938 catalog, to market a 410 for 3-inch shells. It was styled with a lovely fully clothed lady holding a double 28-inch 410 with "no recoil" [11].

By 1952, their beige 5-1/4-by-8 3/4-inch catalog no longer offered a 410 shotgun. However, one post-World War II 410 has surfaced, SN 103156, a boxlock non-ejector double with 26-inch barrels, which auctioned at Christie's in 2000.

Two English-made back-action hammer double 410s with miniature frames bear this name, SN 11391 and SN 10095 (Photo 14). Another English-made Gallyon 410 (SN 11448), a "Best" A&D ejector and whose action was supplied in 1922 by Webley & Scott, illustrates the high quality of a well-made Gallyon ensemble (Photo 15). Another A&D boxlock non-ejector, SN 11414, has also recently surfaced.

The juxtaposition of Midland and Gallyon is illustrative of one key fact of British gunmaking. That is Gallyon, like the firms

∧

Photo 15: A Gallyon 410 given as a gift to a landed gentry's son for finishing "college," SN 11448.

Paul Goodwin photo

of Hellis, Jeffery, Rigby, Lancaster, Evans, Atkin, Lang, Churchill, Dickson, Boss (Robertson), Holland & Holland, and many others, relied upon contract trade craftsmen to make gun components, especially actions.

Midland supplied many of these makers with serviceable actions or whole guns, usually boxlocks. An example appears to be a plain Radcliffe 410, which has a Midland-made action (Photo 16). Interestingly, a correspondent to the British magazine *Sporting Gun*, P.W. Pitt, tells of a "first–class craftsman," Harry England, who made the Midland Gun Company's "Best" sidelocks in the 1930s.

John Harper, Wright & Sons, Arthur Ilsley, Joseph Harkom, Charles Osborne, J. Saunders, and especially Webley & Scott supplied makers with "Best" actions, boxlock or side-lock. The Blackmores of Walsall and Edwin Chilton of Wolver-Hampton supplied many "name" firms with locks, ejectors, and springs.

John Harper, who built barrels and actions and finished many guns for London makers, including many of Boss' "Best" 410 Robertsons, was described by Richard Gallyon as a dapper-dressed Victorian-type country gentleman, barely over 5 feet tall with remarkable visual-motor coordination [12]. Fittingly, he made many small-bore guns for the London and provincial trade. Until he died in the 1960s, he had a machine shop and three to four workers producing many magnificent English 410s. He was one of many wonderful British artisans of 20th-century gunmaking.

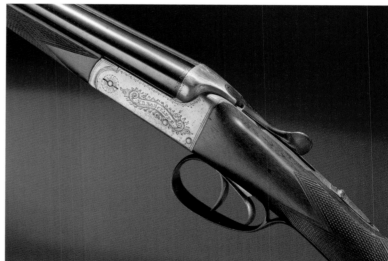

Photo 14 (top): Two Gallyon back-action hammer 410s, SNs 11391 and 10095.

Cameo photo

Photo 16: A plain Radcliffe 410. ∧

Cameo photo

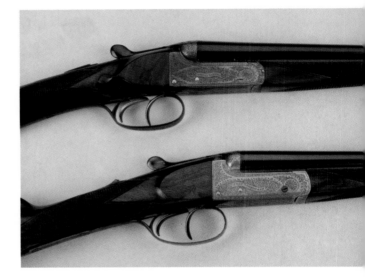

^
Photo 17: A "Best" Boswell 410 ejector, circa 1931, SN 17920.

Paul Goodwin photo

Photo 18: Comparing the Boswell 410 with a Harper-actioned Robertson, SN 7871.

Paul Goodwin photo   ∨

Charles Boswell, a London company, began in the last quarter of the 19th century and moved to 126 Strand, London, in 1884. Charles was a standout live pigeon shooter, which helped him gain prominence for his guns. He sent guns to various parts of the British Empire. The firm temporarily closed in 1940 when bombed out [13]. Subsequently, it reopened and did business until the early 1960s on Connaught St. It is therefore difficult to authenticate specific 410 guns since the records were destroyed (Note: They have subsequently been recovered and reside in Florida [17].) One 410 ejector, SN 17920, with heavy engraving and 27-inch barrels, was auctioned in London in 1998 and is in pristine condition (Photos 17 and 18).

Other Boswell 410s have surfaced, including SNs 6130 and 4139 (these low numbers are not recorded). The latter is a sidelock, the former a boxlock. Another 410, a boxlock with ejectors, SN 146670, was said to have been made in Canada in 1955 and

^
Photo 19: An original high quality William Moore & Grey 410, SN 4453.

Paul Goodwin photo

Photo 21: A typical Harry Morris game scene.

Ray Roy photo   ∨

has a maple leaf inscribed on the forend. It was proofed in Birmingham. The high serial number is inexplicable.

Many other firms such as Reilly, Carr, Ford, BSA, Radcliffe, Rosson, J. Blanch, and Thomas Bland & Sons have had representative 410s appear on the resale market. They are usually either a hammer back-action or a boxlock of variable quality (Photo 19).

For example, a Harry Morris-engraved James Carr & Sons A&D boxlock, SN 46102, has surfaced (Photo 20). The engraving was confirmed by a former student of Morris, F.J. Wiseman, a well-regarded gunmaker from the Birmingham area. The action was from Harper, a "Best." The Morris engraving elevates this gun into the realm of industrial art (Photo 21). Indeed, Harry Morris is considered one of the greatest gun decorators of the first half of the 20th century. He even sold guns under his

Photo 20: A James Carr & Sons A&D boxlock 410 engraved by Harry Morris, SN 46102.

Paul Goodwin photo

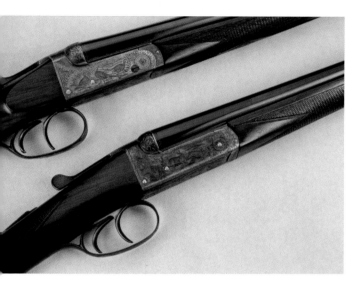

Photo 22: A Carr 410 with Morris engraving, SN 46102, is shown above a "Henry Morris" 410 with the classic Morris game scene, SN 1914.

Paul Goodwin photo

own name. One such is a one-of-a kind 410 ejector, engraved in the classic Morris fashion, SN 1914 (Photo 22).

For a short time before and after World War II, many London, Birmingham, and provincial firms imported Belgian guns in the white and finished them in England under their own name. Evidence includes the architecture of the action, the type of walnut used for the stock, the quality and weights of the barrels, and the inscription on the rib that reads "Made for..." and, often, the proof marks. This period, thankfully, was short lived.

Birmingham Small Arms Company (BSA), founded in 1861, began mass-producing firearms with interchangeable parts in the latter part of the 19th century [14,15]. Their first shotgun, made in 1911, was a "modified Lee Metford" bolt-action 410 bore. In 1920, with over one million square feet of factory workspace and a reported over-five-figure number of workmen, they made the "first British machine-made double-barreled shotgun." Production continued through 1939 with over 48,000 shotguns made. They introduced, in a 1935 catalog, a single-barrel ejector 410 for a 2 1/2-inch cartridge [16]. This writer has yet to see a BSA smoothbore on the open market. There must be some still in existence.

Every nook and cranny of British gunmaking provides fascinating aspects of one of the most important stories of world weaponry, a human tool, which, like the horse and later fusion-fission, changed the course of human civilization.

Other British Gunmakers References

1. Roberts, Paul, personal communication 1997.
2. Boothroyd, Geoffrey, *S.T.C.M.* March 26-April 1, 1992.
3. The Jeffery Record Book located at the Holland & Holland firm.
4. McIntosh, Michael, "Mister Beesley, Life & Times," *The Double Gun Journal,* Summer 1994, Vol. 5, Issue 2.
5. Baker, David, *Sporting Gun,* Jan. 1995.
6. Lancaster Records provided by J. and T. Boydell, 1995.
7. Powell Records provided by David Powell.
8. Tate, Douglas, *Birmingham Gunmakers,* Safari Press, Inc., 1997.
9. Boothroyd, Geoffrey, *S.T.C.M.,* Aug. 4-10, 1994.
10. Baker, David, *Sporting Gun,* December 1997.
11. Baker, David, *The Double Gun Journal,* Summer, 2002.
12. Gallyon, Richard, personal communication 2000.
13. Boothroyd, Geoffrey, *S.T.C.M.,* Dec. 13-19, 1990.
14. Knibbs, John, *The Golden Century,* 2002, John Knibbs Publications, Birmingham.
15. Harriman, Bill, *S.T.C.M.,* 15 August 2002.
16. Harding, C.W., Birmingham Proof House Historian and Archivist, personal communication, 2003.
17. Brown, Nigel, *London Gunmakers,* 1998, Christie's Books, London.

CHAPTER TWENTY FIVE

INTERESTING TYPES OF SMOOTHBORE 410S

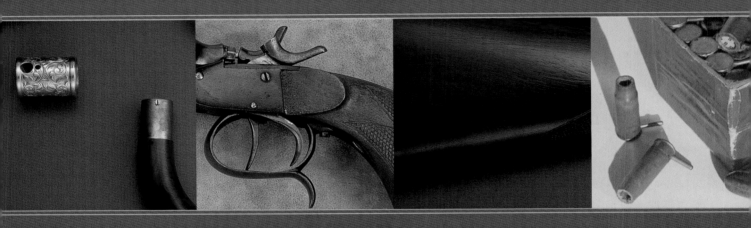

The Cane (Walking Stick) 410

The origin of the smoothbore cane is shrouded in the opaque mists of the past. However, flashes of illumination appear from time to time. John Day of Barnstaple, England, invented the first percussion lock cane gun with an underhammer. He patented this in 1823 and sold these guns for at least 30 years [1,2].

Fifty years after Day's invention, the "London Notices of Importations" show that Robert Hughes imported 16 "walking stick" 410 guns from Europe on September 30, 1874. A month before, in August 1874, William Whitmore imported "410 guns" [3]. These are the first 410 references found in the gun literature.

Cogswell & Harrison, a prolific gunmaking company in the late 19th and early 20th century, recorded its first "stick gun" in 1880, SN 10308, probably a 410 smoothbore. The firm's first specified "410 walking stick" was cataloged March 30, 1880, SN 10311. From then until January 11, 1989, SN 15080, they recorded over 200 410 "walking stick" smoothbores. A few stick guns were 28 bore and fewer still were "rifled" to throw a slug or a "ball" [4].

The Cogswell & Harrison "stick-guns" were of the breech-opening Dumonthier patent type. The action was opened by a "pull and twist" of the handle exposing the chamber and cocking the firing pin simultaneously. A.M. Clark, acting for the Parisian Celestin Dumonthier, patented this

gun in 1876, a marriage of the walking stick and the percussion ignition. This was a 12-mm (a 410 equivalent would be 10.414 mm) smoothbore, an example of which is preserved in a French museum [5]. Another example, one belonging to Colonel Richard Meinertzhagen, was located at Marford Mill, England, in the headquarters of the British Association of Shooting and Conservation, one of the United Kingdom's answers to the anti-gun and anti-hunting ethos that contaminates much of the modern British soul [6].

Crudgington & Baker report that this patent covers three versions of the breech-opening cane, all having an outer sleeve to the barrel. The barrel is pushed forward to reveal the open cartridge chamber, then pulled back to close it. The three versions relate to the firing pin stem and its release. The third variation is quite eccentric and involves blowing the firing pin into the cartridge base with lung power.

Greener, in 1881, refers to the naturalist's "walking stick 410 shotgun" to collect birds and small mammals [7]. He dismissively recommended that this bore be reserved only for smaller birds, much preferring the "24 to 28 shotgun" and a "small rifle" for the collector-taxidermist. He noted in 1881 that the 410 bore had "lately been introduced." We earlier noted that Edward Booth, the Victorian bird collector, used a 410 walking stick between 1865 and 1884 to collect over 250 specimens.

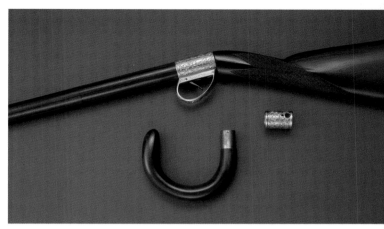

Photo 1: Typical English stock for a cane 410 smoothbore.

Paul Goodwin photo   ∨

Photo 2: A Wilson 410 cane smoothbore.

G. Allan Brown photo

Greener further elaborated that the walking stick gun was usually made in Belgium and France and sold in quantity in London. The barrel inside the cane was of "inferior iron or brass" and brazed together from end to end. Occasionally, the barrel would "burst with the ordinary load." The "mechanism" was poor in both principle and quality. He wondered why there were not more "numerous" accidents.

The 9th Edition in 1910 reveals a kinder disposition towards the walking stick 410-bore shotgun [8]. He describes the "English"-made cane 410s as the "better article" and the 410 as the most popular bore for the walking stick. The English canes are made entirely of iron, except the stock, and British proofed as a breech-loading gun and are "trustworthy." The 410, he noted, had a "killing range" of 25 yards and was in demand by the naturalist, gamekeeper, and though not stated, the dreaded poacher. He still had little use for the Belgian- or French-made walking stick gun (Photo 1 and see Photos 1 and 2 from Chapter 3).

Catherine Dike, the world's doyenne on the cane and its artifacts, reports that these were not furnitured initially in leather or veneered wood, as so many cane guns eventually would be in the later 1800s [9]. Dike's photographic essays, brilliantly conceived and executed, include gun canes made in 19th-century America. They appeared as early as the 1829-1851 period by "A.D. Cushing" of Troy, New York, patented in 1831. "Dr. Lambert" patented a cane gun in 1832. Both Remington Arms Company in 1858 (eventually the most popular American maker of the cane gun) and Henry Deringer of Philadelphia patented a percussion system cane gun for the American market. There is no evidence that these early cane guns were in 410 bore.

By 1890, over 100 patents had been filed in England and America for the cane gun using cartridges with three different firing systems: rimfire, pinfire, and centerfire. Thousands of European-made cane guns of all types had flooded the British market by the turn of the 20th century.

Although the 410 in England and the 12 mm in Europe were well known, there is no evidence that the cane gun existed in America in the 410 smoothbore before 1900 or, for that matter, until well into the 20th century. They were built in other bores

certainly, and often of singular design. For example, Marcellin Daigle of Louisiana designed, patented in 1877, and built a repeating cane gun where the breech was fed by a tubular magazine [2].

In Europe, "Manufrance" made cane guns in the 12-mm bore from the 1800s up to 1950. In America, Remington, with a splendid dog's head for the cane's ivory handle, made these guns well into the post-World War II years.

The cane or walking stick 410 shotgun was available in America until post-World War II, after which the configuration became illegal. It was routinely owned and used in Britain until 1992 when new law made it illegal to own, except in the hands of a licensed collector. Alas, a great and romantic era has essentially vanished.

John K. Wilson

Before this period was finally extinguished, there was a brief but incandescent renaissance of the cane gun in England. Made by John K. Wilson from 1977 to 1992, these modern cane guns for modern ballistics were of the most exquisite quality. He still makes them but only for export to Europe.

His father, Lewis Wilson, started as a part-time gunmaker in the 1920s. John became a full-time maker in 1967.

They rebuilt or serviced guns and made barrels for the trade. In 1977, John built his first cane umbrella 410 and, as of 1986, had made 620 410 single-barrel smoothbore guns for 570 canes and 50 umbrellas.

The barrel action is of heat-treated, solid, high-quality steel alloy with nickel chrome. Generally, it was covered with leather or goatskin morocco or other more exotic skins such as snake, lizard, or crocodile. On rare occasion, the barrel was encased by ebony from Africa or Burma or rosewood. The safety was a "true" safety on the "button," not on the trigger. The action of the pictured gun is covered with 22-karat gold plate engraving. Wilson does all the work save the engraving (Photo 2).

Much of his daily work had been building and proofing big bore double rifle barrels for such firms as Purdey, Holland & Holland, and Westley Richards. The walking stick challenge hit him in the early 1970s when he found two antique cane 410s. He

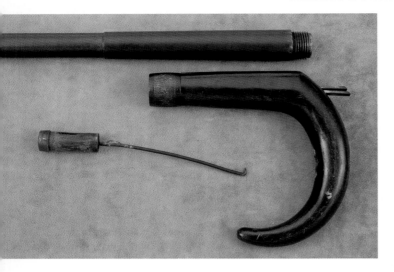

Photo 3: This cane gun was made by a remote uncle to the author in the Redoubtable Mountains of Lebanon.

Paul Goodwin photo

Photo 4: The French pinfire 410 smoothbore with Eley pinfire cartridges and loading tool.

Ronnie Crowe photo ∨

took them to Reginald Bedford, the Proof Master of the London Proof House at the time, and Bedford proceeded to blow them up. The Proof Master said that the 410 bore could not be built today in the walking stick configuration because modern loads are too powerful for the thin-barreled cane. Wilson, a gunmaker par excellence, proved him wrong.

The John Wilson cane gun shown here has a 3-inch 410-cartridge chamber with a button trigger and safety. The ferrule is game-scene engraved with the owner's initials. There is an extra ferrule with a trigger. The gold plate is to 3 microns. There is an interchangeable conventional stock of rosewood. The gun barrel and action are covered with rosewood. The wood was bored from a solid piece and glued to the barrel. The wood was then "turned

to size" and polished to a magnificent luster. The stock grip and heel are checkered. This work of art, however real and deadly, is a visual banquet (Photo 2).

Epilogue

This writer's interest in the cane gun began as a 12-year-old boy in 1949 when my dad brought home a cane "410" from a trip to his ancestral home in the Christian-controlled coastal mountains of Lebanon. I inspected the gun with wonder as dad told the magical story.

It had been hand-tooled in 1880 by a long-dead great-uncle, Antoine Pasha Akiki. At that time, the Levant, including Lebanon, was ruled by Turkey, a decentralized, inefficient and unforgiving Islamic tyrant. Christians were allowed no weapons of any form. So, "camouflaged" firearms were made by artisans in secret blacksmith shops found throughout the valleys and mountains of this ancient world. A number of Middle Eastern cane guns are pictured in Snyder's elaborate book on the cane [10].

Dad found this forgotten cane in the cellar of an old rock house of a cousin in 1949. He idly picked it up and it seemed odd. Boyishly waving it about, he suddenly realized it was too heavy to be just a cane. His curiosity peaked and he began to work with the handle, which suddenly loosened. To his wonder, it slowly unscrewed in his probing fingers, revealing the open breech of a cartridge chamber. The muzzle end was corked with a steel-framed wood plug that yielded to his touch! He discovered that the hook attached to the wood plug would cock the hammer and the trigger, a flat, long, rectangular stem, protruded through the cane handle (Photo 3).

As dad's cousin explained, it was last used by the great-uncle, who pointed the muzzle at the head of a hated Turkish tax collector and flicked the stem. The man instantly expired in a pool of blood on the eve of World War I, the last days of the vast Turkish dominion that once girdled much of the Mediterranean world. Reprisals were forgotten when Turkey recalled its vast legions to participate in the Great War with the Axis powers, hence, the losing side. Thus ended the last great Islamic Empire.

Dad had told me that it held a 410 cartridge, a further cause for infatuation since I had shot game with a single-barrel 410. It was not until many years later that this belief was shattered. John Wilson examined the gun and pronounced it a 38-caliber rifled barrel. So much had the young boy's faith been in his father's casual comment that he never tried to fit a cartridge into the chamber.

It is a prized possession, the romance not dimmed but enhanced with knowledge and time.

Pinfire

The only single-barrel pinfire smoothbore 410 that has publicly surfaced to date is owned by a photojournalist living in Essex, England. He provided photos of this unique single-shot hammer gun with hexagonal barrels, which is of French origin without British proof marks or maker's name (Photo 4).

∧ **Photo 5:** An English 410 smoothbore pistol.

Paul Goodwin photo

The ingenious pinfire cartridge is a single self-contained unit: shot, powder, wad, and ignition. This did away, in one stroke, with the inefficient though picturesque paraphernalia of the muzzleloader: powder flask, wad systems, short flask, and ramrod.

The Parisian Casimir LeFaucheux patented the first pinfire cartridge in 1835. He exhibited his patented breech-opening pinfire smoothbore at the Great Exhibition at Crystal Palace in London in 1851 to the amazed but skeptical public. Joseph Lang may have been the first Britisher to market it in England in the same year, 1851.

The cartridge was both dangerous to handle and difficult to load. But this was the transitional gun between the muzzleloader and the breech-loading centerfire gun that superseded it within 10 to 15 years. However, the pinfire gun appears to have been made or at least was still used in Europe well into the early part of the 20th century, for pinfire cartridges were advertised in Europe as late as the 1930s.

The 410 pictured was almost certainly made late in the 19th century and may be a converted 300-plus-caliber rifle in view of its barrel configuration.

∧ **Photo 5:** An English 410 smoothbore pistol.

Paul Goodwin photo

British firms such as Purdey, Rigby, Reilly, Lang, and Greener converted many of their pinfire guns to centerfire as soon as the latter cartridge was developed and became readily available circa 1861.

Smoothbore Pistol

The short-barrel smoothbore pistol is discussed briefly in the Ithaca chapter. There are a number of 410 pistols of British make, which can only be held today on a special firearms dealer's license in the United States and in the United Kingdom. The Watson chapter illustrates a British "Best." Shown here is a typical English hammer double smoothbore 410 (Photo 5).

Despite the convincing data that support the aphorism: "More guns, less crime," the urbanized western world has shown an increasing aversion to firearms [11]. Hence, it is increasingly unlikely that eccentric or unusual forms of firearms for personal use will be developed in the future.

Interesting Types of Smoothbore 410s References

1. Logan, Herschel C. *Underhammer Guns,* 1960, The Stackpole Company. Harrisburg, Penn.
2. Harriman, Bill, *STCM,* Nov. 26-Dec. 2, 1992.
3. London Proof House Records reviewed 1984 by author with kind permission of the Proof Master.
4. Cogswell & Harrison archives reviewed 1993 by author with kind permission from Farlow's of Pall Mall, London.
5. Crudgington, I.M. & D.J. Baker, *The British Shotgun,* Vol. 2, 1871-1890, pg. 168-169, Ashford, 1989.
6. Meinertzhagen, Colonel R., *Middle East Diary,* The Cresset Press, London 1959.
7. Greener, W.W., *The Gun and Its Development,* 1st Edition, Cassell, etc., 1881, pg. 368.
8. Ibid, 1910, 9th Edition, pg. 387 and 517.
9. Dike, Catherine, *Cane Curiosa,* Les Editions de L'Amateur, Paris, 1982.
10. Snyder, Jeffrey B., *Canes,* Schiffer Publishing, Ltd. Atglen, PA 1993.
11. Lott, John R. Jr., *More Guns Less Crime,* 1998, The University of Chicago Press, Chicago.

CHAPTER TWENTY SIX

ROOK RIFLE/410 SMOOTHBORE CONVERSION STORY

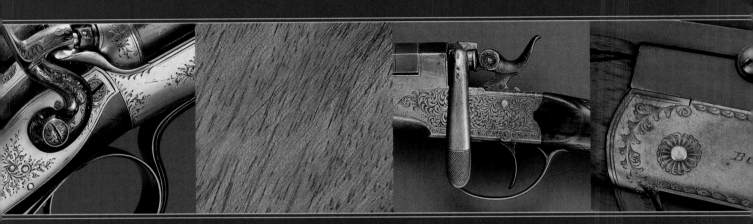

T his chapter is about guns defined by barrel caliber and use. Many single and a rare double-barrel rifle were designed to harvest rook and other wing or ground game and were made in many calibers. The true "rook and rabbit" (RR) rifle ranged from the 22 to the 380 caliber with most in the 295/300 caliber, shooting a 40- to 134-grain bullet [1]. They were built to be accurate and lethal up to 200 yards, although blackpowder residue was a limiting factor if allowed to accumulate. Thereafter, the bullet would rapidly spend itself into a harmless projectile. The RR rifle was manufactured from 1870 to well into the 1930s. It was patented in 1866 by William Tranter as a 380-caliber "central-fire" gun [2,3].

They were all breechloaders with top-, side-, or bottom-lever openers. They were manufactured with either rebounding back-lock hammers or were hammerless (hammer was inside the lock). It was usually a single octagonal barrel. They came in all action lock types, usually back, box, or Martini action'. They

were rarely manufactured in a bar-in-the-wood type action. The gun sold for 6 to 15 guineas at the turn of the century. (Six guineas at that time are now worth 450 pounds or 700 dollars.)

A good quality original rook rifle is now hard to find. Most were destroyed or rotted to death in wet barns. Most of those few that survived were converted to the 410 shotgun bore.

The reasons for the demise of this interesting and useful caliber and gun are threefold. First, there is the development of the 22-rimfire rifle and cartridge. By 1910, this rifle sold for less than one-half the cost of a RR rifle, some as cheaply as one guinea, and the rimfire cartridge was a third of the cost of the centerfire cartridge.

Second, the 1920 Firearms Act required police registration of the RR rifle [5]. This resulted in large numbers being destroyed by police, who made it difficult for people to easily own such a gun. However, many good citizens did not register their RR rifle. Many are now considered "antique," for which ammunition is no longer made, and occasionally may be seen at an auction house.

The third reason was due to the change in English proofing laws in 1925, which made it more difficult to reproof a blackpowder RR rifle [6]. Therefore, many were re-bored to a 410 smoothbore.

Pictured is a Holland & Holland, SN 10925, octagonal single-barreled rook rifle converted after 1925 to a 410-bore shotgun. The barrel is marked "Winner of all the Field Rifle Trials 1883." It is a hammerless boxlock action with a top-lever breech opener. Scroll

---

1 After the 1870s, the Martini action was often combined with the Henry barrel rifling, siring one of the most used military weapon ensembles of the next 50 years. Marcott's introduction of the push-forward under-lever hammerless shotgun in 1871 closely resembled the Martini-actioned Henry-barreled rifle adopted by the British Army in 1871. [4]

Photo 1: A Holland & Holland octagonal single-barreled rook rifle 410 conversion, SN 10925.

G. Allan Brown photo

Photo 2: A Purdey double 410 conversion, circa 1871, showing the remarkable workmanship of the times (SN 8625).

Cameo photo

∨

engraving covers the metal works. Plain pistol grip stock and forend are very finely checkered with over 28 lines to the inch. Originally a 290-caliber blackpowder rifle, it was converted to a 410 nitro-proofed shotgun for the 2 1/2-inch cartridge (Photo 1).

A similar single-barreled Holland & Holland conversion, SN 18312, went to auction in England in 1966. It is a top-lever Anson & Deeley (A&D) boxlock ejector gun with an octagonal 26-inch steel barrel for a 2 1/2-inch cartridge. Scroll engraving and a cheek piece on the stock complete the gun. A third single-barrel Holland & Holland rook rifle, SN 10976, has surfaced which, wonder of wonders, has not been converted and must be a rare bird. It is in the 295/300 caliber and is a top-lever hammerless ejector gun with an octagonal barrel built on a trigger plate action housing the mainspring, hammer, and trigger. It has virtually identical markings to the Holland & Holland (SN 10925) gun noted above. The boxlock action body is fully and finely scroll engraved with panels of foliage and 95 percent case-hardened colors. This is a most beautiful example of a high quality rook rifle of the late 19th century. It is the Ross model, Holland & Holland's "Best" rook rifle, and is an example of their "semi-smoothbore rifling" introduced in approximately 1880, according to Greenwood [7]. The accuracy of this rifling was unparalleled.

A third Holland & Holland ensemble is a "ball and shot" gun with two barrels, a smoothbore 410 and a rifled bore (see Photo 5 in Chapter 18).

Another famous name in gunmaking, James Purdey, manufactured a rook rifle in 1896, SN 12863, which was subsequently converted to a 410 bore after 1953. It is a double steel 26-inch-barreled gun with rebounding hammers of back-action type. It is an "E"-quality gun with fancy scroll engraving and originally made as a 300-caliber double rifle. It is now bored to a 410, 3-inch shotgun cartridge, and was reproofed after 1953 (after having been blackpowder proofed originally). It was shipped with extra-fancy wood and the stock was nicely checkered with a cheek piece now replaced by a steel plate.

An earlier Purdey RR double rifle (SN 8625) with back-action locks and an underlever opener exemplifies the remarkable wood used on guns of that era (Photo 2).

A third Purdey conversion was made when Purdey was at 314-1/2 Oxford Street (Photo 3). Made in the early 1870s, it is the oldest rook rifle/410 conversion known to the author. It has an unusual hammer side-lever configuration with scroll engraving.

Many of these rifles, double side-by-side or single-barreled, were made but only a limited number have surfaced bearing the name of a great British gunmaker such as Purdey, Boss, Holland & Holland, Westley Richards, Greener, Rigby, or Henry Atkins. Most were made before World War I and converted thereafter to a 410-bore shotgun after 1925, usually to a 2 1/2-inch cartridge when the English Proof House changed the rules of proofing. Some were returned to the original maker for a set of 410 barrels or were re-bored and reproofed to 410 specifications. Some were re-barreled by individual barrel makers attaching a privately made side-by-side or single barrel to the existing action, such as a doc-

Photo 3: A trio of Purdeys: Purdey double, SN 8625 (top); Purdey single-barrel 410 conversion, SN 87 (middle); and Purdey single-barrel 410 conversion circa 1900, SN A558 (bottom).

Paul Goodwin photo

<

>

Photo 5 (opposite page): The Boss 410 conversion, SN 6181, shown with the Purdey single-barrel 410 conversion, SN 87 (bottom).

G. Allan Brown photo

umented Rigby rook rifle, SN 13951. This back-action hammer gun was originally a 360-caliber double rifle shipped in 1873. The current barrels have no markings and were proofed according to the 1925 rules for a 410 shotgun, clearly a non-factory add-on.

There is the rare rook rifle of a later vintage, such as SN 9419 from Henry Atkin of 27 St. James Street, London. The address indicates that this gun was made after 1951 and before 1960 as they moved to St. James Street in 1952 and moved again in 1960 when amalgamated with Stephen Grant and Joseph Lang. According to the 1954 Rules of Proof, it was converted to the 410 2 1/2-inch cartridge. It is a top-lever boxlock hammerless shotgun, part octagonal barrel, with foliage engraving on the action. This is the latest rook rifle/410 conversion publicly recorded, and I would appreciate information of any additional ensembles that may have been built and converted subsequent to this gun.

Almost all such rifles made by quality gunmakers were of boxlock or back-action sidelock type with or without exposed hammers. However, there is a documented Westley Richards (SN 17127), a "Best"-quality drop-lock hammerless double barrel shipped in 1910 as a 300 caliber that was converted after 1953 to

a 3-inch chambered 410 smoothbore. It has a single trigger with automatic ejectors, partial beavertail forend, a straight grip stock, and a horn butt plate. The frame is miniature with several well-done gold inlays. There is no other public record of a bar-in-the-wood sidelock action rifle conversion to a 410 smoothbore.

An interesting "G.H. Daw & Company" (another famous name in 19th-century British gunmaking) 410 shotgun surfaced and appeared to have been an original blackpowder-proofed 410 manufactured before 1904. It was re-proofed by 1954 rules for nitro powder and 3-inch cartridges at 5 tons. It is a non-numbered, single-round-barrel, top-lever, back-action hammer gun. It is covered in fancy scroll and the stock is pistol grip and well checkered. The possibility of an original 410 is belied by its thick walls, the inscription "Henry's Rifling," and a flip-down rear sight. Henry did make smoothbore barrels! Based on the maker's inscription, it was probably made between 1882 and 1889. Boothroyd reviewed the data and judged it to be a rook rifle conversion, notwithstanding the visible proof marks. I list this gun in this section in deference but reserve judgment on its pedigree.

∧

Photo 4: A Boss single-barrel 410 conversion, SN 6181.

Paul Goodwin photo

An interesting boxlock Boss 300 single-barrel RR rifle sold in 1910 (SN 6181) was converted after 1954 to a 3-inch 410 smoothbore with a hammerless action (Photos 4 and 5).

A "Best" Boss & Co. profusely engraved double rifle 410 conversion, SN 4057, was made just before the end of the 19th century (Photo 6).

A final example is a Stephen Grant double-barrel "Best" RR rifle with a duke's crest on the stock, SN 3981. It is a back-action hammer gun with exquisite engraving and unparalleled wood (see Photos 2 and 3 in Chapter 11).

The conversion saga continues, seemingly unending, in the auction houses of England, a small but important byway in the 410 drama.

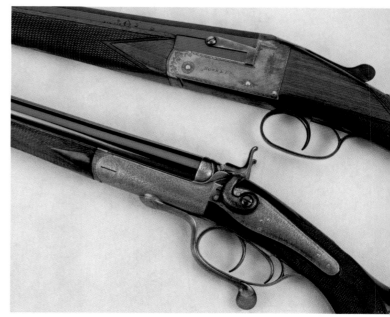

Photo 6: This "Best" Boss double-barrel rifle conversion to a 410 (SN 4057) is an example of the quality of guns from the 1890s (bottom). On top is another Boss 410 conversion, SN 6181.

Paul Goodwin photo >

Rook Rifle/410 Smoothbore Conversion Story References

1. Greener, W.W., *The Gun and Its Development*, Cassell, Petter, Galpin & Co., London 1881, 1910.
2. Boothroyd, Geoffrey, *STCM*, May 31-June 6, 1990.
3. Boothroyd, Geoffrey, *STCM*, November 14, 1996.
4. Crudginton, I.M. and D.J. Baker, *The British Shotgun*, Vol. Two, 1871-1890. Ashford 1989.
5. Greenwood, Colin, *STCM*, May 25-31, 1995, June 1-7, 1995, June 15-21, 1995.
6. Nelson, Archie, of Dickson & Son, personal communication 1994.
7. Greenwood, Colin, "A Popular Pest Controller," *The Shooting Gazette*, May 2002.

INDEX